Ysenda Maxtone Graham

BRITISH SUMMER TIME BEGINS

The School Summer Holidays 1930–1980

Little, Brown

LITTLE, BROWN

First published in Great Britain in 2020 by Little, Brown

3 5 7 9 10 8 6 4

A CIP catalogue record for this book
is available from the British Library.

ISBN 978-1-4087-1055-5

Typeset in Garamond by M Rules
Printed and bound in Great Britain by Clays Ltd, Elcograf S.p.A.

Papers used by Little, Brown are from well-managed forests
and other responsible sources.

Little, Brown
An imprint of
Little, Brown Book Group
Carmelite House
50 Victoria Embankment
London EC4Y ODZ

An Hachette UK Company
www.hachette.co.uk

www.littlebrown.co.uk

For Michael, Toby, Charles and Francis

Contents

Prologue

'You're writing a book about summer holidays?'

'Not just summer holidays: *the* summer holidays.'

Note the distinction. Summer holidays are a small, glamorous subset of *the* summer holidays. This book is about the latter. *The* summer holidays are the vast stretch of untimetabled time that begins as soon as you emerge through the school gates on a July morning, and goes on until the moment in September when you return, two shoe sizes larger and somehow changed.

When you step into that balmy ocean of time in mid-July, released from lessons and uniform, you feel as if you're stepping into infinity. You can't even imagine September; it doesn't occur to you that such a brown, lugubrious month will ever arrive. All you can see before you in your imagination is sunlight shimmering on grass and water.

It's this stretch of time that I'm aiming to capture through the recollections of men and women I've spoken to, who were actually there, being children, in the fifty years from 1930 to 1980.

The summer holidays might, if you were lucky, *contain* summer holidays – a week or more at a faraway place, to get to which you were crammed in the back of an overloaded car, not wearing seat belts, feeling sick as your chain-smoking parents drove along a succession of urban high streets towards a coast, dale or moor, suitcases tied down onto the roof rack. There will be 'going on holiday' in this book, I promise: tents will be erected, and bare feet will touch the ground of Majorca, 1969; but going-away-type holidays are only a part of the story.

'Tell me about the non-events of your childhood summers as well as the events,' I pleaded with my interviewees, who ranged across the social spectrum from those for whom the word 'tea' meant sandwiches and cake in the nursery at 4 p.m. to those for whom it meant a hot meal at 6. I was just as interested in the hours spent sitting on the pavement rolling melted tar into balls, or the long dusks hitting a tennis ball against the back wall of the house, as I was in what was on the menu at seaside boarding houses or French restaurants in 1965, though I was fascinated by that, too.

When no adult was taking any notice of you in those long summer weeks ('my parents,' as countless people said to me, 'had no idea where I was'), you were properly being you in a way you could never be at school, where the tendency was always to conform in order to fit in. So this is really a book about how we discovered who we were, through how we chose to spend our free time, until someone called us in for whichever kind of tea it was. It's about the formation of the childhood mind in the weeks when no one was barking at us. It's about families, small or extended, and what really went on in them, not behind closed doors, but behind open doors. How did those summers form us and shape the way we lived the rest of our lives?

If my previous book, *Terms & Conditions*, about life in girls' boarding schools between 1939 and 1979, was the non-fiction *Mallory Towers*, this one is perhaps the non-fiction *Famous Five*. Enid Blyton's novels shaped both term-times and holidays: while children spent the holidays reading *Mallory Towers*, and then begged to be sent to boarding school because it all sounded so exciting, they then spent their term-times reading *Famous Five* books and vowing to model their summers on them.

In real life, were children really 'famous', in the old-fashioned meaning of marvellous? Were there, typically, five of them? What was the truth behind the lashings of ginger beer and the unsupervised rowing-boat trips to deserted islands? Did food really taste better out of doors?

My cut-off date for *Terms & Conditions* was 1979, the date of the arrival of the duvet, which put an end to the spartan existence that had made boarding schools the character-forming institutions they had been. In this book, my cut-off point is the arrival of the video game, which gave children pre-packaged alternative worlds to consume their hours, and thus lessened the need to invent ones for themselves. Binatone tennis, played on a Binatone TV Master with two paddles to make the ball bounce back and forth across the net, was released in 1976, but it wasn't till 1978 that it started infiltrating the British playroom. I decided to nudge my cut-off date to 1980, the year before IBM introduced its first Personal Computer.

I'm going back to the 1930s, a decade further than I did for *Terms & Conditions*, because I wanted to meet people who were old enough to remember what they were doing at 11 a.m. on Sunday 3 September 1939. It was bad enough, surely, that it was early September so the dreaded end of the summer holidays was coming into view; now they had to deal with the fact that a war had broken out as well.

It might seem that some of my chapter titles and sections are rather negative: 'Nothing Much Planned', 'Not Going Abroad', 'The People You Were Stuck With', and so on. I'm aiming to reflect the truth. Summers were more a matter of stasis than travel. But, as we'll see, it was a particular kind of stasis. And who even needed abroad, when journeys in Britain took so long that (as the Radio 3 presenter Ian Skelly recalled, describing his family's annual journey and change of climate from Lytham St Annes in Lancashire to Branscombe in Devon when the M5 only went as far as Bristol), 'it felt as if you were going all the way to Australia'? 'Abroad!' said Sir Nicholas Soames, outraged when I suggested he might have gone somewhere more exotic and warmer than the north of Scotland for a month every August in the 1950s. 'Certainly not! No one went abroad except to fight a war.'

Although the events (and non-events) described in these pages happened so recently, this was a Britain scarcely recognisable today. For one thing, when people did travel they lugged enormous, bulging, wheel-less suitcases – suitcases so heavy that in order to carry one in your right hand you needed to do a counter-bend to the left for the sake of balance, permanently warping your spine. It actually made things easier if you were carrying two suitcases of equal back-breaking weight: hence a generation of fathers who said, 'Here – let me carry them both'. Why it took so long between the invention of the wheel (3500 BC) and the invention of the suitcase on wheels ('rolling luggage' was patented in 1972) remains a mystery. The halfway stage was the suitcase-trolley onto which you fixed a suitcase with a bit of stretchy elastic, but it was useless. Suitcases flopped off these as soon as you turned a corner at normal walking pace.

For another thing, the whole country was crawling with loose children.

Whom did I interview for this book? Well, everyone I could, for eighteen months, travelling the length and breadth of the country, buttonholing market traders, visiting men and women in day-care centres, chatting to people brought up on farms, in castles, on council estates, in back-to-back houses and in suburban houses with lawns and rockeries. This is not a book of hearsay. In order to be eligible to be mentioned in this book, the thing mentioned has to have happened directly to the person who talked to me. The sample here is, of course, only a tiny fraction of the millions of people I could have interviewed. But the few speak for the many; individual recollections represent general trends among classes and types. There's a sprinkling of the famous – politicians, writers and broadcasters whose childhoods I was nosey about – but their recollections are just part of the great mix, and, remember, they weren't famous when they were children – they were just moping about trying to avoid boredom, like everyone else.

This is a book about lashings of time – as well as of ginger beer – in the pre-digital age. As we remember from having been children ourselves, in order to discover who you really are while you're growing up, and whether you're genuinely talented at something, it's no good setting yourself precisely thirty minutes to 'practise' your extra-curricular activity of the moment. That's the dismal term-time restriction. It's even worse if a parent is making you do the thirty minutes' practice and keeping an eye on the time. That's death to enthusiasm: torture by Suzuki. The urge needs to come from the child. A child needs to vanish deeply into whatever it is: to lose track of time passing: to sit at the piano, or read through a whole adult library, or work out the guitar chords, or write a first novel on lined paper, or build something, or dam something, or play with a bat and ball, for days and weeks on end, so that time itself becomes the vast landscape he or she lives in.

That total immersion was made possible during those long childhood summers of – as we'll see – astonishing levels of unaccounted-for time. What really happened inside those hours of which everyone lost track? And did those bare feet in ancient time really walk upon England's gravel drives and tarmac pavements for so long that by the end of the summer the bases of millions of small feet were as hard as paws or hooves?

Before any of this could start happening, the summer term itself needed to come to an end. This book opens with that glorious prospect.

PART I

SUMMER OPENS OUT

I

Summer Term Ends

A sort of ecstatic craziness took over in schools at the very thought of the approaching summer holidays. The excitement started building as soon as exams were over. It was as much as the staff could do to keep a lid on things.

For children, always hopeful that life is about to get better around the corner, the prospect of imminent release is even more intoxicating than release itself. L. P. Hartley put his finger on this phenomenon in *The Go-Between*, describing the moment when Leo Colston comes up to his dormitory and sees his trunk with its lid pushed back, its tray 'foaming with tissue paper in which were wrapped my lighter and more breakable possessions'. That, for Leo, was 'a supreme moment: nothing that came after it surpassed it in pure bliss'. In the sight of that packed trunk, the whole of a child's unalloyed optimism was encapsulated. It was pure anticipation of pleasure, untarnished by any reality.

That fictional scene took place in 1900; but in the non-fictional mid-twentieth century, summer-holiday-excitement reached just the same pitch. The daily drudgery was almost over. 'No more Latin, no more French, no more sitting on the old school bench', as the terrible rhyme went, chanted in playgrounds and corridors. There was a feeling in the air that life was about to change for the even-better (if you liked school) or for the infinitely-better (if you hated it).

Although every school had its official last day and moment of term, summer terms seemed to peter out towards their end, in the way a tarmacked road on the edge of a village peters out into a meadow. Windows were kept open during lessons, allowing the warm, scented air to waft in and mingle with the smell of chalk dust.

Teachers began to lighten up a bit – but the mid-twentieth century was a time when the purpose of school being in any way 'fun' had still not really occurred to most staff. So the young and the old were pulling against each other.

Hot weather in late June brought a tiny bit of loosening of the formalities. At boys' schools, the first sign that there might be any possibility of release came after half-term, when a notice went up on headmasters' noticeboards with the title 'SHIRT-SLEEVE ORDER'. 'From the Headmaster. From Monday 9th June, boys may come to school wearing shirts with the *top button only* undone, and wearing no tie and no blazer. Shirt-sleeves must be rolled up to *below the elbow*.' So limited were schools' concepts of relaxation that rolling up the sleeves was not an option. It was a rule.

Schoolteachers' ideas of lightening up were different from pupils' ideas of lightening up. Sports day was another of the teachers' ideas of lightening up: a day of ruthless competition to the sound of starting pistols. The athletes enjoyed it, but it was an ordeal for the smaller children who couldn't jump over a hurdle without knocking it over, or make much headway along the long-jump sand.

Meanwhile, in classrooms, it was time for a bit of classroom 'fun'. This was the time of year when schoolmasters and mistresses were given the brief freedom to stimulate their pupils with their own closet enthusiasms, whether for comic writing, bridge or cryptic crosswords. History masters who never normally showed any sense of humour started reading aloud from *1066 and All That*

and chortling over their favourite bits. Tired old maths masters –
some of them wearing gowns – came bumbling into the classroom
and organised arithmetical games, such as 'Fizz, Buzz, Miaow',
where you had to go round the class counting upwards and say
'Fizz', 'Buzz' or 'Miaow' instead of the number if it was a prime
number, divisible by three or divisible by five. Again, this was not
exactly fun, but it was fun compared with a normal maths lesson.
On blackboards, long-drawn-out games of hangman were played,
the mystery words reflecting the subject speciality of the setter:
'CONSTANTINOPLE', 'HYPERBOLE', 'PYTHAGORAS'.

The pupils longed to have lessons out of doors. Benign English
teachers took whole forms of excited pupils out onto the lawn for
a double lesson under a tree. No one listened. Everyone just made
daisy chains or tied the grass into knots. Any teacher who tried
to carry on teaching normal lessons after exams ('getting ahead
on next year's syllabus') was reviled.

It was in these few weeks of the year that boarding schools in
the middle of nowhere – places that had felt bleak, isolated and
imprisoning for the rest of the year – briefly turned into paradises
of midnight swims and tennis games at dusk, with the poplar
shadows lengthening across the courts.

Classroom windows gave a view onto the world everyone
yearned to be let out into. Post-war state schools, designed by
architects obsessed with plate glass, had windows going down to
the ground: ideal to gaze out of, but they made the heat inside the
classrooms in early July unbearable. In their sweltering classroom
at the Catholic primary school Our Lady of Mount Carmel in
Blacon, Cheshire, in the last week of the summer term of 1978,
the sweating nine-year-olds gazed out of the windows during Mrs
Hayden's lesson. 'She was furious that we weren't electrified by
her lesson,' the university lecturer Derren Gilhooley recalls. 'She
got a large piece of semi-opaque Fablon and stuck it all along the
bottom half of the windows. So we couldn't look out any more.'

That seemed a brutal act of daydream-snatching. Mrs Hayden

knew that if she lightened up too much, the whole system would implode.

The concept of 'mufti day' or 'no-uniform day' was another small gesture of lightening up that schools felt they could just about risk. In the sweltering heat of that classroom, Derren chose to wear his black velour jumper with '77' appliquéd on the front, 'because it was my favourite top and I wanted to wear it for all my life. I took my style cues from the presenters of *Tomorrow's World.*' He was boiling hot. The broadcaster Caroline Wyatt, on mufti day at her Primary School in Bangor, Northern Ireland, in summer 1976, wore (instead of the usual grey skirt, white shirt and stripy tie) a sleeveless cotton dress sewn for her by 'Nana Ward', her parents' former landlord in Chislehurst, who was an honorary grandmother to Caroline and made all her home clothes.

Mufti day, 1976. Caroline Wyatt outside her primary school in Bangor, Northern Ireland

Sensing that the hold these establishments had over them was loosening, pupils pushed the boundaries, and they did so more and more as the 1950s and 1960s turned over to the more anarchic 1970s. At the more innocent end of the boundary-pushing spectrum, convent girls became so overexcited that best friends had to be separated and put into different dormitories. At the less innocent end, a group of 1970s Benenden girls kidnapped the headmistress's West Highland White and dyed it pink. They were expelled for this. At Glenalmond in Perthshire, on the last morning of term in summer 1980, Mark Dunfoy recalled, a full food fight broke out in the dining room at breakfast, and spiralled out of control. 'It began when the fifty leavers turned the top table onto its side and used it as a barricade, from which they hurled their cornflakes bowls at the three hundred and fifty non-leavers. It escalated ten minutes later when the dinner ladies came in wheeling their trolleys laden with the main course: four hundred soft-boiled eggs.'

Behaviour on day-school buses became anarchic, the thuggier boys spitting great gobs of saliva onto the floor and bursting the lightbulbs. The sixth-formers at Nottingham High School in 1977 removed the wheels from the sweet but ineffectual chemistry master's car and padlocked it to the railings. There was a sense that civilisation was breaking down. The staff didn't want much more to do with these pupils; and their parents weren't much looking forward to taking them on.

At boarding schools in the dying days of the school year, boundary-pushing escalated. The seniors at Hatherop Castle climbed out of windows to meet the opposite sex and drink cider, or sometimes get pregnant, at the far corners of the tennis courts. Etonians, as the Scottish landowner Jamie Blackett recalled, climbed onto the roof of the school library. 'The convention was to leave something up there (such as a lavatory) to prove you'd been there.'

The only revenge the staff could take on rule-breaking

pupils – apart from expelling them – was to send them home with a long summer reading list that would haunt their summer. It was a futile gesture. Not a single book on those reading lists would be read, least of all *Moby-Dick*. Actually, I did chat to one man, the publisher Simon Winder, who, one summer, did sit down and read every book on the Westminster School reading list, 'just as an experiment'. It blew his mind.

School staff, at their wits' end trying to keep their pupils on the straight and narrow till the final day, needed to come up with tasks to keep everyone busy. The nuns at the Convent of the Holy Sepulchre near Hungerford in 1960 devised an ingenious outlet for harnessing their girls' frivolous energy. 'Each girl was given two blanket squares that they had to tie round the bottom of each foot with string', one Old Girl told me. 'Then, for the next hour, we were set to "sliding": cleaning the wooden floors of the vast Georgian house by sliding about on them with those blankets attached, spreading the floor polish that the nuns had tipped out of a tin.' It was a balletic scene.

Depending on how happy or unhappy you were at school, you didn't or did make a chart to count down the days, hours and minutes till the end. Children who were moderately happy made an 'end-of-term worm' out of coloured card, each segment denoting a day, and they cut a segment off each day till there was nothing left but the worm's head. Felicity Shimmin, miserable at Clarendon School in Abergele in Wales, strictly run by the Plymouth Brethren, kept a handmade chart inside the lid of her desk. 'I didn't just tick off the days; the colours with which I obliterated each day got brighter towards the end. I was just longing for warmth and comfort and being nurtured.'

*

For boarders, the imminent change from one life to another was particularly acute. Here is Elizabeth Millman, recording the final moments of summer terms at The Laurels near Rugby in her diaries

in the 1930s. It was a five-year diary, so on the same page she records
what she did on five consecutive 28 Julys from 1935 to 1939. The
handwriting gets more grown up each year. Note that summer terms
ended later than they do these days: the summer holidays lasted
from late July to late September.

28 July 1937: Packing day. Prayers in hall, then last singing.
Sad. Last call-over. Then pack. Then play tennis. Too hot.
Tea in the garden, ices. Weighing. I am 7 st 13 lbs. Last
drawing-room.

27 July 1938: End of term, school photo taken. Colours
given. I got school gym and dancing. Last mending in
common room. Last singing. Joanie Parker leaving, sad.
Tidied out desks. Weighing. I weigh 8 st 2 lbs. Last drawing-
room. Said goodbye to early people.

Last this, last that. It was as if you were about to die, which
in a way you were – to that life. Nothing would ever be the same
again, after Joanie Parker had left and you'd been through a whole
English summer.

The girls at the Laurels, in Rugby, around the time of the
end-of-summer-term weigh-in, 1937. Elizabeth Millman is
the girl in plaits, far left, second row from front

'Early people': those were the ones given special permission to leave a few hours early because they were going off by ship or primitive aeroplane to spend the summer with their parents in far-flung bits of the Empire. The Foreign Office and the British Raj paid for one journey home per child every two years.

Trunks were equated with homegoing to such an extent that they acquired a mystical aura of their own. The smell of the inside of a trunk would always be associated with the change of life from one existence to another. At Queen Mary's, Duncombe Park in Yorkshire, on the last night of term, the girls curled up to sleep inside their empty trunks. That was a symbolic act: to sleep in the container that represented going home, the 'vessels of salvation', as L. P. Hartley called them.

Schools differed in methods of giving out school reports. Some handed them out on the final day of term, which had the advantage of getting the agony over with. Others posted them to the parents a week later. For Jilly Cooper, just as she was properly settling down into the bliss of being at home, her life would be ruined because her school report arrived, reaching its long, nasty finger into her paradise. 'It was always terrible,' said Jilly. 'The reports said I was "horribly lazy, useless and disruptive". My parents took several days to forgive me.' It was less cruel to have 'closure' on the last day of term: a tricky meeting with your tutor in which he or she 'went through' your report with you, and you took it home to show to your parents, tearing out a page or two on the way, or changing a 'D' to a 'B' (the easiest of the letter changes).

*

The final morning arrived in the bare-walled schools. Chairs were put upside down on desks, blackboards given a final wipe, removing the last traces of gibbet beams. Only an hour to go: but nothing was over until the whole school had sung. Schools were clever to come up with this wheeze: they knew that communal

singing would lift everyone onto a higher plane and bind them
together. In boarding schools, the final sing-song usually took
place on the penultimate evening. Hilaire Belloc poems were
recited and specially written poems were read out, full of in-
jokes, and then everyone sang songs from *The Oxford Song Book*,
followed by the school song, and the jollity ended with 'Auld
Lang Syne', everyone trying not to cry as they said their final
goodbyes to the leavers.

In day schools, singing was a final-morning thing. 'And did
those feet in ancient time ...' could be heard coming from
red-brick halls across hot towns. It was a strange hymn, if you
thought about it. It began in mid-sentence with four questions
in a row, all of which would be given the answer 'no' if you took
them seriously, and then it went into a gearing-up-for-war passage, before building towards the climactic phrase 'Till we have
built Jerusalem'. No one did analyse the words. Sung to Parry's
setting, the elevated vocabulary of Blake's poem stirred up deep
patriotism and a sense of loyalty to the school that was about to
be said goodbye to.

At the boys' grammar school in Kirkham, Lancashire, which
Ian Skelly loathed, the final hymn was 'Lord, dismiss us with Thy
blessing'. At last, He was about to.

Then, after the distribution of last soiled items of lost property
scraped up from changing-room floors, and a short lecture by the
headmaster or mistress about how not to waste the summer – it
was all over. At Westminster School in the late 1940s, at the end
of the final service in Westminster Abbey, the organist let rip
with the final voluntary, which was, by tradition, 'The Teddy
Bears' Picnic'. The sound of that jaunty tune ringing out along the
Gothic vaulting was exhilarating for the boys walking down the
nave towards freedom.

At a 1950s end-of-term assembly, the headmistress of Clarendon
School, having seen girls exhibiting unseemly shows of emotion
when running to greet their parents, announced: 'Girls should

NOT rush across the courtyard into their parents' cars. Girls should be cool, calm and collected.'

Cool, calm – and collected at last. Unless they weren't. A child's worst dread – worse even than being the last to be picked for sports teams – was to be the last to be collected because your parents had either run out of petrol or put the wrong date in their diaries. It did happen that a forlorn child would sit on his or her trunk on the gravel long after all the others had left. 'I sat on my own in the drive of my prep school, Ludgrove,' said Jamie Blackett, 'very anxious because my parents were so late.' Parents were so out of touch with the daily lives of their children in those days that they did get the date wrong.

As soon as the parents arrived, you stepped seamlessly from one world into the other. 'The moment I got into my parents' car,' said Phoebe Fortescue (at St Margaret's, Bushy, in the 1970s) 'I took off my navy outer-knickers – the navy "bags" we had to wear – and waved them out of the window. We all did. No one could stop us. We were free.' The girls of St Leonards in Fife, crossing the Tay to go north or the Forth to go south, threw their hats into the river if they were leaving. It was a glorious sight, but if it was windy, which it usually was, the hats got caught in the spars of the bridges and stayed there.

One of the few personal items you'd been allowed at boarding school was a photograph frame or cube with photographs of your parents, your pets and your house. Everyone had spent hours during term-time gazing not only at their own photographs but at their friends' photographs. Starved of home, uncertain of their social status in the group, they needed to study those photographs to remind themselves of the other world that awaited them, and to fantasise and dream about the grander life they could be living. It was to their own houses that pupils were now returning: to a small house with dormer windows, or to a vast house with a portico, or to an urban or suburban house, or (for colonial children) to a funny looking house with a tin roof.

*The house with a tin roof that Steph Worsley
would be going home to*

Day pupils walked up the path, opened the door and arrived home, at an unusual time of day. It might not seem dramatic: some of them had done a paper round that very morning and would do another one tomorrow, as they in fact did on 364 mornings a year.

But it would be different, because British summer time had begun.

2

Stasis (1): Home, But Nothing Much Planned

You arrived home in a state of pre-summer excitement – and, slightly disconcertingly, no one took much notice. Your parents were pleased to see you but ten minutes later they expected you to vanish, so they could get on with their lives.

Entertainments weren't laid on. The division of each day into forty-minute periods with precisely timed breaks had dissolved away. It was hard at first to adapt to the new regime-less regime. Boys found themselves leaping out of bed at 7 a.m. and calling their fathers 'sir' at breakfast. Boarding-school girls found themselves frantically stripping their bed down to the mattress and folding the sheets on the bedside chair.

Time was suddenly handed to you in a vast chunk. What on earth were you going to do with it? Would the flatlining of the calendar be soul-destroying or liberating?

'Unpacked,' wrote Elizabeth Millman in her diary, on the day of arrival home in July 1935. 'Tidied room all afternoon. Tea in garden, wrote long letter to Auntie H. Listened to wireless.' Thus began weeks of muted, unplanned activity. 'Went for walk across fields with Anne and Jonathan. Game of tennis. Sewed.' 'Finished *Wuthering Heights*.' 'Finished lots of sleeve but ran out of wool.'

'Wrote reams to Annabel.' 'Last ride in JB343.' 'Read after breakfast, did gardening, mowed lawn.' 'Taught Rosemary to play chopsticks.' It didn't occur to her that she needed to be having a more exotic time. 'I didn't wake up every morning asking myself, "How am I feeling today?" I just got on with it.'

So this, as I mentioned in the prologue, was a particular kind of stasis. It did not mean 'physical inactivity' or 'torpor'. It meant a situation of staying local, with a vast amount of physical and mental activity built in. I call it 'kinetic stasis'.

Having been wrenched away from home after a rushed breakfast every morning of the school year, or having been forcibly removed from home for months at boarding school, you could bask, at last, in the fact that you were now allowed to stay put. 'One of the best things about those first days of the summer holidays,' said the counsellor Felicity Shimmin, 'was lying in bed and listening to the radio every morning. We weren't allowed to listen to any pop music at Clarendon School.' (This was the early 1960s.) 'Our father had died, and our mother was working as a psychiatrist, so my sister and I had the house to ourselves. We stayed in bed all morning and had what we liked for breakfast.' The bossy voices of their schoolmistresses receded into the distance – although Felicity found it hard to get rid of the witchy voice of her headmistress, who had written a letter to her mother saying, 'I'm afraid Felicity must have her hair cut. It's bad for the morale of the form.' She took particular pleasure in not getting her hair cut in the holidays.

The sudden silence was so deep you could hear it. A wasp buzzing at the window; a lawnmower in the distance; a ticking clock; but otherwise, silence after the din of term-time. 'I found it very hard, actually,' said Lucinda MacDougald, who came home from her jolly boarding school, St Michael's Burton Park, where she and her friends chatted and laughed their heads off non-stop, to the utter silence of home.

'A shaft of sunlight coming through onto the carpet in the drawing room of our house in Tunbridge Wells, and me just being there, reading at funny angles' was how Simon Winder summed up that silence. 'I waited for the television to come on at four. In fact, I put all the clocks in the house forward so I'd be allowed to switch it on before four.' That was a futile act, as there was still nothing to watch until Big Ben itself struck four.

Then, out into the fresh air you went. Through my many conversations, I deduced that the calibre of children's summers in the mid-twentieth century didn't depend so much on whether their family was rich or poor; it depended more on whether the doors were open or closed. Doors in the plural, that is: the back door and the front door. If they were open, whether they were doors onto private lawns and gravel drives, or onto back gardens and a street, those open doors spelled freedom.

The fewer possessions worth stealing, the more the doors were open, so it was the poorest who were the freest. Front doors in Belgravia and Knightsbridge weren't open all day. But in towns across the country, whole streets of front and back doors were open all day. Dwelling places were not boxed-in units. The open doors at both ends transformed them into havens with through-draughts in which to pause briefly for meals before going back out. Children spent their days in liminal spaces – 'liminal' meaning 'occupying a position at, or on both sides of, a boundary or threshold'.

To test this 'open-doors' theory, I interviewed two people from the extreme ends of the social spectrum, both born in the 1930s: Malcolm Innes, who was Lord Lyon King of Arms (Scotland's chief herald), and the long-serving former Labour MP Dennis Skinner, whose coal-mining father was sacked after the General Strike, until he got his job back a decade later. Those two men couldn't have had more different childhood summers: one in a fully staffed castle on a 7,000-acre estate in Aberdeenshire, the other in a tiny rented house in the coal-mining town of Clay Cross in Derbyshire. But, because the doors of both houses were open at front and back, all the time, both experienced that extraordinary freedom.

Dennis Skinner was running out of the open doors of his

house and up to the top of the slag heap, 300 feet, and back again, from the age of nine. 'I was running circuits round the backs of the houses – I fancied myself as a long-distance runner.' He was simultaneously building up political awareness: 'My friends were telling me that the royals had "blue blood" in them, and I was saying, "Don't be daft! Blue blood! It's the same colour as ours."'

Malcolm, having had his bedroom curtains drawn open by the housekeeper, was running out into the grounds and taking the goats from the stables to the field to graze. 'The front door wasn't even locked at night,' he told me. 'Even in our Edinburgh town house, our front door was left open all day and the inner door was not locked.' In Aberdeenshire, he spent all morning out helping the grieve (estate manager) with the milking and churning at the home farm. 'Two Italian prisoners of war were billeted with the grieve. My father invited them in for tea and cakes, and he always drove them to the Catholic Mass in Aboyne.'

Dennis went in to lunch with his mother who sang all day (songs such as 'Sally, Sally, don't ever wander away from the alley') as she washed and ironed, not only the family's washing but also Mrs Langley's washing from down the road. Malcolm, on hearing the gong ring, went in to lunch in the dining room prepared by Mrs Cheyne, the cook. 'A bottle of whisky was kept under the sideboard,' he told me, 'but it was only used on wasp stings and bee stings. I thought that was what whisky was for.'

Both interiors were places of kindness. Neither boy ever went abroad. Malcolm said, 'The Daimler was on bricks for the duration of the war and in the years after. The only way we could travel to the village was by tractor.' Dennis said, 'We never had any money for a day out.' He didn't see the sea till he was sixteen. He foraged for mushrooms and berries and knew where all the best places for foraging were. 'I could take you to them now.' Malcolm foraged in the fields for sheep's wool, which he put into sacks to be turned into socks by local knitters.

Malcolm said, 'We had complete freedom to wander – and no

governesses in the holidays.' Dennis, arguably, had even more freedom: for Malcolm, it was a two-mile walk down the private drive to
the village, whereas Dennis was interacting with the world beyond
the demesne, playing football and cricket on 'the welfare' – the two
pitches owned by the pits. Summing up his childhood, Dennis
said, 'Romantic past? Don't give me "romantic past". It was sheer
poverty.' Yet I sensed great spiritual and physical freedom in both
of those childhoods.

A minor burglary at Malcolm's Edinburgh house in 1953 ush-
ered in a new era of inner-door-locking when in town. But open
doors persisted for decades in working-class streets. The lost nor-
mality of whole streets of houses having their front doors open
all day long was reinforced to me when Frankie Devlin, ex-boxer
brought up in a Catholic street in Belfast in the 1950s and 1960s,
described the way things worked in those small houses sprawling
with children. 'No one came in to steal anything, because we all
had the same, that is, nothing. All the doors were open all day.
You'd go into any house and say, "My ma needs some milk" – and
all the mothers had big families and their breasts were full of milk,
and they'd just squirt a bit of it over you for a joke. That was till
the Troubles started. One day in 1971 – that was just after the first
soldier had been killed – a policeman came down our street and
said, "You must keep your front doors shut in the future." That
changed our whole lives.'

*

It was not only houses that had thresholds that you lived on
both sides of. Towns and villages did, too. Again and again, the
people I interviewed painted a picture of topographical infinity.
'Our garden backed onto a meadow with a stream at the bottom.'
'Our garden in Leigh-on-Sea backed onto the woods.' 'Our house
was at the edge of the village so we just went out to the meadow
at the back and stayed there all day.' 'Sheffield had these fingers
of green coming into it, so it was so easy to get out into the

wilderness.' Those back doors led into gardens, and those gardens had gates at the back of them which led onto meadows, which led onto streams – everything led onto something else, and you were allowed out into it, all day. These were the edgelands, before today's edgelands of business-park car parks. Houses were porous, and the gardens behind them were porous, with fences you could climb over into the garden next door. Towns and villages were porous, with children passing in and out of the boundaries.

Even in the middle of towns, far from the edges, there were bits of wasteland all over the place: patches of grass or back alleys, and children spilled out into these and played there unsupervised. A single eccentric feature, such as a small hillock of dried-out tarmac left by the pavement builder, became a focus for hours of entertainment.

If no grown-up had filled in the days for you by arranging official activities, you were thankful. No child looked forward to being landed with an unwanted cousin, or a French exchange girl or boy to entertain, with all the visits to museums that those acts of hospitality would make necessary. 'Punitive trips to the Shell Museum in Glandford', as the poet and children's author Kevin Crossley-Holland summed up those rare enforced excursions (although he did later add that the Shell Museum is well worth a visit).

Generally parents did not arrange such tiresome situations, or at least not until the end of the holidays. It was the convention that children should entertain themselves.

'We were thrown out onto the street.' 'We were thrown out onto the greensward of South Shields.' 'We were turfed out into the back alley.' Being thrown out was how gaggles of children found each other and stuck together. 'Our houses had just been built in 1946, for young families,' said the writer Valerie Grove (thrown out onto the greensward of South Shields). 'There was Rozzie, Anne, Mauveen, Tony and Edwin, and my sister Ali. We went around looking for horses to feed sugar-lumps to.'

The habit of being allowed out unsupervised started young: Susan Gardham in Hemsworth, Yorkshire, told me she was first sent down to the corner shop by her mother to buy sugar in 1954, when she was two and a half. 'My mother saw me across the road, and off I walked, down to Mr and Mrs Miles's shop.' She dutifully toddled back home, with the sugar.

From the age of four, it was normal to be out all day, intermingling with the world. 'We roamed around knocking on doors, asking whether we could take the baby out for a walk,' said Alice Allen, brought up in Newton-le-Willows in Lancashire in the 1940s. 'The mothers always said yes.' This was a symbiotic activity, beneficial to three age groups: the mother, the girls and the baby. It was an example of (to use Director of Civil Exchange Caroline Slocock's phrase) children being 'good social pollinators'. The girls did not expect payment for walking the babies. They mainly wanted to be seen taking a baby out in a high-end pram. 'My friend Margaret and I always wanted to take a baby out in a big Ascot pram,' said Alice. 'We always brought the baby back safe.'

It was the convention for parents to treat their children more like cats (allowed to go in or out as they pleased) than dogs (taken for walks).

'Didn't your mother ever take you on outings?' I asked one baronet's daughter.

'Certainly not! Our mother would have thought it rather déclassé to take her own children on outings. I mean, she might take the gardeners' sons for a day's outing to the zoo, but she wouldn't have dreamed of taking *us*.'

In towns and villages, the system of freedom to roam worked on trust, and on a network of children looking out for each other, with a bit of curtain-twitching from neighbours and sometimes a network of aunts who lived nearby and kept their eyes open for trouble. Susan Brown, brought up in Bradford in the 1940s, told me that at her father's draper's shop, Hartley's, net-curtain material was the top-selling item.

'Woe betide you if you weren't back in time for tea,' many recalled. Though few had watches, they knew instinctively when the tea-moment was, and it could be any time from 4 p.m. in the middle-class Home Counties to 10 p.m. in Orkney where it never got dark. 'I was embarrassed to be called in at five o'clock,' said Morag MacInnes, brought up in Stromness in the 1950s, where the children ran all day through the streets. 'Others would be out till goodness knows when. At midsummer you could play golf at midnight.'

*

It was amazing how fit you could get, officially going nowhere but in fact running everywhere. Here's an example of kinetic stasis in Scotland: 'I pictured myself winning Wimbledon and the Open Golf championship and climbing Everest,' said the retired businessman Charles Fraser, son of the manse at Hamilton, Lanarkshire, in the 1930s. 'I had incredibly active summers. After morning prayers and a cooked breakfast, I shinned up beech trees in our large garden and came back into the house, Mansewood, where the kind maids were getting lunch ready to the sound of the gramophone. During the war, twelve evacuees from Greenock came to stay with us. I thought they were great, although I could hardly understand a word they said. The tennis lawn made a great football pitch.'

This was Beanpole Britain: a nation of children who had not an ounce of fat on them because they were running around in the same place all day (after tea as well as before tea). 'If you'd had your tea,' George Oaks (farmer's son in Suffolk) said to me, 'the first thing you wanted to do was to go back out again.'

Everyone used the props available, to get better at things. If there happened to be a low wall in the garden, you'd get good at gymnastics. The BBC journalist Caroline Wyatt did. 'Our front garden had a red-brick wall along the front. The summer of 1976 was the first summer that I learned to do a handstand into a crab.

My friend Anne could do a cartwheel on the wall. She was my tall, thin, capable friend.' The two girls did gymnastics on that wall and in the local park all day, inspired by Bella the gymnast from 'Bella at the Bar' in the comic *Tammy*.

Caroline practising her handstands in the local park in Bangor

Caroline had been adopted by a diplomat father married to a Swiss nurse, both 'super, wonderful, lovely, kind'. Her mother was to die of illness in 1978, when Caroline was eleven, so that summer of 1976 lives, blazing, in Caroline's memory.

There was nothing glamorous about it, but, again, there was an overwhelming sense of freedom, and of free time, most of it spent playing in her front garden on a new estate in Bangor in Northern Ireland (thirteen miles from Belfast, so doors still open). The new houses weren't built to cope with the highly unusual heat. 'Next door had a small paddling-pool, so we piled into it and cooled down with the hose.'

The chief props of her urban freedom were (1) a gaggle of children living in proximity, and the parents 'having no idea where they all were'; (2) a nearby building site with a ruin on it 'said to be haunted'; (3) a half-built shed you were not meant to climb on; and (4) a stream running along the back of the gardens, from which you could fish out golf balls, sell them and buy sweets with the proceeds. Other groups of children had variations on these props.

Whatever you were doing, you did it interminably. There was nothing else to do except carry on doing what you were doing until you got good at it, or at least learned that you'd never get good at it. It might be pointless or thankless activity. For Ben Thomas (now principal of Thomas's Schools), it was lying on the grass at the edge of the stream in his grandparents' garden all day, trying to catch minnows in a jam jar. 'I caught a minnow about three times in two weeks.' For Jenefer Tatham, in Sidmouth during the war, it was dressing up a litter of real kittens in her doll's clothes, lining them up in the pram and taking them out for a walk, or at least trying to. For Jackie King, in Jersey, it was 'writing words on marrows, such as "I am the greatest" – Muhammad Ali's catchphrase – and seeing the letters gradually growing huge over the days as the marrows grew'. All these occupations were surprisingly educational about the behaviour of flora and fauna, while seeming to be thankless. They certainly taught these people patience and perseverance.

Such freedom – and the boys carried knives. I found it surprising, as a twenty-first-century dweller in a city riddled with youth knife crime, that in Arthur Ransome's *Swallows and Amazons*, as a reward for learning to swim, Roger's mother gives him 'a knife with a good big blade'. Knives were viewed as improving, wood-whittling or rope-cutting tools, something every boy should carry.

*

This picture of the British landscape thickly populated with small children running wild grew more convincing, the more I talked to people. So many people's first comment about their summers was 'we were allowed to roam free' or 'we ran wild'. They can't all have been making it up – although memories are selective and edited according to a person's natural optimism or pessimism. (I learned to separate the optimists from the pessimists with the Weather Question. Some who spent their childhoods in Scotland said to me, 'I can't remember a single rainy day.' Others said, 'I can't remember a single day when it wasn't raining.')

But physical freedom was the overriding memory. Some told me that their parents, who themselves had been brought up under Victorian house arrest, gazing longingly out of windows and yearning for freedom and comfortable clothes, made it their business to give their children the freedom they had been denied. This was the case for Alice Renton, tomboy in wartime Ayrshire. 'My mother believed girls should do everything that boys did – she had felt deprived of freedom herself as a child. I wore shorts, or my brothers' cast-off kilts. I refused to wear a skirt. My mother gave me a 2.2 rifle when I was eight. I shot rabbits – my grandfather gave me a penny for every rabbit's tail I brought to him. I crawled through the rhododendron bushes in the evening at the side of the fields, shooting them when they came out to graze. It was such fun.'

Alice's friends (like Charles Fraser's) were 'the Vacs' – the evacuees from Glasgow, Jessie, Nellie, Cathy, Ina and Chrissie, among others – who lived on the top floor of the vast house. All the children roamed around in a gang, making two-storey houses in the rhododendron bushes. Alice quickly adopted their Glaswegian accent. 'I was summoned to the drawing room one day because I'd misbehaved. My mother said, "Go to bed now." I replied, "Ah'm no' frens wi' youze."'

'I have a vision of golden summers,' Alice said. 'All out of doors, doing things by ourselves, with gun, rod and pony. Terrific freedom.'

In happy homes, that freedom was life-enhancing, but for those growing up in less-than-happy homes, such as Caroline Slocock, it was life-saving. Caroline's parents in the 1960s were going through a nasty separation, and there was a lot of anger as well as a sudden lack of money. 'My mother cried when the electricity bills arrived,' Caroline said. 'My attic bedroom was insulated with metallic plates from my parents' printing business – they'd run *Wimborne News* in central Wimborne together, and splitting up had taken away my mother's job. It was like having her heart ripped out. She went to work as a secretary. We had very few possessions. What we did have, though, was the immense richness of the garden, which we could get out of by climbing over a fence, and we went into the fields down to the river, which I did from the age of five. I worry that children in unhappy homes nowadays can't get out.'

*

There could be a surprisingly wide radius for the kinetic stasis. Bikes (ideal vehicles for travelling for miles without officially going anywhere) were the chief enablers of this phenomenon.

It was rare for your bike to fit you. It was either too large, so you had to stand on the pedals or fix blocks of wood onto them to reach them from the saddle, or too small – the bike you'd had last summer when you were tiny. 'All the bikes in the Old Laundry were adult bikes, much too big,' said Ann Lindsay, daughter of a tenant farm manager in Aberdeenshire, where the children had the run of a huge estate in the 1950s, and where (Ann said) 'washed-out pale pink was the colour of my summers – the washed-out pale pink of Elastoplast, and Germolene, and the gravel at Laurencekirk station, and the bras hanging in the laundry room.' She said, 'I never learned to sit on a bike. We just stood on the pedals and freewheeled down the drives, which were both a mile long.'

Bikes were things you tended not to buy new: you had them handed down if you were lucky. A few people told me they were given a bike – 'I got a bike as a present for passing my 11-plus,' said Susan Brown. But mainly, they arrived in your life in a rusty state. If you were not lucky but were good with your hands, you made your own. Here's retired miner Ian Oxley, born in 1945 into a mining family in South Kirkby, near Pontefract:

'My bike was a "BSA". That officially stood for "Birmingham Small Arms", but for us, "BSA" stood for "Bits Stuck Anywhere". I found two old wheels lying in the road, and a frame in a shed, and I worked at the florist and earned 7s. 6d. a week so I could buy a couple of tyres. I found a rusty old chain at the bottom of a stream. I went into my mam's pantry – everyone had a basin they kept the fat in. I put the chain into a pan with the fat, warmed it gently and the fat got into the rust and I made the chain work again, with a repair link from Hutt's garage.'

Having made the bike, eleven-year-old Ian and his friend Johnny Owen cycled 'all the way to Doncaster', twelve miles away on the Great North Road, 'taking treacle sandwiches. The treacle soaked into the bread and it tasted lovely. We actually saw lorries. We collected the number plates: they were that rare.' They're still best friends.

Paradoxically, it was almost *because* self-improvement wasn't the purpose that it became the result. An eleven-year-old quietly worked out the deep physics of how to build a bike. Everyone was getting better at something without anyone telling them to.

Unsupervised and not hovered over, Peter Susman (now a QC) was cycling all over London by the age of ten. Ben Thomas, at the age of eight, was cycling up and down his street in Chelsea as usual when he became so intrigued to work out how the marching band 'turned the corner' in formation on its way to Buckingham Palace for the Changing of the Guard that he followed the band all the way there. 'I got lost on the way back and asked a policeman. He didn't take me home: he just pointed the way.' No one worried. 'Trainspotting and church-crawling on a bike became a fixed habit,' said the historian Nicolas Barker, who grew up in

Cambridge during the war. 'My first solo expedition, in 1943, when I was eleven, was to a place nine miles away between St Neots and Huntingdon, where I could watch the Scotch Express on the main line: there's one point where you could see for two miles, so you got the prospect of the train coming towards you. The siren went as I cycled along and I hid in a wood. I heard gunfire sounds, and there was a piece of shrapnel in my bicycle basket when I came back.' Shrapnel – along with the jam sandwiches and the notebook to record the numbers of trains.

The other chief vehicle for kinetic stasis was the pony. When Jilly Cooper summed up her childhood summers with the words 'the incredible freedom to roam', she meant on horseback. 'I said goodbye to my mother and got on my pony, Willow, and went off for the whole day. My mother didn't expect me back until seven. I liked to have the pony's gymkhana rosettes on the nearside so everyone could see them as I trotted back home through the streets of Ilkley.'

Jilly Cooper with her brother Timothy, her pony Willow, and their dog Simmie, in 1948

'Our grandmother's only rule,' said riding coach Lucinda Sims, who was allowed to ride bareback from morning to dusk, 'was that the ponies must be brought back calm and not sweating. The worst thing you can do is to come back from a ride with an overheated, mad horse.' 'My sisters and I would go off on our ponies for a whole day,' said the artist Miranda Johnston, 'taking the dachshund with us on a long lead.'

Freedom came with danger. This was not a world without its dark and tragic sides.

'There were proper flashers in those days, with raincoats,' said writer Libby Purves, who grew up in Walberswick in Suffolk in the 1950s. 'They would open their mac and show you their erection. We failed to be traumatised.' The university administrator Abby Scott, who spent her early 1970s summers on a council estate in Harlow hanging around on the tops of garages plaiting her friends' hair, said, 'Endlessly there was this bloke saying, "Let me get in your knickers". He was known as a kiddy-fiddler. His phrase was, "If you don't shut up, Jim'll fix it for you."' Which dates him, as *Jim'll Fix It* started in 1975, and the fiddler was more accurate than he knew in his appropriation of Jimmy Savile's euphemism. The classic retort from the children to this kind of advance, Abby said, was, 'You pervert!' Evelyn Armstrong, now a retired teacher, said there were men exposing themselves all over the place in Saltcoats in Ayrshire in the 1960s, inviting you to their houses, which you learned to decline. 'We were out solving our own problems,' she said. Nor was it only out on the streets that dirty old men were up to their tricks. I asked Lizie de la Morinière whether, during her teenage summer holidays from the boarding school Hatherop Castle, she'd had any boyfriends, and she said yes, she'd done a fair bit of flirting and frolicking in the hay bales with the high-born sons of her parents' friends. That made a change from the swarthy village boys (known as 'the VBs') who were the only males on offer in the grounds of her school. 'But the main problem,' she said, 'was the dirty-old-men friends of my father offering to "give me a swimming lesson" and then grabbing my bottom and propelling me up and down the swimming pool. I was chased around the garden by several of my father's friends. I just ran away as fast as I could.'

Meanwhile, in gardens and on streets, accidents happened all the time. Scabs, bruises and scars were notched up as tokens of fearlessness. People showed me great gaps in their mouths where their teeth had been knocked out by heavy swings on long chains or by falling out of trees. Children fell off climbing frames onto the gritty tarmac and had the bones in their feet pulverised by seesaws that thumped down to the ground with the full force of gravity as soon as the person at the other end got off. One person I spoke to said a friend of his had been seriously injured on a trainspotting outing, when he fell off a bridge while hanging down, trying to read the number on a passing train.

And children died. *Guardian* writer Joanna Moorhead's childhood was torn into two halves on one idyllic, blue-skied day in Whitefield, Manchester, in July 1972, when she was eleven. Her four-year-old sister Clare had just got out of the paddling pool at a friend's house and was crossing the road in her swimming costume with her group of little friends when she – and only she – was run over by a passing van. She died the next day. Joanna told me, 'I vowed never to trust a clear blue sky or a sunny day again, and indeed I never have.'

3

Stasis (2): Playing

'There were good games, and there were *bad* games,' said the Revd Dr Giles Fraser, priest, theologian and *The Moral Maze* panellist – and admirably honest about his and his brother's childhood 'bad games', one of which was to put a worm onto a large leaf and set it off across a lake.

When I asked him to expand on 'My brother and I would just leave the house and go and bugger about', he mentioned the good and the bad games. 'We made *good* versions of cricket: if you hit the shed you got three points, if the ball went into this flowerbed you were out.' For the bad games, 'we found imaginative ways to kill wasps and worms. There was definitely a bit of the psychopath in us, especially with wasps.'

Unwatched, and with 'boredom the mother of invention', as Giles put it, swathes of loose children were playing out their dark fantasies. These were acted out not on screens, but for real. In the post-war period there was still a lot of 'working out the trauma' going on, and this provided an excuse for children to experience the frisson of inflicting cruelty or having it inflicted on them. 'My friend Chris's father,' said Ali O'Neale, 'had been a prisoner of war under the Japanese; he'd worked on the River Kwai and had been starved, and he walked with a limp. Chris's brother Colin made us run behind his bike tied to a rope until we were exhausted. Or he tied us to a pine tree in the garden and lit a fire under our feet. Or he dug a hole and dropped us into a pit.' During the Troubles in Northern Ireland, Caroline Wyatt and her friends played 'Soldiers and IRA', 'and I always had to be a soldier, being a Brit'.

Playing always went further than it did in the *Janet and John* books. You'd be innocently playing in a treehouse and suddenly find that your brother had kicked the ladder away so you were imprisoned 'in Colditz' for the rest of the day. 'My brother used to tie me and my sister down to the cattle grid – we were spreadeagled down there, waiting for the next oncoming car,' said Heathfield Old Girl Bolla Denehy. This was seen as a perfectly normal act of play.

'Slaves' was another favourite game: someone goading a whole retinue of underlings, flicking a whip. Even in a game as innocent sounding as 'schools', there was always a dominant child who assumed the role of sadistic teacher, bullying and terrifying her victims. It was a jungle out there.

For horsy girls, the outlet for sadism was to play show-jumping games: creating an arena of jumps with bamboo sticks over flowerpots, and with one of them over the goldfish pond (that was 'the water jump'). 'We put ropes round our friends' necks, with reins made of old washing line, and made them jump the jumps,' as Ali O'Neale recalled. (Not 'asked' them to jump the jump: made them.)

Children were creating ammunition out of nature and using it to shoot other children in the eye. Suffolk farmer's son George Oaks drew me a diagram: take an elderberry branch two inches thick, push the pith out, get a piece of hazel to make the handle, shave it with your penknife so it would go through the middle. Get acorn, cut acorn in half. One half in far end, one half in the other end, and you had a compressed air gun.

It was not done to show fear – 'not even,' as Jackie King

recalled, 'when you were being chased by Christopher Martin-Jenkins with his sheath knife'. 'We sat on a roller skate with an annual on it and cascaded down the steep road,' said Evelyn Armstrong: a typical fearless pastime. You were a 'chicken' if you were too much of a chicken to play the game called 'playing chicken'. On an unsupervised camping trip in Ireland in the 1970s, Mark Dunfoy and his eleven-year-old friends, having been dropped in a field by Mark's father and left to fend for themselves for four days, 'played chicken' for hours, first by aiming knives and then by hurling axes at each other. Then, pulling out the wooden fencing round the field for firewood, they built a bonfire so enormous and hot that they couldn't get anywhere near it to cook the supper.

A favourite game of Ben Scrimgeour and his brother (aged thirteen) was to take turns driving their grandfather's battered old disused car round and round the field at high speed with the windows open: the aim was to score a 'goal' by kicking a ball through an open window as the car careered past, skidding.

Games were physical, violent, cruel, dangerous, varied and long-drawn-out. Everyone was being dramatically and brutally toughened up.

In urban settings, after a satisfying morning of laying trails of footprints in wet concrete on building sites, and dirtying other people's washing on the line, children went around knocking on doors and running away. Whether this game was called 'knock-down ginger' (as it was in London) or just 'knock and run', as it was everywhere else, it was the scourge of towns and cities, along with the other favourite game, 'stealing the milk money'. Even in 1950s Stromness, where you might have thought the children would be playing sweetly in the heather, they were in fact divided into three gangs: the North-Enders, Middle-Towners ('Middle-Tooners') and South-Enders, all trying to capture each other, and 'dreeping' (sliding) down the sides of buildings. 'The South-Enders had a reputation for being the real toughies,' said

Morag MacInnes. 'They were not playing in the heather but setting fire to the heather.'

The most-played games in Stromness, Morag said, were ones passed down from the Vikings: one was called 'Knifey', where you threw your open knife between the other person's legs and then threw it to the side of them and they would have to reach where it landed. (I was disappointed that no blood was shed in this rather tame-sounding Viking game.) Another was throwing stones in the air and catching them in the back of your hands: a kind of Viking 'jacks'.

Children were hurling themselves off walls and over the brows of hills, convinced they would be able to fly. 'My mother spotted us out of the window,' said Elfrida Eden (who spent her summers living in the school her parents ran in the New Forest) 'on a high wall, holding two corners of a sheet, intending to parachute. We jumped off, and we were somehow so relaxed and trusting that we didn't injure ourselves.' Edward Hall, theatre director son of Sir Peter, did injure himself. 'At the age of seven I was very excited about the idea of flight. With a straw waste-paper basket and a sheet I made a parachute. That took two hours of very focused work. I squished myself into the waste-paper basket on top of a chair on top of the table in the playroom. I remember the shock of hitting the ground *so* hard. In my mind there had been no doubt that I was going to float gently down.'

This was accidental self-education.

*

In through roads and cul-de-sacs, street furniture provided playing props. End-of-terrace windowless walls were ideal for rhythmic ball-throwing: 'Betty Grable is a star: S-T-A-R!' was the example Susan Brown gave me from her 1940s Bradford child-hood, 'the air full of the smell of lanolin from the woollen mills and the clatter of the looms'. Paving stones laid in hopscotch-ready formation removed even the need for chalk. A small dip in the road with an old puddle in it enabled weeks of repeated cycling stunts.

Along with 'sitting on the curb, watching the tar melt as entertainment' in their 1970s cul-de-sac in Oxford, Colin Burrow, now a Fellow of All Souls, and his brothers used to 'see if we could get from one end of the road to the other on our bikes without turning a single pedal. You were allowed to kick off once, but you had to do the rest by swinging your legs.' It was surprising how many hours of fun could be got out of such a simple and pointless challenge.

Children did a great deal of 'playing round the lamp-post'. This happened in (for example) Random Street in Alexandria, near Glasgow, where former Primus of the Scottish Episcopal Church Richard Holloway grew up in the 1930s and 1940s. 'I was a pale Scottish child and I got sunstroke from playing out,' said Richard. (So, a Scottish-weather optimist.) 'There was hardly any traffic – just occasionally the horrible van that emptied the dry lavatories and left a trail of brown damp.' I pressed him on exactly what game you 'played round a lamp-post' – you couldn't swing from it, surely, without smashing your whole body into it – and he admitted he couldn't be more specific, except to say that they did play round it, well into the evening, in the days when gas lamps didn't banish the darkness but just provided pools of light in the darkness. I think it was really just chatting round the lamp-post, attracted by its light. 'I told my friends stories about films I said I'd seen but hadn't – I'd just seen the advertisements for them in the paper.'

Back lanes were good playing zones, even if they reeked of the rubbish in the bins. Neil Herron, who grew up in Cooperative Terrace, Sunderland (and who in 2008 would become a champion of the Metric Martyrs who'd been arrested for daring to sell fruit by imperial weights), described a 1960s playing paradise in the back lane behind Cooperative Terrace. Cricket and football were enhanced by having Paul Pang, an all-round sportsman and son of the local Chinese takeaway owners, living further down the street.

'A dustbin was the wicket,' Neil said. 'It was six and out if the ball went over someone's wall. Straight back past the bowler or wicket-keeper was best. With Paul Pang there, we could have an international cricket match in the back lane. We bought a Chinese takeaway supper from the Pangs' takeaway every Friday evening after my dad came back from his two pints at the working men's club. My mother wasn't into anything exotic – she'd have the omelette and chips.'

Football was if anything even better, as Paul Pang was better at football than cricket. 'One of the garages was exactly the shape of a goal, and there was a streetlight next to it, so we could play late into the evening.'

With the limitations of it not being advisable to hit a ball over a wall, boys developed venue-specific skills. 'Smash a window and you got a minus-score,' said Archbishop of York Stephen Cottrell, brought up in Leigh-on-Sea.

*

If you went out of your back door rather than the front door, the entertainments were more muted, hemmed in by home rules about what you were and weren't allowed to throw at what. In back gardens with low walls into the next gardens, children did what they could with the props provided. They built dens against the back fence, with three chairs and a sheet.

'Home was dreary,' said the historian Juliet Gardiner, brought up in 1950s Hemel Hempstead by unloving adoptive parents, 'but I did have my friends Susan and Sandra round to play, and cousins came and visited. We had a tin bath in the garden that my father had filled with the hose. We just sat in it, aged six, seven and eight. I longed to have a dog but we had a tortoise. We'd drilled a hole into the tortoise's shell and tied it to a meat skewer on a long string so it could go round and round in a large circle.'

*Juliet Gardiner and her cousins playing in the back garden
in Hemel Hempstead. (Tortoise out of shot)*

No one was scintillated, not the children and not the tortoise.
In 1960s photograph albums I've seen photographs of girls as old
as sixteen sitting in paddling pools in back gardens, while their
fathers read the newspaper in a deckchair. They weren't going on
holiday any time soon, and this was as close as they were going to
get to any sense of being in a resort. Someone would eventually
get up and put up the badminton net (homemade with a length of
strawberry netting), and they plick-plocked the shuttlecock over it
for a while. There was always one damaged shuttlecock that didn't
fly properly and made a muffled thud.

There was a remarkable lack of expensive toys. The only
bright-red modern item of playing furniture in 1970s gardens was
the partially deflated space hopper (introduced into the UK in
1969) – perhaps the most optimistic name ever for a toy. A large
balloon-shaped object designed to be sat on, it lifted you just a few
inches off the ground before plummeting down under your weight
plus the pull of earth's remorseless gravity.

If you happened to get on well with your siblings or to have 'James from across the road' or 'Susan from round the corner' to play with, your summers were vastly enhanced. You were lucky if (like Valerie Grove's), your parents had thoughtfully bought a house on a new estate especially because it was 'full of young families'. As a young child in Causeway Head near Stirling in the 1950s, Ali O'Neale had no friends and nothing to do except 'sit on the pavement all day playing with stones'. When she was eleven the family moved to Bridge of Allan, and at last she had friends and bikes. The fun started: as well as playing Japanese prisoners of war, they played cowboys and Indians, preferring the Indians, painting their faces and drawing red circles round their nipples and cycling to the grocer's. Two years later they moved to Dunblane: 'only three miles away but might as well have been three hundred. I was removed from all my friends and couldn't go and see them as there were no buses and my mother couldn't drive.'

*

Just as gardens and roads had side bits, back bits and hidden bits to play in, so did the interiors of houses. Corridors became bowling alleys, landings became the domestic equivalent of village greens – common ground for everyone to play on, where no one felt territorially threatened.

With his friend Nick who lived 'in the white house with the flat roof across the road' on Straight Road in Colchester, the journalist Giles Smith played the football game of Subbuteo on the landing for days and weeks of his 1970s summers. He took me through the intricacies of the game, and reminded me of the deep immersion such games could suck you into.

'Subbuteo was played on a cloth pitch that needed to be laid down on top of another carpet of exactly the right consistency to prevent it from slipping or rucking up. Wood or tiles would have been a nightmare, and the brown shag-pile carpet in my bedroom would also have been hopeless. The landing had the right kind of carpet – a cheap, hard, nylon, shallow one – and there was just enough space to spread out the pitch, although it didn't leave much room round the edge, 'so you were constantly kneeling on players and breaking them'. (More than one ex-Subbuteo addict I spoke to recalled the 'broken' players in their sets, who then had to be thought of as the 'disabled' players.)

The teams were tiny models, all standing in exactly the same pose on round-bottomed, button-shaped bases: 'perhaps they *were* buttons,' said Giles. 'The ball was ludicrously out of scale, coming up to the players' chins. You didn't flick the ball with finger and thumb – that would have sent it shooting off into the bathroom; you flicked it with just your forefinger – a subtler movement than a flick. If the ball hit the base of an opposing player, you lost possession.' Goal-scoring was never an act of surprise: you announced your intention of shooting by saying 'Shot!', which gave your opponent time to go round and control his goalkeeper, who was attached to a long stick, from behind the net.

This was another case of developing venue-specific skills. The boys contorted themselves on that small landing and spent hours perfecting their flicks. 'We were developing wild skills to make our players swerve round the obstruction of the opposing player and pick up the ball on the other side of them. More than any spectacular goals, it was that swerve of a player round another that was the extreme skill. We spent a lot of time practising on our own.'

Giles's family lived ten miles from the sea, but they only went to the seaside for one day per summer holidays, to visit some friends who had a beach hut at Walton-on-the-Naze. Their existence of nothing-much-planned and not-going-anywhere was brought home (literally) to Giles one Saturday morning, when his father went out to the front garden to photograph the traffic jam. 'People were heading for the coast and Colchester Zoo in unusual numbers, and my father went out to take a photo of it.

It is, in some ways, the most poignant holiday snap in the family album: a picture of other people heading off to have summery fun while we stayed at home.'

Giles's street in Colchester
on a normal (non-traffic-jam)
summer's day

The bliss of summer stasis:
Giles's father, Alan Smith,
happily not travelling anywhere

In his whole childhood, the family only went on holiday twice, once to Cornwall and once to Somerset. For weeks, they were just at home – and happily so. They liked the stasis. The detached house had a garden big enough to kick a ball in, and there was a large enough windowless patch of back wall to hit a Slaz ball against. 'Slaz balls mimicked the properties of a tennis ball but were made of foam so they weren't as destructive. They radically changed the whole world of hitting a tennis ball against the back of a house.'

'Were you bored?' I asked Giles.

'I don't recall being bored. I recall being under-occupied, but it wasn't like boredom.'

Thus it was, in houses on straight roads everywhere in those days of extended periods of non-travel. Full records of the dates, matches and half-time and full-time scores of those Subbuteo games were kept in exercise books. There was ample time to play whole seasons with your imagined teams, thinking yourself into the players' minds.

This was the borderline where 'playing' became as much about the mind as the body. The life of the mind is the subject of the next chapter – and developing the mind during those summers was about far more than just reading books.

4

Stasis (3): The Life of the Mind

A game of cricket in the back garden is just playing. But if you're imagining you're 'being' England versus the West Indies, acting the part of each of the players in turn, that's the life of the mind. For siblings living in close proximity for whole summers, that life-of-the-mind version of playing was a useful ploy for defusing competitiveness. If you were 'being' a bad or boring player, you positively tried to play badly or boringly. If you were being someone you didn't like, you deliberately got yourself out. Whole games, whole series, were acted out, everyone talking non-stop in the accents of the players. This was a mixture of sport and 'improv'.

Away from school, with nothing to watch on television apart from the never-to-be-finished noughts-and-crosses games on the Test Card F (first broadcast in 1967), children had ample time to escape into scenarios like that, and to live inside them. Thus, minds were shaped and imaginations honed.

Reading was the fastest way to escape into someone else's scenario, and comics were the quickest way of reading. You could just curl up and drop out. *Battle Picture Library* addicts, such as Peter Witchlow in Plumstead in the 1960s, spent their summers absorbed in graphic war scenarios with speech bubbles: 'Gott im Himmel, Englander, for you ze war is over!'

The *Beano* and the *Dandy* were both selling two million copies a week in the 1950s. The day when the comic you were addicted to landed on the mat was the best day of the week. Summer was the best season, because the Summer Specials came out: a bumper edition to see you through August. Jamie Buxton, ex-comic addict brought up in Lincolnshire in the 1960s, said that for him comics were far from ephemeral: 'I read and reread them and they became dog-eared, in the way that my daughter would later watch and rewatch *Friends*: with addiction and total devotion to the characters.'

Parental disapproval helped. Grown-ups fretted that comics were rotting their children's brains, lacking as they did the essential element of prose in proper paragraphs. Nor did they like the violence – the endless 'pow', 'wham', 'bam', 'biff' and 'ooh-yah'. Jamie disagrees about the brain-rotting: 'There's an inbuilt assumption that words are somehow "better" than pictures, but I don't buy that. Comic strips in some ways do things better than prose. Reading stimulates the imagination, but pictures feed it, and sometimes that is just what you want. Sometimes, especially in the lazy summer holidays, you just wanted to gorge.' As for the violence, 'boys like violence because it echoes their real life. Schooldays are the most violent time of your life. I wanted the baddies to be punished – imprisoned or blown up. I craved the satisfaction of seeing justice done.' 'Seeing' being the operative word, as there was a picture of it happening.

Comics started to merge in a dispiriting way for their addicts in the 1960s. *Girls' Crystal* merged with *School Friend* in 1963, and *School Friend* then merged with *June* to become *June & School Friend*. *Scorcher* merged with *Score* to become *Scorcher & Score*, and then that merged with *Tiger* to become *Tiger & Scorcher*. It was hard to keep up.

Books enabled you to escape with more parental approval: to sink into deep, immobile, antisocial absorption. A bookworm wasn't any fun to be around, as Rachel Johnson recalls. 'We desperately wanted our elder brother Boris to play with us, but he just said, "Let's play reading".'

The discovery that there was not just one Willard Price Adventure novel but fourteen in the set, not just one Mallory Towers book but six, not just one *Jill and her Pony* book but nine, not just one *Doctor Who* novelisation but sixty, not just one Agatha Christie murder mystery but eighty-two, brought relief to those who had both insatiable story-hunger and a collecting urge. Their twin dreads were running out of reading matter and not completing the set. This was binge-reading in the age before binge-watching. Peter Susman, aged fourteen, listed more than 100 books he'd read in 1956, including those by Somerset Maugham, Evelyn Waugh, C. S. Forester and Joseph Conrad. 'I'm well known for having an enormous number of facts in my head,' he told me as we sat in his flat in the Inner Temple. 'People have said, "What about feelings, Peter?"'

Children curled up in contorted positions, oblivious, reading in trees, under trees, on window seats, on deckchairs, under the arm of the sofa or in bed with a torch. The books were by no means always novels. 'I read my way through my father's whole childhood collection of bound copies of *The Boy's Own Paper*,' said Joanna Barker. 'There were really good experiments, such as "how to make gunpowder".' 'My pride and joy,' said Miranda Johnston, was *The Reader's Digest Book of the Countryside*.' 'My grandmother had given me *The Hamlyn All-Colour Cookbook*,' said Debora Robertson, 'and I studied it hard and spent all summer cooking from it: banana curry, quiche and vol-au-vents.'

Rereading seemed a valid approach to the world of literature. No one was stopping you from going back to the beginning as soon as you reached the end. Repeat-readers grew up knowing a great deal about a little, while new-material readers knew a little about a great deal. As we'll see later, the 'repeat' urge extended to holiday destinations.

Libraries were a godsend to the voracious readers, some growing up in bookless households, who were allowed into the adult section at a young age by kind librarians (and there were legions of them) who empathised with their thirst to move up. Rowan Williams, the former Archbishop of Canterbury, told me he went through books so fast that he had to go back to the library in Swansea for new ones not once a week but once a day, in order to quench his thirst for history and mythology.

I met two people whose families had been so bookish that all of them – parents and children alike – read in silence during mealtimes. One was Anne McMullan's family, in Hampstead Garden Suburb in the 1960s and 1970s, a quiet domestic paradise with seventeen guinea pigs. 'We came in from the garden for supper, got our books out at the table, and read.' The other was the biographer Philip Ziegler's family, in the New Forest in the 1930s. 'As a family we all read at mealtimes. We each had a bookrest at our place at the table. I was amazed when I went to visit families and they didn't read during meals. My father always put on a velvet smoking jacket for dinner. He had a passion for Henry James novels. He was a slow eater. He would pick up a tiny bit of food on his fork, and it would drop off, and he put the fork into his mouth and looked slightly baffled. So meals were a rather long-drawn-out process.'

Long-drawn-out – and silent. 'Did you make conversation with each other?' I asked.

'Only if you had something important to say. You were interrupting family reading.' It's a habit Philip has kept up all his life. 'Both my wives reacted with some horror to my habit of reading at the table, but they came round to it.'

Did reading inspire the way you lived? It did. Devouring adventure novels reminded you that, compared with the characters in the novels, you weren't having an exciting enough time.

The fictional scenarios became a template for what you ought to be doing. Tara Odgers (now a civil servant in the Ministry of Defence), having read *Swallows and Amazons* during one late 1970s summer, set about building a raft of her own and trying to float it on the moat of the house of some friends. She managed to fix four plastic barrels onto an old door with some netting. 'And, amazingly, it floated.'

Tara Odgers (left) with her father, her sister Octavia, and the Swallows and Amazons-inspired raft that floated

Jayne Ozanne, who grew up in Guernsey and is now a leading campaigner for LGBTQ+ rights in the Church of England, modelled herself entirely on the tomboy George in the *Famous Five* books. She and her friend Simon ran wild across their corner of Guernsey, a sort of Famous Two, building a den with a periscope in the hayloft, re-enacting the wartime Resistance on the Channel Islands, running into maize fields to get lost on purpose, and jumping off the harbour wall when the tide was high 'so it was like jumping off a two-storey building'. That was the life of the body – but also the life of the mind, because they were 'being' the Blyton characters. 'I was a really good Number 2 to Simon,' Jayne said. 'It was the healthiest relationship I've ever had.'

Literature reinforced the idea that islands were exciting. If there was a real island in sight, even just a sandy hummock in the middle of a lake or pond, everyone wanted to sail to it and spend the night on it. The allure of islands – the sense that they were unclaimed, ungoverned wildernesses where you would be cut off from the rest of the world with its parent-imposed mealtimes and conventions, was irresistible. Edward Hall said, 'my friend Johnny had an old rowing boat. We dragged it down to the lake and got it out to a little shit-scarred, duck-infested island and we spent the night there, freezing cold.' There was a trail of inspiration for this: children were inspired by the island-obsessed Famous Five, who were inspired by the island-obsessed Swallows versus Amazons, who were themselves inspired by Robinson Crusoe. 'They always eat everything they find in a captured ship,' Titty says excitedly in *Swallows and Amazons* – she had read her *Robinson Crusoe* and wanted to live by the book.

A brief authorial paragraph of literary criticism here: Enid Blyton's novels have been pilloried for being sexist and racist. In the period of this book, no one noticed any of that, and nor did they notice that the books were quite clunky. Timothy, the dog, is far too clever for a real dog, carrying notes to specific people as instructed. Storms begin and end with biblical suddenness. The Five have ideas far too quickly at moments of crisis: 'Wait a bit! Don't interrupt me! I'm thinking!' They fall asleep far too suddenly, for example at this moment at the end of *Five on a Treasure Island*: '"Won't the boys be pleased? I do feel so ha ..." But before she could finish, the little girl was asleep.' As for *Swallows and Amazons*, Arthur Ransome's celebration of the childhood imagination can sometimes be toe-curling. 'Roger could not run straight against the wind because he was a sailing vessel, a tea-clipper, the *Cutty Sark*.' But the fact that these were well-plotted stories about unsupervised children on islands made them irresistible.

Television, as well as being a sop for boredom, was a springboard for imaginative action. First you watched a programme, then you went outside and acted it out. 'We needed nothing,' said Edward Hall: 'just space and an idea.' As soon as he and his friend had watched the animated puppet programme *Stingray* (1964–5), they put on their swimming goggles, went out of doors and started feeling their way around in the garden in slow motion, as if they were divers from the eponymous submarine. Brought up in Yardley, Birmingham, the dentist Celia Burns and her friend Louise spent whole days acting out television shows. 'We did the whole of *New Faces*, one of us being each of the ten contestants, and the other one the judge, Mickie Most. When I was eleven, my friend Antonia and I loved *The Sweeney*. We set up entire episodes. She was Regan and I was Carter. We had a replica gun and kept a black notebook in which we wrote down the car registration numbers of suspects.'

Already in the early 1970s there was an anti-television television programme called *Why Don't You Just Switch Off Your Television Set and Go and Do Something Less Boring Instead?* – a programme that lasted until 1995, so forty years of trying to wean children off itself – but the children didn't need prompting. They were doing it already.

They were producing their own books and magazines, usually with a print run of one. Children wrote (or at least started writing) novels on Basildon Bond pads, which seemed right because the pages were the same size as the pages of a real book. Valerie Grove, pony-mad in North Shields, produced (and finished) 'The *June* Books', 'illustrated by the author', at the dining-room table, 'all plagiarised from Ruby Ferguson's *Jill* books', as Valerie admitted, showing me a copy of one of her *June* books she'd kept. The story began, 'I was feeling like the happiest person on earth, cantering down the sunny lanes of Ashwood, where I live, on my pony I had hired for three months, Conqueror, or Connie for short.' It continued breathlessly for 100 pages, never wavering from the pony theme. The stories were, Valerie said, 'terminally banal', but 'I vividly recall waking each day longing to get back to writing.' The handwriting was firm and mature, the spelling flawless.

She and her neighbour Rozzy also produced a magazine, *The Horse & Pony Times*. They brought out seven issues of it in 1957, on an old Remington typewriter her father's office had got rid of, so they could go into red for the headlines.

Jilly Cooper was building up romantic capital for life by going to see films, as well as by reading romantic novels. 'I liked to go to bed straight after getting home from the cinema,' she said, 'so I could just dream about gorgeous Rock Hudson. Matinées were not so good.'

*

'Three sets at tennis club. Played dominoes, monkey and snap. Combed tangles out of hair. Ironed night-dress case. After supper, lexicon, bezique, bagatelle. Had Ovaltine.' That's the teenager Elizabeth Millman again, at home in Northamptonshire in the mid-1930s, reminding us what pursuits there were to fall back on in those home summers – and reminding us of the importance of indoor games to while away the evenings and rainy days.

A game of Monopoly (the English version came out in 1936) could last for five hours or more on a rainy afternoon; indeed, it was designed to. This was a similar phenomenon to extended Sunday sermons in Bach's day. There was nothing else for the congregation to do, so why not string it out?

Monopoly captivated children's imaginations to an extraordinary degree. A brutally capitalist game in which the aim is to enrich yourself while bankrupting others, and during which everyone spends at least one spell in jail, it ignited in children an unquenchable acquisitive urge, in violent contrast to the non-acquisitiveness of their day-to-day lives. Beans on toast for supper – and buy up half of London. The genius of the game was you could own the square you landed on, if no one else had bought it first. The game caused catastrophic family rifts. The fact that you were 'being' the boat, dog, car, hat, shoe or thimble didn't alleviate this. The game was too toxic. It was sibling against sibling, friend against friend. Someone was always stubbornly refusing to do the side-deal that would allow someone else to complete their set. The hours hunched round the Monopoly board would instil a lifelong sense of Mayfair being dark blue and coveted, and Regent Street being dark green, hidden away in a north-eastern corner, and not worth the expense.

The long arc of time could seem miserably endless if you were a captive at a friend's house for an afternoon and he or she was making you play a long, complicated board game you weren't familiar with. Friendships came to bitter, bored ends as an enforced board game petered out five hours later. The host knew the rules and tricks, while the guest was baffled and at a disadvantage. The lid illustrations were misleadingly exciting – swarthy adventurers fighting off pirates, with a tag line such as 'An exciting game of adventure against all the odds' – making the box's actual contents (a folding board and some conical plastic protagonists) seem anticlimactic by comparison.

Board-game rules were complicated and often directed solely towards boys – for example in the game called Drive (1960) – glamorous in the early days of mass car ownership:

A player is chosen to start the game. He takes the top card from the face-down pack and places it face-up alongside his own Start position. He then 'drives' his car along the road on the card he has just played. If there be (*sic*) a small black Triangle on the roadway it must be played with the 'Triangle' side touching the 'Start' card . . .

Drive was an example of a game that took you away, in your

imagination only, from where you were to a vehicle, on a road, with a roundabout. Travel Go (brought out by Waddington's in 1961) was another game that fulfilled the urge to imagine you were travelling, when you weren't. The map of the world was laid out before you on its brightly coloured board, with dotted lines between the continents: you could buy tickets when you landed on the Thomas Cook square, and choose your destination and mode of travel. It was a flawed game, as well as a long one. You planned your global journey, but your plane or boat could be blown off course by a 'hazard' card, and you were then stuck in the Falkland Islands for ages, waiting to throw a six.

In games-playing households, jigsaw puzzles were laid out on tables in corners of rooms: another 'long arc of time' pastime, designed to take days or weeks to complete, family members drifting past and having a desultory go. The edges were easy; it was the middles that made the heart sink. 'The Prince of Wales jumping over a hedge'. 'Hunting scene.' 'HMS *Queen Mary*.' Those were the quaint 1930s jigsaw scenes, all containing vast demoralising swathes of sea or sky, that Elaine Ashton remembers from her childhood in wartime Wales in a house thick with her father's cigar smoke. 'My mother and brother played chess and dominoes and they kept a running tally of their scores for the whole summer.'

*

Without even realising they were doing it, or being told by anyone to do it, and with no agenda of self-improvement, children were broadening their minds, absorbing whatever was on offer in print or sound. The *Times* columnist and peer Daniel Finkelstein caught the politics bug at the age of twelve. 'Central to that was Watergate. Nixon resigned when we were on our Scottish holiday. I talked to my father about it, and lay on the floor reading about it. There was no football during the summer so I read the papers from the front.'

Others caught the music bug. 'I got my Wagner craze over

with early,' said Rowan Williams. 'As well as borrowing books every day from the public library, I borrowed the complete operas of Wagner.' Ian Skelly, who grew up in the 1960s and 1970s in Lytham St Annes, Lancashire, was rescued (spiritually at least) by the record library on the railway bridge at Squire's Gate station, where he, too, borrowed box sets of Wagner.

'My parents couldn't "get" me,' Ian said. 'They weren't asking me to turn my pop music down – they were asking me to turn my Wagner down.'

The only hills in that bleak Lancashire coastal landscape, Ian said, were the railway bridges at the various stations. In a bookless, piano-less household in grey Lytham, with its whining gulls and lethal rip tides ('It was my father's ambition to live by the sea – sadly he wanted to live by *that* sea'), Ian's spirit was kept going by four things.

The first was the longed-for annual family holiday to Devon (see the later chapter on the seaside, where his monochrome life goes into dazzling colour). The second was the record library, a welcoming haven run by Ivan Marsh, who happened to be the co-author of *The Penguin Guide to Classical Music*.

The third was listening to the radio. Ian emphasised the importance, to a rather lonely boy, of the illusion of the one-to-one relationship between presenter and listener. 'I loved radio, particularly Radio 2. I listened to Terry Wogan and to Ray Moore. Ray Moore had an uncanny ability to make you feel he was talking to just you. He treated his listener as someone he knew. I remember the shock once, when I heard someone else on a train saying, "Did you hear Ray Moore this morning?" I could hardly believe they'd heard him, too.' Now a radio presenter himself, Ian Skelly makes sure he never, ever says on the radio, 'Good morning, everyone.' The whole point of radio, he feels, is that the listener should feel that the presenter is talking to just him or her, and not to 'everyone'. 'Listening to the radio as a child,' he said, 'was a form of escape from that deadness, into the world of the possible.'

The fourth thing that kept him going was the sign he saw when the local train pulled into Lytham station, rain hammering on the window. The sign on one of the platforms said, 'TO KIRKHAM AND BEYOND'.

'How I longed to go beyond!' he said. The very thought of 'beyond' gave him hope.

5

The Lack of Luxury

When it came to luxury during those mid-twentieth-century summers, it was much more a matter of 'lack of' than of 'lap of'. Across the social spectrum, whether due to genuine poverty or mere thrift, luxury was strikingly absent from children's lives. The usual state of affairs was that you didn't buy new clothes, you didn't have many possessions and you hardly ever went to a restaurant or café.

It was either pre-war, in which case the country was recovering from the Depression and, anyway, no grown-up would dream of spoiling children with possessions or expensive food, or it was wartime, in which case there was nothing to be had, or it was post-war, in which case there was still nothing to be had, or it was the 1960s and 1970s, in which case you were being brought up by parents who'd lived through the war and were allergic to waste and extravagance.

There was no convention that 'going out' meant 'spending money'. 'Going out' meant taking your own sandwiches wrapped in greaseproof paper, eating them on a rug, and spending the day in a place in the open air that didn't charge for entry. So deeply ingrained was the habit of not eating out that when, in 1968, Judith Kerr concluded her story *The Tiger Who Came to*

Tea with the sensational event of Sophie's parents spontaneously taking her out, in the dark, to a café for sausages, chips and ice cream, it took the child reading population by storm.

I had my antennae out for luxury-lack as I talked to people, and it was everywhere, at the heart of existences, all the way from Shirley Cotter (brought up in working-class Fulham in the 1940s) having to unravel her jumper when she'd grown out of it and roll the wool into a ball to knit into a new one with a bit of extra wool to make the new one a size larger, to Rachel Johnson and her siblings going about in semi-rags at the family farm on Exmoor.

I expected lack of luxury among the working classes. What surprised me more was the deeply ingrained habit of non-materialism among the middle and even upper classes. Summers were spent in ragged hand-me-down clothes with little or no cash in the pocket. Three successful adults I spoke to, all brought up in middle class or above families, looked back on their luxury-free childhoods with a sense of pride at their early decades of unspoiltness. There was a deep feeling that it had been good for them and had taught them to appreciate treats in later life. 'My mother bought a cottage next to a pigsty in Ireland for £300 in 1964,' said Libby Purves. 'It had nothing in it. Just camp beds, a camping stove, and a chemical lav out the back. Putting the stove on top of two breeze blocks counted as "improvement".' Here the family spent their summers, having driven from east Suffolk to Fishguard in their mother's 2CV, 'the least lucky of us having to sit on the middle bar of the back seat', camping on the way, and the children sleeping on the deck of the ferry, to save money. That seemed completely normal.

Rachel Johnson showed me a photograph of her family assembled in the farmyard of her grandparents' hill farm, one August morning in 1970. They all look happy, but the children look quite grubby, with muddy knees and unwashed, unbrushed hair, clearly wearing any old ragged, stained item they'd found on the floor and managed to pull on. It was all gumboots, dirty gym shoes or bare feet on the scrubby ground. 'I wore hand-me-downs till the age of sixteen,' Rachel said. '"Neglect" doesn't do it justice. We were hungry all the time. We ate stale digestives that had been put into the Aga. It didn't make them fresh, it just made them taste burnt.'

The Johnson family assembled in the farmyard on Exmoor, 1974.
Rachel, front row, barefoot in trousers and T-shirt. Boris behind her.
© Johnson family archive

Meals in the farmhouse consisted of three chief recipes: rice salad made with tinned tuna and roughly chopped onion; apple crumble; and Carnation-milk ice cream. 'That was made by mixing Carnation with cocoa powder and putting the mixture into a pewter-coloured ice tray. The ice cream would lacerate your mouth, as it was basically milky ice with jagged shards.'

Those ready-worn clothes, passed down through siblings, were threadbare and diaphanous with overuse. It was usual to live in one pair of hand-me-down shorts or corduroy trousers and one jumper for the whole holidays. 'We had the same holiday clothes for years and years,' said Libby Purves. 'There was none of this stuff about new summer wardrobes. I never had more than one swimming costume in a summer. Putting the same wet costume back on is a vivid memory. And wearing it again and again the following summers: it was a very long time before your mother would admit you had breasts. Also, I had the same tar-stained beach towel till last year, which dated from my early childhood. I am sixty-eight.'

Libby Purves and her brother, in old clothes, messing about in their dingy, Triton, in the local creek at Walberswick, 1963

It was simply not done, among the thinking classes, to spend money. Even for Daniel Finkelstein's middle-class family in Hendon, whose lives were 'revolutionised', he told me, 'when Brent Cross Shopping Centre opened in 1976 and we could get there without crossing a road', the greatest treat for his parents in old age was 'to set off to have coffee at Tesco'. 'When he died, my father left me his watch. It was a Casio.'

A summer's day out with Daniel's father was 'heading to the beach in hiking boots and a big anorak. Sandwiches with real sand in them, and for me beef burgers in a thermos.' They did have a television, but 'my parents were always having to hold the aerial up'. They did listen to music, 'but we only had six records, which we played over and over again.' The records were: *The Sooty Show*, Sousa's Military Marches, Beethoven's *Pastoral Symphony*, Doris Day's children's songs, *The Young Mozart* and *The Young Beethoven* — the latter being child-friendly introductions to the lives of the great composers, and on the Beethoven one someone shouted, 'Beethoven? BEETHOVEN!' to illustrate that he was deaf.

Daniel satisfied his urge to accumulate material objects by collecting World Cup coins and FA Cup coins from the Esso petrol station. The single great purchase of his whole childhood was (eventually) a record player of his own with speakers recommended by his father who had a PhD in audio-electronics.

Oddly enough, there was no sense of deprivation. 'My parents were extremely generous. They just had no interest in material things.' The life of the mind was what mattered.

There was an assumption of non-possession and non-wastefulness. Ann Lindsay and her sister wore pale-blue silk underwear sewn by their mother out of the material from the parachute she'd used when she'd been a pilot. Over the underwear they wore kilts made by their mother from a roll of old Gordon Highlanders tartan she'd picked up in the army reject store in Aberdeen.

*Ann Lindsay's mother had been a pilot, hence the
parachute silk for her children's underwear*

*Ann and her sister practising the Highland Fling in the garden, kilts
made from an old roll of army reject store tartan*

Whatever you had, you were considered lucky to have it and should not ask for more. 'I washed my doll's [NB 'doll's' in the singular] clothes a lot,' said Juliet Gardiner, 'and laid them out on the stones to dry. I did have a spade and a round bucket, but I longed for a castle-shaped bucket. I wasn't allowed one.' A castle-shaped bucket, enabling corner crenellations on her sandcastles, would have been an indulgence too far.

'My sister and I had one kitchen drawer each to keep all our things in,' said Sue Sabbagh, brought up in respectable Harrogate in the 1940s and 1950s. 'We just used to sit on the stairs above the only telephone in the house, which was in the freezing hall, imitating my mother having telephone conversations.' Lots of people told me that the family dressing-up box contained not a single item of official dressing-up clothing. They were just full of parents' moth-eaten old cast-offs. Amateur dramatics were put on by children wearing old waistcoats down to their knees.

You might think the sign of the line being crossed from thrift into genuine poverty was when your father cut holes in the toes of your too-small school shoes to convert them into sandals for the summer. This did happen to entrepreneur Douglas Addison, who grew up in a council house in Alva, near Stirling, in the 1960s. 'Sandals or Wellingtons, summer or winter, that was all we wore on our feet,' he said. 'So I improved my own shoes: I cut out car tyres and glued blocks of rubber to the soles and heels to make them into Gary Glitter shoes. That did make them quite heavy to walk about in.' But, actually, people from all walks of life were cutting holes in their shoes to convert them into sandals. It made economic sense.

'What was the weather like during those Scottish summers?' I asked Douglas Addison, to gauge his position on rose-tinted-specs scale.

'Crap all the time. I just wanted to get out of it. We lived on porridge, tripe boiled in milk and pigs' trotters. The tripe was sickly and disgusting, but it was almost free from the butcher's. There was a surprising amount of meat on the pigs' trotters. You knew they were cooked when the toenails came off.'

Those luxury-free childhoods trained children in the use of initiative. 'My sister Mandy decided to paint her bedroom pink, but buying coloured emulsion was out of the question, so she painted her whole room pink by adding tomato ketchup to the white paint. My brother and I went and caught pigeons in an old mill. The top storey was full of pigeons. We climbed along the beams with a torch in our hand. If you shine a torch on a pigeon it won't move. You just put it in a bag and wring its neck. We came back with a bag of dead pigeons and our mum made pigeon pie.'

They did at least have a black-and-white television, but only one family member could watch it properly, due to the stick-on screen. 'When colour televisions first came out, a chap came round selling a screen with rubber suckers at each corner. You stuck it on the black-and-white television and it made the picture go into colour. Well, it gave red, green and blue tinges to everything. But it only worked for the person sitting directly in front of it.'

There were only two channels, and his father made the whole family watch the wrestling all Saturday afternoon. This was another aspect of life that made Douglas long to 'get out of the whole circle. I knew I could do better.'

As with cutting holes in shoes, it wasn't just the hard-up families who subsisted on offal. The well-off could find themselves living on offal, or on winkles and grubs, through the summer, but for different reasons. There was a bit of a playing-at-being-poor urge among the upper-class 'Tiree set', who spent their summers on the Scottish island of Tiree and, who, while there, liked to live as if they were subsistence farmers, for the satisfying, thrifty fun of it. 'I think we will *have* to try slugs,' Alex Renton remembers hearing his aunt saying to his mother, in the late 1960s. 'Foraging for food was very much part of my holidays,' Alex said. 'I think we spent 80 per cent of our time foraging. The first thing my mother did when we arrived was to start collecting snails and putting them in a bucket. We ate everything: winkles, shrimps . . . my sister ate a jellyfish once.' They were unwittingly blazing the trail for the 'locally sourced' and farmers' market crazes.

Offal appeared with dismal regularity on upper-class nursery tables. It was all part of the doctrine of non-spoiling. Bubble Carew-Pole, who spent her 1930s summers in a stately home in Cornwall, remembers the horrible feeling of a piece of veiny liver going round and round in her mouth in the nursery, and being unable to swallow it. 'And the next day, lunch was brains. But it was the liver that finished us,' she said. That was a life of luxury (the food was brought up to the nursery by a kitchen maid) but sometimes it didn't feel very luxurious to the children.

There was a deep suspicion, among the grown-ups, of anything expensive or bought. 'Even crisps were seen as a wicked indulgence,' said Ann Lindsay. 'A van came to Clatterin Brig once a week, and we were allowed to go and buy a bag of crisps if we'd been extraordinarily good. But one day my mother weighed the crisps, and then she sliced up a potato and fried it, and realised you only needed about an inch and a half of potato to make a packet of crisps. There was much more disapproval after that.'

For picnics, the central item was the ham sandwich. Not even the ham, mayonnaise and lettuce sandwich: just ham. 'And the Spam sandwich,' added Celia Burns, recalling her family's annual car journeys to the rented cottage in Yorkshire in the 1970s. 'Their generic name was "pressed-meat sandwiches". Till I was sixteen in 1980, those were what we lived on, on journeys, plus thermoses of tea and coffee: we never bought tea or coffee in a café. By 1980 we might stop just once per summer at a café for a cup of coffee and a slice of cake.'

The excitement of a café stop was enhanced by its rarity. For Celia, her main treat of the summer was a trip to the Wimpy Bar in New Street, Birmingham, with her older siblings. 'That might happen once during the summer. They would buy me a

knickerbocker glory and I could never finish it.' The name 'knickerbocker glory' shone out in the imagination, glittering in its
ice-creamy, tinned-fruity different-ness from the normal currency
of life. Celia's experience typified the pattern: over-excitement at
the thought of a knickerbocker glory, followed by defeat when
confronted by the cornucopia of a portion.

The rarity of going out to eat caused butterflies of excitement on
the day of actually going to a restaurant. Many I spoke to recalled
the single trip to a restaurant per year, and the unbelievable thrill
of it. 'On the evening we arrived in Herne Bay for our vicarage
swap,' said vicar's daughter Phoebe Fortescue (swapping vicar-
ages for holidays was common practice among the cash-strapped
clergy), 'we went out for a meal at the local hotel. It was the only
time we ever went out. For the starter you could choose pâté, soup,
or pineapple juice. I was tempted by the pineapple juice, but I
always chose the pâté for the triangles of toast. It was the highlight
of my year.' For the rest of the holiday they lived on home cooking
and picnics.

There were exceptions to the not-going-to-restaurants rule: cosmopolitan Londoners and the nouveau riche were beginning to eat
out, in the 1960s and 1970s. Those people did things differently.
They were the first to dip their toes into the waters of materialism,
and they liked it.

To the normal thrifty masses, it seemed extraordinary that any
family would go to a restaurant for no proper reason – just because
the mother didn't feel like cooking. Imagine! To be taken out by
such a family, to a restaurant where 'chicken in a basket' was on
the menu, was something to fantasise about, even if the reality
turned out to be sawing into a bony piece of chicken on a paper
napkin, pushing against the edge of the plastic round-bottomed
basket which wouldn't keep still. On the rare occasions when
normal families did go out to a restaurant, to celebrate someone's
birthday or exam result, the experience was usually agonising
because, having looked forward to the event for weeks, they then

had to wait ages for the food to arrive – sometimes an hour or more. Conversation ran out in hushed dining rooms. Everyone watched the waiter emerge once every half-hour carrying a tray through the green-baize door, but it was to bring long-awaited food to other famished diners who had arrived after you, which seemed grossly unfair. Fathers, not used to having to wait for food to be put in front of them, became tetchy and sometimes furious, summoning the manager for a showdown. Then, at long last, the 'curry Madras' arrived and it was a daunting heap of brownness.

There were other aspects of luxury-lack in Phoebe Fortescue's 1960s and 1970s vicarage childhood in Ham Common. 'From the age of ten I made all my own clothes, on a hand-cranked Singer sewing machine. I loved clothes, but we never had any money. I made turquoise hot pants – I thought I was the bees' knees. Also a pink cheesecloth layered ruched skirt.' She and her siblings all helped with the cooking every day, and there might be a crowd for lunch, as any tramps who came and helped in the vicarage garden in the morning were invited to lunch and given their train fare back.

The vicarage had eight bedrooms but only one bathroom, and the bathroom had the one and only loo in it – which made for morning queues, as the house was full of lodgers, many of them African students studying medicine.

I've lost count of the number of non-luxurious lavatorial situations I heard during interviews. Having to queue for the single loo in a vicarage was mild, compared to the privies in yards in other earlier childhoods. Bill Halson loved going to stay with his grandparents in their cottage in Woolhope, Herefordshire, in the 1940s, but the loo-going was primitive. His grandfather, born in 1871, had saved and saved from his first days as an apprentice, and had managed to buy property. 'When the bedroom ceiling collapsed, my grandmother mended it with newspaper covered in flour-and-water paste: the mice loved that. There was no running water, only a pump from a well; no electricity; a range in the kitchen; and a privy at the end of the yew-tree avenue. We called it "Alleluia Avenue" and we walked down there in the dark, crunching snails all the way. There was a pile of cut-up newspaper squares on a string. Every now and then we had to empty the contents, carry them to the back end of the garden, dig a deep hole and pour them in.'

Bill Halson and his brother, staying with their Herefordshire grandfather, 1936

The whole experience of having to see, and indeed revisit, one's own and one's family's excrement was a remarkably common theme. Earth closets were everywhere. Digging a hole was what you did on arrival in a camping field. All public lavatories were revolting, even worse than school ones. Railway-station lavatories stank of disinfectant and urine, the floors were wet with spillage and the hard-loo-paper dispensers were empty.

You just had to shut your eyes, hold your nose and get on with it. Worse was to come, if and when you ever ventured across the Channel.

One touch of glamour beginning to seep into English gardens in the 1970s was the new concept of installing one's own swimming pool. But these were hardly the kidney-shaped azure pleasure-pools you saw in foreign-holiday brochures, if ever you looked at them. They were mostly homemade and underheated. 'My father commandeered the operation,' said one woman I spoke to, brought up in rural Somerset in the 1960s. 'Building the pool involved weeks of hard labour. All of us children had to carry stones all day from one end of a muddy clay hole to the other. First it was a hole, and then, gradually, it became a pool. It wasn't heated, and the water was green – but it transformed our lives. All the local families came.'

The first glimmers of envy entered the summer-holidays consciousness: swimming-pool envy, or, if you were lucky enough to have a pool, temperature envy. A typical home-built pool would reach 76° Fahrenheit at its very highest in the summer of 1976. Mostly, it hovered around 67°. There were rumours that some very rich people – the kind who had pools with shallow steps in the semi-circle at the shallow end – reached 84° on a regular basis. For those who lived through this, the number eighty-four is forever associated with unattainable luxury.

'The crowning glory of my English summers,' said Simon Winder, 'was being invited to swim in the pool of a friend of mine who lived at the housing-complex end of Tunbridge Wells. His father was in oil, and they had a swimming pool *and* a Volvo Estate: so glamorous, it was almost unbearable.'

PART II

THE PEOPLE YOU WERE STUCK WITH

6

Yourself

Let's not pretend that no one was bored or lonely. Or, if not exactly lonely, alarmingly solitary for months on end. This is a chapter about summer solitude, both voluntary and involuntary. It's about being stuck with yourself.

It has been established by his biographer Douglas Botting that by the time Gavin Maxwell went away to board at prep school aged eight in the early 1920s, he had only ever met ten other children, three of whom were his own siblings. That's extreme and is explained partly by the fact that he was brought up in a remote corner of rural Wigtownshire. But it was not unusual for bookish children in the mid-twentieth century to shun the company of other children, or for sociable children somehow never to encounter them. Sometimes you went out into your road or cul-de-sac and there simply weren't any other children around. Or you were an only child stuck out in the country, miles from anywhere and anyone. So, you had the freedom, but not the company.

Take the historian Nicolas Barker, brought up in Cambridge in the 1930s and 1940s – he was the one we met earlier who cycled off on solitary trainspotting expeditions with sandwiches and a note-book. He was not lonely but he was friendless. The family lived at 17 Cranmer Road, 'and in the whole road, only three houses were not occupied by professors'. All the professors were well past middle age, so any children they might have had had long ago fled the nest. 'The only other boy still around, Eli Lauterpacht, was five years older than me, but he might has well have been a hundred. I didn't have any young friends.'

This was partly due to the war, he said: 'social relations were suspended. But I was entirely happy.' He did have a sister, Juliet, who became a violin-maker, and they had the run of the next-door eight-acre garden of Leckhampton after its fence blew down in 1940. They made friends with Spoulton, the gardener. That was all the non-family company they required.

Their house was stuffed with books and Nicolas spent hours on his own, reading: 'I read everything from the *Army & Navy Catalogue* to the whole of Scott, Dickens and Thackeray and the *Heimskringla*. I did read *Swallows and Amazons*, and stories by Aubrey de Sélincourt about children mucking about on the Norfolk Broads. The idea of other people having friends and doing things together was attractive, but it was not something that happened to me.'

One day, a desperate local mother tried to engineer a friendship. 'Queenie Leavis asked my mother if she could bring her son Ralph to play for the afternoon – he didn't have any friends either.' Those two boys, one the son of a professor of Political Science and the other the son of two great literary critics, behaved civilly enough to each other 'but we did so without much enthusiasm. It was very disconcerting. I was being used as a social experiment.'

Rather than friends, Nicolas preferred to collect things: minerals, coins, botanical specimens, butterflies, seals and stamps. We can imagine young Ralph Leavis feeling compelled to make admiring comments about these items during that long, awkward afternoon. For children happiest with their own company, bedroom museum items, lined up on shelves around them, became their friends. Eli Lauterpacht down the road (who was later to become the renowned scholar and international lawyer) took enough notice of Nicolas to give him the foreign stamps from registered envelopes that came in the post throughout the war, containing raw diamonds sent by (or for) escaping Jews as payment for their transport and so they would have something to live on when they got out of Nazi Europe. Eli's father Hersch Lauterpacht, helper of escaping Jews, played a crucial part in this scheme.

Nicolas stuck those stamps lovingly into his album. Stamp-collecting was another means of inhaling a whiff of abroad, for children who weren't going there. A tiny illustration of an exotic bird on a perforated stamp – a stamp that had actually touched the warm air of abroad, and had the name of a foreign country in its own language along the edge – was a powerful travel substitute.

Double summer time – the clocks going forward two hours rather than one, which happened from 1940 to 1945 in order to give people longer to get home before the blackout – meant even longer hours of solitary playing in the garden, before going to bed in the daylight. Social relations were indeed suspended, said Walter Balmford, who lived in Handsworth, Birmingham, during the war. 'I just went into the wood and lay down and watched the little creatures. I was on my own most of the time, going into the wood and talking to nature.' This didn't seem weird at all. We underestimate the longing of children to be left on their own, so they can talk to insects and worms and invent their own imagined worlds. 'I had a secret society with only me in it,' said Libby Purves. 'It was called The Lone Wolves. I imagined that the word "Mobo" – the brand name written on my scooter – was a secret message to me.' This was proper daydreaming, and if you were doing it on your own you never needed to feel embarrassed.

For children who liked sports but weren't good at them, voluntary solitude was an attractive option because it let you off having to play sports with other children. You could play against yourself instead. 'If I played with others,' said Daniel Finkelstein, 'I always lost. I'm really bad at games. You wouldn't have found me, my sister and my brother playing touch football like the Kennedys. I ran around on my own in the garden, playing imaginary football matches – defending against myself, and I was very good at scoring against myself.' On rainy days he did the same indoors with Subbuteo: 'I had a five-a-side set with walls. I could play it on my own for hours – two teams against each other: Peru v. Watford, or Brazil v. QPR. You couldn't do Brazil v. Wolves because their colours were too similar.'

On your own, you could fix the outcomes and mould the universe to shape your vision of how life should be. In gardens all over Britain, children were playing cricket, football and wall tennis against themselves, or playing dice versions of those games in which a good deal of cheating (the rethrowing of dice) went on if the underdogs weren't doing well enough. On your own, with no one watching, you could play God (a more benignly interfering God than real God) and engineer justice.

In Ruislip in the 1950s, Nicholas Sagovsky, who was to become Canon Theologian of Westminster Abbey, played hours of cricket by and against himself through much of the summers of his childhood. 'We had a side passage where you could bowl with a tennis ball and try to hit the centre part of the gate. In the back garden, there was just enough room for a cricket net, so I could use a hard ball. I became a slow bowler, because there was no room for a run-up. I learned to bowl very straight. I could hit the stumps five times out of six. But I had difficulty getting my colours at school, because I could bowl but hadn't had enough friends to bat with.'

This was involuntary solitude. Nicholas was lonely for two reasons: one, because he had been sent away to boarding school aged thirteen, as had all his local gaggle of friends (all to different schools), and by the time they came home for the summer they'd grown apart and lost touch with each other. Quite a few people said the same to me about going to boarding school. 'You lost contact with all the local boys and girls.' That was a small but crucial consequence of sending children away to boarding school, and one not always considered by the parents.

The second reason was Ruislip itself. 'I find it hard to say "Ruislip" without a certain edge in my voice,' Nicholas said. 'Unlike

for Betjeman, the Metropolitan Line doesn't do it for me.' He felt
trapped and friendless in suburban no man's land: far from the
beauty of the countryside and far from the excitement of the city. The
London suburbs, supposed to be the best of both worlds, seemed to
him the worst of both. Very occasionally, the family would 'go up
to town' for the day, only sixteen miles away along the Metropolitan
Line but it might as well have been the other end of the country.
'Town' was seen as intrinsically expensive.

It was his maternal grandmother who had decided that Ruislip
would be the perfect place for her daughter to bring up her grand-
son. The grandmother came to live there with them, which brought
its own strains in the kitchen and made for stilted, stifling indoor
Sunday lunches with the 'good' silver and china, a meal Nicholas
dreaded and vowed never to inflict on his own children. 'For my
grandmother and for my mother,' Nicholas said, 'moving to the
suburbs represented arrival: being able to get out of London to a place
with a leafy garden.' For Nicholas they spelled summers of boredom.
It didn't help that his parents wouldn't let him read the kind of books
that would have got him into reading. 'They disapproved of Enid
Blyton, the *Beano* and the *Dandy*. What was missing was the sense
of being *carried away* by reading.' Hours hung especially heavily on
the solitary non-bookworms. As soon as he could, Nicholas started
hitchhiking across the country to visit school friends.

That glimpse of indoor dining-room lunches on hot summer
Sundays reminds us that families didn't eat main meals out of doors,
as a rule, until the mid-1970s. There wasn't the garden furniture for
it. Nor was there the hedonistic convention. On a hot day a family
might carry out some old deckchairs and put up a small folding tin
picnic table for tea. The deckchairs were much too low for the table.
Leaning forward in them while trying to reach up and eat a cucumber sandwich was a physical strain and caused bad indigestion.

On a vast coastal expanse of rural Lincolnshire, ten miles south
of Cleethorpes and twenty miles north of Skegness, near a village
called South Somercotes, Jamie Buxton, having devoured his comics,

wandered about on his own for endless long summer days of the 1960s and early 1970s. There was no one else around: 'only two boys in the village my age, and I didn't know them.' Jamie was another boy home from boarding school. He relished the solitude: 'a massive contrast from school'. He was vaguely aware that he had meals at different times from the rest of the village: when his grandmother clanged the bell installed to summon him in to lunch at the middle-class hour of 1 p.m., everyone else had already had their lunch an hour earlier.

Both his parents had died of cancer – his father when he was nine and his mother two years later. In the years before those deaths, the family had lived in Germany and gone on thrilling family holidays to Austria by train. After their parents' deaths, Jamie and his older sisters had gone to live in Lincolnshire with their eighty-year-old beekeeping grandfather and his second wife Dorothy, both of whom were kind but perpetually busy. Jamie's sisters left to live elsewhere as soon as they could, so it was just Jamie, on his own, in an outhouse of his grandparents' old rectory, where he had all his parents' old books to read his way through (as well as comics), and got 'heavily into *The Lord of the Rings*'.

'I just walked up and down the beach all day. It was a mile and a half's walk to the beach; then you went over a sea wall and across another half-mile of mud, and then it was just sand for miles. I didn't really feel lonely. I daydreamed. I was presumably processing stuff. We were brought up not to talk about what had happened: it was never brought up in conversation. I think my grandparents thought, If we don't talk about it, they won't kick off.'

Was he bored on those long solitary days?

'Maybe I was, but in my brain, boredom and discontentment are not the same thing. You can be bored but not discontented. I got into a kind of transcendental state of boredom. It was a state of mind rather than something to avoid. And, remember: I had the heat. If you didn't have many possessions, as I didn't, just the fact that you were out of doors in the heat was a real thing,' (As Leo Colston in

The Go-Between put this very phenomenon, 'I felt I had been given the freedom of the heat, and I roamed about in it as if I was exploring a new element.')

That shimmering Lincolnshire heat was itself a possession and felt like company. At the age of fifteen Jamie at last got hold of a second-hand NSU moped, which he pushed all the way along the road to the beach and then spent all day revving up and going backwards and forwards along the miles of deserted sand. 'When I look back on it, it does seem very strange. It was a real backwater there.' He admitted that if there was ever any opportunity to go to any town – the nearest one being Louth, eight miles away – he jumped at it. His step-grandmother, in her WRVS uniform, occasionally drove him there in the car.

'What did you do once you got to Louth?'

'I went into the army surplus store. I don't know what it was about army greatcoats, flashlights, canteens and camping stoves: I just loved looking at them. I'd save up for weeks to buy a khaki-painted old torch.'

Jamie Buxton in 1965, in the days when his parents were still alive, gazing out of the train window on a family journey from Germany to Austria. Photo by his sister Rachel Buxton

As the writer Miranda France said, telling me about her solitary days wandering around and daydreaming on the family farm in Sussex in the 1970s, 'Solitude was a good preparation for knowing how to sink into yourself.' It turned out to be a useful skill for adulthood. She read for hours, and longed to watch *Magpie* in the afternoons, but was not allowed to watch ITV: her parents considered it a bad influence and banned *Magpie*, the lowbrow equivalent of *Blue Peter*.

The young Marnie Palmer yearned for siblings and friends. Little did she know, in the early 1960s – a solitary, lonely girl living an unglamorous life with her grandmother who ran a B&B in Paignton – that she would one day marry John 'Goldfinger' Palmer, gold-smelting entrepreneur and later timeshare criminal, who would become richer than the Queen, and they'd sail around the world together in their yacht before he was convicted. Life was as flat as anything for the young Marnie. The only glamour was when she watched the television and was so sure the handsome newsreader could see her, just as she could see him, that she sat in front of him coyly crossing her legs.

'During the summers I waited at table in my Nan's B&B, serving breakfast to guests, and I had to give up my bedroom to the guests and relocate to the garden shed. I liked the shed. There was a trough of water in there, and I lay in the trough and stitched up my jeans in the water with big criss-cross stitches, to make them look skin-tight every day. I was mostly happy at my Nan's, but I was alone. I did hours of walking to and from anywhere, with my transistor radio in my hand, just walking up and down the front at Paignton, looking at the rude postcards, thinking of meeting someone, anyone. I was never bored, though, because I would go into my dreams, but I was lonely.'

Marnie Palmer in the garden of her Nan's house, with Alsatian Rex.
She longed for brothers and sisters

Daydreaming was a central occupation for these solitary people. They made friends with the hidden alleyways of their minds. Marnie Palmer was daydreaming about meeting her prince – and she later did, and the daydreaming had prepared her for that moment. 'I can't say I put my solitude to a single moment of good use,' said Jamie Buxton; but he did grow up to become a thriller writer and children's fantasy fiction author, so who knows? *Lord of the Rings* and Dan Dare scenarios were swirling around in his head. Lots of people I spoke to said they hadn't put their summers to officially good use. But in those empty hours, they were building up imaginative capital to sustain them through life.

In the chilly garden of Southdean Lodge, her parents' remote inherited shooting lodge in Bonchester Bridge just over the Scottish border from Northumberland, Markie Robson-Scott wandered around alone for six weeks of every summer in the 1950s and 1960s (we'll hear more about the annual journeys there in a later chapter). An only child, she was on her own for countless hours and days. 'Slates fell off the roof of the house in the gales,' she said. 'I remember writing on a fallen slate, "I'm lonely".' She was so solitary that she played games not only in but *with* the grass. 'I had names for certain kinds of grass. "Cloudy Light" was one. In fact, "Cloudy Light" then became a kind of fairy who accompanied me.' There was a fallen silver birch tree in the wood beside the house. 'I sat on the silver birch and I had a relationship with it. I even wrote it postcards later, when I wasn't there.' In the depths of solitude, she was willing inanimate objects to life.

*An only child in Scotland: Markie Robson-Scott,
and the grass she made friends with*

*

If lonely children or teenagers said, 'I'm bored!' their mothers had a selection of fierce retorts up their sleeves. 'Go and do a puzzle', 'Go and tidy your room', and 'Go and clean your hairbrush' were popular ones. Far from cleaning their hairbrush, *Top of the Pops* addicts (from 1964 onwards, when the programme began) went up to their room and sang into their hairbrush, holding it vertically. 'Go outside and run your head along the railings: that'll sort you out.' That was what Cockney mothers said to their sons, as recalled by Bill Carroll who grew up in Stepney in the 1950s.

Ali O'Neale remembers her younger brothers, bored to tears in their bungalow in Causewayhead in Stirlingshire, chanting, 'There's nothing to do! There's nothing to do!' out of the window. It was a sort of SOS to the public, who took no notice. Their mother just told them to 'run along'. She hadn't been played with as a child and had no intention of playing with her own children.

'The boredom of it all!' said Catherine Mould, remembering arriving home for the summer holidays in Wales in the 1970s: the euphoria of the first evening, and then the anticlimax of the prospect of the weeks stretching ahead. 'I said to my mother, "I'm so bored", and she said, "Only boring people are bored. Go outside". So I went outside, but quickly sneaked up to my bedroom and listened to Cat Stevens and felt sorry for myself. It was good for me and my sisters in some ways, because we vowed that in adult life we would never be bored.'

In her case, she slightly blamed Wales. 'We were just over the border in Wales, and all the fun seemed to be happening in Gloucestershire. Gloucestershire felt like a Mecca. Our only social life was a Reel Club run by a colonel in the village hall.' There was one other family of friends nearby. 'The brother in that family had a chemistry lab in the stables, so we made "legal highs" with the chemicals, and stole cigarettes from their parents' cigarette boxes that lay around on tables over the place and were easy to help yourself from.'

Out of the four categories – solitude, loneliness, boredom and misery – you were fortunate if you only ticked a selection and not all of them. Amazingly, not many children did tick all of them. The lonely ones weren't always bored, the bored ones weren't always lonely and solitary ones weren't always miserable.

7

Siblings and Cousins

The cuts, scars and black eyes didn't just come from pre-health-and-safety playground equipment, or from falling out of trees or skimming roof-slates at other people's faces for the fun of it. They also came from sibling violence.

'When you're grown up,' Colin Burrow remembers his father patiently explaining to him and his two brothers as they sat squished together in the back of the family Austin Maxi on the way to Berkshire, punching each other, 'you won't have to talk to each other at all. But now you do.'

The three brothers certainly did have to talk to each other: they were stuck together every summer through the 1960s and 1970s in the family's cottage on the Berkshire Downs – only seventeen miles from their term-time house in Oxford, 'but the journey felt as if it took a day and a half', partly because, as Colin recalls, 'there was always a bottleneck in Abingdon', but mainly because of the fighting.

'I was the youngest of the three,' Colin said, 'which was the worst position because I always had to sit in the middle. Dad would lash out at random – a random swipe in our direction from the driver's seat, and I got the worst of it.'

Once arrived at the cottage, which had no mains drainage and no television, the brothers roamed free, returning only to be fed.

They played cricket on the village green, where the disputes about lbw could get 'very nasty', and they played Monopoly on rainy days, which involved 'ritual screaming'.

They bought perforated notepads from the post office, in which they scribbled their interpretations of mysteries going on in the village. 'I think we genuinely did spend an awful lot of time out of doors being quite nice to each other,' Colin says. But 'I honed my verbal skills winding up my middle brother. He was particularly pleasing to wind up because he had a temper. You know exactly how to annoy someone, and you do, deliberately – because what else is there to do?'

What indeed? The deliberate annoying of siblings was a pastime in itself: cathartic and satisfying. Enforced proximity meant an increasing skill at knowing exactly which buttons to press to cause an eruption of fury. Colin is now a professor of English Literature, so the verbal-skills-honing clearly worked. Fighting was the background music to their existence. 'You could hit my eldest brother on the shoulders as hard as you could, but he didn't flinch. He set himself up as a monument of strength, and we put him to the test.'

We've met the too-lonely children; these were the not-lonely-enough ones. 'Later on, in my teens,' said Colin, 'I just wanted to read. I wore a black polo neck that had a black badge on it that said 'Piss off' in very small letters. You had to come quite close to read it.'

Whether or not siblings got on well was entirely a matter of luck. Out of a mother's tummy could pop brothers and sisters with similar interests, or ones with totally different interests and temperaments that didn't mix. Almost on purpose – partly to avoid unbearable competition but also partly to spite each other – siblings developed opposing interests. When it came to dabbling in the nearby stream, for example, Colin recalled, 'my middle brother and I had incompatible desires. His principal interest was damming watercourses, while mine was fishing. He was upstream ruining my fun, and I was downstream ruining his by whingeing, which was how I spent most of my childhood.'

Living together for weeks entrenched these differences and

confirmed for life each child's sense of his or her position in the family. In families where siblings didn't get on well, there was nothing exciting about waking up each day and thinking, Oh goody – I've got ready-made companions to play with. Siblings were just a daily, boring, predictable reality. You knew exactly what they were going to say at breakfast, and the fuss one of them would make if rhubarb was served at lunch, and exactly how they would try to ruin your day in countless subtle or unsubtle ways, leading to pinches, punches or Chinese burns. In a closed world, cut off, with no outsiders watching, siblings felt free to exhibit the very worst of themselves in appalling tantrums, not edifying to anyone.

'I hated my sister,' said Jane Adams (b. 1956), who now runs a gallery in Cornwall but grew up in Chesterfield. 'She was about as opposite to me as you could get. She was a completely alien being. And the worst thing was that our mother dressed us in matching clothes all summer. She modelled us on how Princess Elizabeth and Princess Margaret had dressed as children.'

At least the Burrow boys were making an effort to play together. They all listened to *Test Match Special* while helping their father (an Oxford don) to re-floor a bit of 'the derelict', the nickname for the end cottage of the three old farmworkers' cottages that were their holiday residence. They were there, re-flooring the derelict, when Brian Johnston was alleged to have spoken the immortal words 'the bowler's Holding, the batsman's Willey'.

The sadder situation was when siblings lived in the same house but didn't play or do anything together, as there was so little rapport that it wasn't even worth trying; or if the age differences were hopelessly huge; or if one of the siblings had gone away to boarding school and thus had grown apart.

'I remember when I was fourteen,' said Archbishop Stephen Cottrell, 'my brother who was six years younger than me, and who I'd always played with, saying, "But can't we play?" And I just couldn't do it any more. I remember his frustration, that I'd left childhood behind.' 'My brother and I were chalk and cheese,' said

Anne Owen, brought up in Shenfield in the 1950s. 'We were determined to do things differently: it was engines, fortifications, bikes,
practical things for him, and music, drama, literature and nature for
me. We fought frequently: I could taunt him and he would respond
physically. I was probably an insufferable sibling.' In 1950s Alva,
Stirlingshire, where Douglas Addison shared a cramped bedroom
with his four brothers, while his two sisters were in the next-door
room, 'we were put together so much that there was no bonding. It
was mostly fisticuffs. There was just no privacy. The only bonding
happened if there was a rival family, and we thumped them.'

Even if siblings had little in common, the weeks of enforced
proximity did give them one thing in common: a lifetime's bank of
shared jokes and shared butts of jokes. One influence that did pass
from sibling to sibling was the sense of humour. However badly you
got on, someone usually knew how to make all the others crease
up with laughter – the richest material for laughter being shared
material, such as the habits of the neighbours or of the more distant,
weird relatives.

Younger siblings tended to be the ones who were routinely teased,
left out or egged on to do terrifying dares. 'As a girl growing up with
two older brothers,' said Alice Renton, 'you were expected to be
tough. I broke my collarbone three times, as well as getting broken
toes from horses standing on me.'

'What did you and your neighbour five years younger do all day?'
I asked Anne Owen. She replied, 'We used to torture her younger
sister.' That was an honest reply. She didn't mean literally torture, but
the friend's sister was five years younger again and seemed a mere
annoyance. They told her to get out of their way, closing the bedroom
door to exclude her, and telling her and go to bed so they could watch
Doctor Who after tea. 'She was intrepid and a natural gymnast. Once,
when we were meant to be "playing nicely" with her, we left her to
her own devices and she climbed to the top of the garden swing and
hung by her legs shrieking until someone (not us) came to rescue her.'

That was a sort of torture by neglect. Kevin Crossley-Holland,

who loved his younger sister Sally ('my only sibling – such an unpleasant word'), said he nonetheless 'treated her in the manner of a slave. I
was always setting her impossible tasks, such as to run up and down
the garden a hundred times.' Sally did as bidden – anything to win
the approval of her competitive, sporty elder brother. 'If I was trying
to cross a freezing stream barefoot for the sixth time in a day, I was
also daring Sally to do the same – and I would be lavish with my
praise when I thought she deserved it. In my perennial efforts to raise
more cash I came up with a novel scheme of picking flowers from
neighbouring gardens, tying them into bouquets and selling them
round and about – that's to say, pushing Sally in front of me to sell
them, "in aid of the poor children". This scheme worked so well that
I moved on to stage two: selling the flowers back to their owners.
Again, Sally obliged.'

*Kevin Crossley-Holland's sister Sally (out of shot) is obediently
bowling at her older brother in the garden of their cottage
at Whiteleaf, Buckinghamshire, 1953*

Thus the sense of each child's role in life became ingrained, and it would not be easy to shift. Sally needed to find a pursuit in which her brother could not compete, and so it was that she eventually went to the Ballet Rambert school in Notting Hill Gate.

*

How lucky were you, if you and your siblings happened to live together in harmony! And how lucky were your parents, who found themselves living according to the premise that 'children cancel each other out' – i.e. the more there are, the more they entertain each other and leave you in peace. It was pure bad biological luck if you happened to be the hated one in a Cain and Abel situation or a Goneril/Regan/Cordelia situation. A single shared obsession could make the difference. If one sibling managed to pass his or her obsession with (say) ponies, or following cricket, to the others, it could provide an inexhaustible subject to talk about and to base games on.

When I asked Jilly Cooper about her childhood summers, the first thing she said was, 'It was bliss, because my brother came home from boarding school. He was a wonderfully glamorous brother to have home. All my friends fell in love with him.' So, no sad growing apart in that sibling relationship, in spite of boarding-school-induced separation. Jilly's brother, Timothy, three years older, was 'extraordinarily good-looking,' Jilly said. He brought his friends from Rugby to stay, and Jilly brought hers from the Godolphin School in Salisbury, and they all had a lovely time. 'He wasn't quite as interested in ponies as I was,' Jilly admits. But 'my mother said, "He'll take you to dances, darling", and that's exactly what he did.'

If you were lucky (extremely lucky), sibling togetherness meant weeks of unplanned fun without having to make arrangements to see anyone else. This was the situation in Vanessa Buxton's family, the Norfolk Buxtons, 'one of the big Norfolk families, like the Gurneys or the Barclays', as Vanessa explained to me. 'My mother, who was a Buxton, had married my father, also a Buxton. They were fourth cousins once removed, which is totally "normal for Norfolk".'

'We were complete,' Vanessa said, 'because there were four of us. Our parents had four children in four years: twins, then me, then my younger brother. We lived on a farm, and we were off in the woods all day, or playing in the barns where we made straw-bale houses with multiple storeys and tunnels. Our parents had no idea where we were.' (That detail again. It was the refrain of the mid-twentieth century.)

Their father, an MP, had installed a bell on top of the house that could be pulled with a rope to summon everyone in for meals, 'and we had to eat what was put in front of us – there was a strong rule of "waste not, want not". The sweets were kept in a tin on the top shelf.'

*The Buxton siblings, Robbie, Peter, Camilla and Vanessa:
a happy foursome, and 'complete'*

The effect of not needing other children to play with was that
the children did not become sophisticated, as they were cut off
from outside influences and fashions (and happy to be so). 'There
was a Pony Club nearby, but we didn't like the competitive side
of all that: all those girls with their immaculate ponies, while
ours weren't. We hung together as a gang, as we were all very
shy.' This was a sort of sibling-company inbreeding to match the
parental-marital one. The furthest they would get from their
inner circle was when they went sailing with cousins (more
Buxtons) in Blakeney, where they all wallowed together in the
black Blakeney mud.

Camilla Buxton wallowing in the Norfolk mud

'We were not grown-up for our age. Just once, we had a German exchange girl to stay for the summer. She was incredibly sophisticated, with long red nails, and her boyfriend had a sports car.' The German girl must have felt pretty stranded in Norfolk with the non-nail-varnish Buxtons.

One thing her close sibling existence did prepare Vanessa for was life in a girls' boarding school. 'My brothers insisted that I learn to shoot, and they taught me to fight. I knew how to land a good punch. I remember slugging a girl at St Mary's, Wantage.'

*

Cousins, likewise, could be assets or they could be liabilities. Because you didn't have to live with them all summer, there wasn't the same level of loathing or physical violence as there was with siblings. But there could be real froideur, during enforced get-togethers organised by parents, aunts and uncles who were themselves siblings and were trying to engineer friendships between their respective offspring.

The pressure that you should be getting on with these cousins, because they were related to you by blood, made the not-getting-on with them feel all the more painful and sad. 'I don't blame the cousin herself,' said the lexicographer Jonathon Green, recalling the time when his mother arranged for a cousin to come and stay for the first fortnight of the summer holidays, without asking him whether he wanted it. 'She [the cousin] may well have found it as tedious as I did, but all I wanted to do was get a few weeks of peace. This was not available when I had to sacrifice my much-beloved role as an only child. The most galling aspect of it was that my mother had invited the cousin as an act of charity – though goodness knows we were hardly rich.' So his mother was feeling virtuous throughout Jonathon's fortnight of enforced sociability.

Juliet Gardiner had her cousin Joan inflicted on her every summer, when Joan came with the family on holiday to Paignton.

Juliet had to share a bedroom with her in Mrs Pollard's boarding house for a fortnight. (There'll be more about Mrs Pollard's
boarding house in a later chapter.) Joan (Juliet's mother's sister's
daughter) was not a blood relative, as Juliet was adopted, but she
still counted as a cousin, and Juliet's parents thought it would be
nice for her to have Joan, the same age, for company.

'She wasn't very nice to me,' said Juliet. 'She would pinch me,
and knock the ice cream out of my hand on purpose: that sort
of thing. She was quite mean. She wouldn't share things. And
she kept saying, "I wish Aunt Dolly and Uncle Charles hadn't
adopted you."'

It didn't help that Juliet's father didn't like "that Horsley lot",
as he referred to the branch of his wife's family from which Joan
came. (They lived in Horsley, Gloucestershire.) As Juliet recalled,
'They were jealous that I'd gone to a Girls' Day School Trust
school: they thought I was getting above my station. I never heard
the end of it.' So, there was tension in the air before the holiday
even started. Rivalry between cousins, unlike between siblings,
was couched in civility, but it was just as rife, and an unself-
confident cousin could have his or her self-esteem damaged for life
by being exposed as inferior or in some way not-normal.

At their best, such as in an extended Catholic family like the
Frasers, who gathered in a castle in Inverness-shire for six weeks
every summer, cousins provided a ready-made vast party of friends
who happened to be relatives.

There were so many cousins gathered together at Moniack
Castle that everyone was bound to find someone of approxi-
mately the same age they got on with. 'One of the *points* of a large
Catholic family,' as Kit Fraser explained to me, 'was that we were
brought up to be nice people. Our parents believed in honour,
duty, good behaviour and being kind and loving. The uncles and
aunts all loved one another. It was a very Catholic household. We
would always have a priest to stay.'

'There were thirty-six of us first cousins who went up to

Moniack every summer,' recalls the artist Olivia Fraser. 'We were all thrilled to see each other. The house was run by my Aunt Philippa – now the mildest of lovely aunts, aged ninety-two, but she was quite fierce in those days [the 1960s and 1970s]. It was a patriarchal household. There was a rule that the boys had the first baths, and the girls then got into their dirty water.'

Fraser cousins gathered in large numbers at Moniack Castle

Everyone took turns with the washing-up: 'Aunt Philippa didn't believe in machines. There was a dishwasher but she didn't think they worked.' Ten boy cousins slept in a dormitory known as 'the badgers' hole', while Olivia shared a room with her sisters, and you'd find cousins spilling out of every room in the castle. 'Fourteen of us would cram into a small Ford car to go ice-skating,' said Olivia. 'I was on the floor under everyone's feet.' There were midnight feasts, and morning shooting and fishing excursions to 'catch the lunch', the children beating while their fathers and uncles shot.

Off to catch the lunch: kilted Fraser cousins Anthony,
Tom, Rupert, Archie and Anselm

Kit, one of the cousins, organised elections to decide who would be allowed to run the house for a day. 'There were posters all over the house: "Vote for Kit" – my election name was actually "Mr Kitler". All of us candidates gave impassioned speeches. One year, the result hinged on a single one-year-old toddler who had to run either towards me or my cousin Rory.'

On the day when the election-winner ran the household, the children sat at the main table in the dining room and the grown-ups at the nursery table.

This was the kind of existence that the lonely only children yearned for. Amateur dramatics were taken seriously, the older cousins writing plays in which each cousin would have at least one line. Everyone spent days rehearsing, making props and doing the make-up. 'I adapted Shakespeare plays,' said Kit. 'We did *Hamlet* one year. It was hilarious for the adults.'

The French have a noun for it: '*le cousinage*', a host of cousins so large that it becomes a whole cloud-like concept in itself. French Catholic grandparents born to vast families, who had six children each, each of whom then had six more, invite the extended family to stay in their grandparental country house for the month of August. The main thing Hervé de la Morinière recalled to me about those vast cousinly gatherings was the ordeal of having to kiss every single cousin, parent, aunt, uncle and grandparent twice, before breakfast.

Le cousinage existed in Britain, too. There could be rivalries between the different branches: as Charles Ropner, who gathered in Yorkshire with great clans of his cousins in the 1970s, recalls, the best trick to play on your gullible, greedy or wet cousin was to 'give him a wasp sandwich'. To make a wasp sandwich 'you slap butter and jam onto a slice of bread, wait for the wasp to be attracted to the jam, slap the top slice down, press hard, cut into two slices, and present to the cousin'. 'There was quite a bit of scrapping between the Strakers and the Darbyshires [two branches of the cousins],' he said. 'Occasional kidnappings: putting a bag over a cousin's head and leaving him in a ditch.' All harmless cousinly fun.

Everywhere in these cousinly gatherings, lack of luxury continued to be the theme. In Moniack, everyone lived on Scotch broth, grouse and jugged hare. The Ropner/Straker/Darbyshire family barbecues down by the river were 'disgusting', Charlie Ropner recalls. 'Burnt sausages that had fallen through onto the charcoal and been picked up and shoved into the river to rinse off. Wet swimming costumes, wet towels, sheep shit, horse shit, dogs everywhere – Labradors, boxers, terriers and mongrels, all shaking themselves off, and they'd eat the whole barbecue if you turned your back for a second.'

A Ropner/Straker/Darbyshire cousins' picnic in Yorkshire, 1970s, with burnt sausages rinsed off in the river

Generally, the rule was the more cousins, the merrier. Cousins seemed to work better in large crowds than they did in small, enforced pairings.

8

Mothers

'Did your mother work?' I asked Elizabeth Millman, daughter of a successful doctor in 1930s Northamptonshire.

'Oh, no! They didn't in those days.'

That was a generalisation, of course. Some of 'them' certainly did work, as we've already seen from Dennis Skinner's mother taking in Mrs Langley's washing, and the sisters whose mother was a full-time psychiatrist. But there was a kernel of truth in Elizabeth's words. Lots of mothers like hers, who nowadays would work, for the independence, status, self-esteem and sheer money of it, didn't in the mid-twentieth century. 'It wasn't the done thing for ladies to work,' said Fred Walker, brought up in 1930s and 1940s Glasgow, the son of the managing director of a furnishing company. Even in the decades after the war, the luxury of not-working remained a status symbol. When Elizabeth said 'they', she was referring to the swathes of wives of professionals who, if they ever had had a job, had given it up as soon as they married, on the understanding that wifehood and motherhood would be their vocations from now on.

This was all very well during term-time, when they could listen to *Woman's Hour* in peace in the daytime, or chat to their friends on the telephone in the hall. But at the moment when the summer holidays began, their own workload dramatically increased. The freedom they generously granted their offspring depended on their own inglorious toil in the background. British drudgery begins.

Nor was it only the middle- and upper-class mothers who didn't work. When I went to Newton-le-Willows to meet a whole neon-lit church-hall-ful of women who'd been brought up as children of factory workers in the 1930s and 1940s, the vast majority told me that their mothers hadn't gone out to work. The household would have fallen apart if they had. There was more than enough work for them to do at home, in the days when you had to lug the washing down to the cellar and agitate the handle of the jiffy-washer. One said, 'My mother ran the pub in Golborne'. But apart from that, their mothers had stayed at home, unpaid, the hubs of their families, managing the cleaning, washing and cooking.

So, if you shut your eyes and think of mid-twentieth-century mothers in summer, the general picture is this: while the fathers were out being the breadwinners – or, if they were 'taking August off', liked to work quietly in their study or shed till someone said 'lunch is ready' – and while even the children of hard-up families got jobs from their early teens and gave the mothers their wages (as we'll see later in the chapter on summer jobs), the mothers were in for a long, hot spell of making everything run smoothly for everyone else.

This involved a great deal of pastry-rolling. 'My mother made apple pies, and steak and kidney,' as Anne Stockton of Newton-le-Willows said; 'mine made bread, fruit pies and fruit cakes,' said Grace McNulty. The smell of baking wafted from open kitchen windows. Mothers had their sleeves rolled up.

The important fact, from the children's point of view, was that their mothers were there. That reassuring baking smell meant 'my mother is at home so all is well with the world'. Even if the mothers were a mere benign presence in the background of their children's lives, 'keeping an eye on us from the kitchen window', as the author and swimmer Jenny Landreth described her mother's default setting in the 1960s, and even if they didn't take a close interest in their children's day-to-day activities or fights, they were there, givers of unconditional love over the undressed salads of lettuce, tomatoes and cucumber and the undressed wounds.

They were too busy with the housekeeping to be very sympathetic if you hurt yourself. 'If we fell over,' said Noreen Rimmer in Newton-le-Willows, 'our mother just scrubbed our knees with a brush. She put vinegar on insect bites.' 'My mum believed all illnesses could be cured with calamine lotion or peroxide,' said Douglas Addison. 'We washed the wound with water and she put peroxide on it and it bubbled up.'

How were the mothers' moods? They varied. It was fine for the ones for whom the vocation of motherhood came naturally. 'I never once heard my mother say, "I wish I'd had a career",' said IT consultant Paul Hansford, brought up at Gorleston-on-Sea near Great Yarmouth in the 1950s, where 'Dad was the moneymaker'. 'My mother liked being a housewife, cooking, doing housework and gardening.' (That was how it seemed from his point of view, anyway.) But, for the ones to whom motherhood didn't come naturally, these could be summers of quiet desperation. 'My mother,' said the author and marriage-bureau proprietor Penrose Halson, 'was one of those women who absolutely wasn't prepared for motherhood. She had four children between 1939 and 1945. She couldn't cook. She was depressed and miserable.'

Colin Burrow's mother did work, as it happened. Her other life was as a successful children's author, Diana Wynne Jones. 'Her second or third novel, *The Ogre Downstairs*,' said Colin, 'was read on *Jackanory*. But she didn't write in the summer. While the school holidays were on, she was there on duty as a mother.'

And 'she spent most of the summer on her knees,' he recalled, 'weeding.' The garden of their Berkshire cottage needed constant attention to keep the bedding plants from being strangled by the overgrowth. 'When me and my brothers smashed a tennis ball into the flowerbed during our games of French cricket, she would cry out, "Me flars!"'

After the torturous seventeen-mile journey to the Berkshire cottage, during which she and Colin's father chain-smoked in the front while the boys fought non-stop in the back, 'our mother was cross by the time we arrived,' said Colin – and one can hardly blame her. During that journey, her status as successful working mother had evaporated – as it did at the beginning of summer for all mothers (such as teachers) who had term-time jobs but reverted to pure motherhood in the holidays.

While Colin's father marked papers in his peaceful study in 'the derelict', his mother toiled away 'making cream teas for visiting Indian academics. I think she felt she was running a guesthouse for nothing.'

Things really turned sour, Colin said, 'when my father's mother came to stay, whom my mother couldn't stick. My grandmother's favoured line at the table was, "Shall I make a fruit salad?" By which she meant "Where's my pudding?"'

One can quite see why his mother might be 'grumpy about the catering', as Colin put it.

The house did have an Indesit washing machine, but there would always be a crisis. It flooded at least once every summer.

That was the problem with second homes in Britain: something always went wrong with a rusty appliance, making what should be a rest into an ordeal, and somehow it was the mother (and perhaps her most mature, household-aware daughter) who had to deal with getting it repaired. It was the same for Markie Robson-Scott's mother when they arrived at the inherited shooting lodge in Scotland at the beginning of each summer. It was up to her to get the house going mechanically. 'My father would go straight into his study and get his typewriter out. My mother's job was to get the Aga going. There were always incredible struggles with the Aga. The whole atmosphere of the house was infused with the misery of the Aga. You had to do "riddling" – shaking the coke with a double-pronged poker. If you didn't riddle it enough, it went out.'

And this was summer. 'But the summers in Roxburghshire were freezing,' recalled Markie. 'Just as cold as winter. The house was in an isolated, exposed position, twelve miles from Jedburgh, with fields in front and behind. All the books were damp. The whole house was damp. The salt stuck together and you couldn't pour it out. The curtains were damp and full of dead or half-dead butterflies. I found that disgusting – *and* sad. It was always windy. My mother spent the day lugging wood from the bothy in a wheelbarrow to keep the fires alight. She had to do all the cooking, and pin the washing out on the line. My father liked to go out for long walks on his own. She buttered Selkirk bannock for him to take with him.'

A typical diary entry from August 1961 goes: 'Beastly weather. Played indoors all day. Daddy's typewriter went wrong.'

Oh, please – not the typewriter. That meant a tedious trip to the typewriter repair man in Hawick. Markie's mother kept a brave face through all this, and at least in the afternoons she had the intellectual stimulation of helping her husband to translate the letters of Sigmund Freud and Arnold Zweig from German to English.

Markie and her mother

Juliet Gardiner's (adoptive) mother spent her 1940s and 1950s summers in a state of continuous low-level grumpiness. It sounds like a bit of a joyless marriage, in Hemel Hempstead. 'My father had never got over his brother's death at the Battle of the Somme,' said Juliet. A pall of gloom hung over the household. 'My father got the coal in and mowed the lawn. My mother did all the housework, which she complained about. Before she'd married, I think she'd been a servant to two bachelor gents. Now she desperately wanted to be accepted as middle class. But we had no char. She did all the washing by hand, clothes hanging on racks or dripping over the kitchen table . . . and she polished a lot. She was always polishing the sideboard. Then off she went shopping with her plastic bucket-bag.'

Tea was served indoors, even on hot days, in the polished dining room: Heinz Russian salad with stale bread, 'followed by my mother's pièce de résistance: chocolate éclairs'. Thank goodness for the chocolate éclairs.

*

I heard it again and again: 'My mother gave up work to bring up her children.' For example, Kevin Crossley-Holland said, 'My mother was a renowned potter, but she gave up her work to bring up her children. And she was intent that we would see England at its best. Every summer, she took us to Wimbledon and to Lord's. She was a wonderful mother.'

'I asked my mother, "Why are you at home?"' Ruth Deech (now the cross-bench peer Baroness Deech) told me. 'My mother replied, "I gave up everything for you."' That exchange happened during the summer holidays of 1953, when Ruth was ten. 'My mother had worked for the London County Council as a town planner, and the rule was that when you were married you had to stop. My mother defied the rule and wore a wedding ring round her neck – but when she got pregnant with me, she lost her nerve and gave up her job. Having seen what her life was like, I vowed I would never stay at home like her.'

To Ruth it seemed clear that her mother was 'a frustrated housewife'. 'She was on her hands and knees cleaning the front steps of our house in Clapham. Our kitchen was so primitive. No washing machine. No hot water – you had to boil the water and wash clothes in the bath. Gas lighting. No fridge – my mother had to go shopping every day, for a quarter of a pound of butter and six eggs. She would queue for twenty minutes at the butcher's for a piece of tripe. When she bought a chicken, she first singed the feathers over the gas cooker, and then smashed the chicken open with an axe, taking out the innards, which usually included a couple of half-formed eggs. I've never liked chicken since.'

It was an intellectually stimulating, German-speaking household; Ruth's father was the Austrian-born journalist Josef Fraenkel, who covered the Nuremberg trials – we'll see more about their father-and-daughter outings in the next chapter. 'The house resounded to the clatter of a typewriter,' said Ruth. 'My mother read Dickens aloud to me, and took me to the Festival Hall as soon as it opened, and to Covent Garden.' She was determined to make her self-sacrifice worthwhile, and she was a dedicated educator of Ruth, her only child. But she got far too excited about days out. 'She put on her best hat and gloves from Selfridges to take me the dentist, Dr Schrotter, in Portland Place. That summer outing was a nightmare. What a butcher! He'd been a dentist in Vienna. With his old-fashioned drill ... it was dreadful. He chatted away to my mother – and she liked that. It was an outing for her.'

Even while doing the daily shopping on Clapham High Street, 'my mother would stop and talk for ages to a passer-by. At home she was on the telephone for hours.'

Hours of talking – and more hours – too many hours of lightweight chit-chat for her clever mother, and it pained Ruth to hear it.

Annabel Heseltine recalls that her mother was 'very lonely' during the long (and blissful for Annabel) weeks they spent every summer in a rented house on the Flete estate in Devon in the 1960s and early 1970s. 'My father was in London. There my mother was – a young MP's wife in the middle of nowhere, and she didn't know anyone. She hadn't passed her driving test, but she could drive to the village on private roads.'

No wonder au pairs came into fashion: a homesick foreign girl to help with the drudgery in exchange for board and lodging, a bit of pocket money and hours of stilted conversation practice in the kitchen.

*

The mothers who did work were all the more heroic. George Oaks's mother had no choice but to go out to work in 1940s Suffolk, because George's father was an alcoholic, so of no use. 'My father was at home. As soon as the pub was open he was down there having a drink. My mother worked on the land all day, picking stones to clear the land or picking peas, and in the evenings she served in a pub.'

His mother was also running their cottage in Eye, which had no electric light; and there was not a penny to spare. 'If a saucepan wore through, she mended it with a double-washer. We were all dressed from jumble sales. My mother did all the mending and darning. She did the washing in an outhouse with a copper boiler. She lit a fire underneath it to boil the water, and put the washing in with blocks of soap. Then she scrubbed it on a washboard and put it through the mangle.'

In search of meat, George told me, all the local mothers became adept at 'throwing the sickle', hitting rabbits when they came out to feed, so the family could have baked rabbit for supper.

How did she keep the children in check? 'Through strictness,' George said. 'If I did wrong, I got a hiding with a slipper. My brother got on my nerves. I put a stick into a bucket of pitch and put the pitch on his head. I got a hiding and was sent to bed with no supper.' A bit of maternal corporal punishment was expected. 'Our mother,' said Jenny Landreth, brought up in a happy middle-class family in 1960s Sutton Coldfield, 'smacked us with the sticks she used for washing. That did not feel abusive. It felt normal. She smacked us for being rude.' She washed up while listening to *The Archers*. 'The drudgery! But she and my father were in am-dram and they did go out to rehearsals on Monday, Wednesday and Friday.'

In 1970s London, the novelist Sabine Durrant's mother, single because widowed, had no choice but to take young Sabine with her to the office for a couple of weeks every summer, once she'd used up her own holiday allowance and the kindness of friends who took Sabine on holiday with them. 'My mother was a bilingual secretary,' said Sabine. 'I was plonked in a corner of the office, and I was both special and a nuisance: a princess and a complete pain. There was a drinks machine, and I made cocktails out of coffee, tea, hot chocolate and chicken soup. They gave me a typewriter to play with. My mother and I brought our own packed lunches: I had a garlic-sausage sandwich and a Ski yoghurt. Then, it was a very long afternoon. I watched the flies trapped against the window, and the traffic below, crawling along Charing Cross Road.'

This immersion in her mother's working life happened every summer for six years, until Sabine was twelve, when her mother remarried and gave up her job. 'That was a mixed success,' said Sabine. 'She always thought she wanted to be the sort of house-wife who played tennis and bridge, and she did all that. But she was always looking for other work to do, such as pyramid-selling Shaklee vitamins, or working for interior-designer friends. I hated the role model she became. I was incredibly irritated by her – though that says a lot about me. She stopped driving, too – her husband did it all. It used to enrage me.'

It was being in close proximity to their frustrated non-working mothers for those long summer weeks that made the majority of the next generation vow that they would not let that happen to them. Quite the opposite, though, in the case of Lucinda MacDougald: 'having my mother at home with us all through the holidays made me decide to be a stay-at-home mother with my own children.'

*

'My mother was quite tough,' said John Julius Norwich. 'She used to say, "Accustom yourself to nettles!" "Accustom yourself to wasps!"'

In spite of that alarming injunction, John Julius's relationship with his mother, Lady Diana Cooper, was one of the closest mother-child relationships I heard about. 'I spent hours a day with her,' he said. 'I was an only child, and she'd had to wait ten years until she had me. From the age of four, I got into her bed every morning, still warm from my father who'd just got out of it. All my lessons were in bed with my mother: she taught me to read by the age of three, and she taught me all the capitals of countries, and arithmetic – addition, subtraction and multiplication, but not division, because she never understood the principle.'

The Coopers spent every weekend from June to September in their large cottage in Bognor Regis. 'I lived across the garden with my nanny and the cook, in the little lodge, but I ran up to the house straight after breakfast. Bed was my mother's control centre. She never had a desk. She wrote letters in pencil so as not to get ink on the sheets. She made things hum. She would suddenly say, "we're going on a picnic today" or "let's take a boat to an island". One August morning she told me she'd hired a caravan, just for the two of us. We hooked it onto the back of the car and did a tour of the West Country, parking in forests.'

John Julius's close relationship with his mother was rare in those days when 'the grown-ups' were usually a separate species, living separate lives and eating superior, richer food in the dining room while the children lived on boiled chicken in the nursery. John Julius did live on nursery food – 'I had chicken and two veg and rice pudding in the lodge, while the grown-ups were having enormous amounts of seafood in the dining room' – but, between meals, he and his mother basked in each other's company. 'My mother and I drove into Bognor each morning to buy lobster and prawns from the blue-jerseyed sailors.'

He was spared the daily ritual that so many upper-class children endured, of having to dress up in party clothes for the daily hour in the drawing room after tea, to 'visit' their parents and be on display. This ritual was described to me in detail by Bubble Carew-Pole:

'We ran around the garden all day with our swimsuits on.' (This was during her pre-war summers at Antony House in Cornwall.) 'Nanny sometimes took us to the beach in her car, and we had our ponies. We had tea in the nursery at 4.30 – always sandwiches before cake – and then we got into our frilly dresses with sashes. Nanny took us down at 5.30 and pushed us into the drawing room. The room was full of parents, aunts, uncles and guests who were staying. We just hoped there'd be a kindred spirit who'd play a game with us. Some of them were too grand to play anything. The most boring question we dreaded them asking us was, "D'you do lessons?" Some of the kinder ones did play cards with us, such as Old Maid. I cried when I was the "Old Maid" – I thought I'd never get married.'

This emotional distance between mother and children was normal in the upper classes. 'We didn't enjoy family life with our parents,' said Elaine Ashton, brought up in a fishing lodge in Monmouthshire before and during the war. 'Not like children do now.' Elaine and her brothers weren't even collected from their boarding school by their parents at the end of the summer term. Ricketts the chauffeur, in black uniform and black hat, was sent to Malvern to drive the children home from their various schools scattered around that school-ridden town.

'We didn't feel at home with our parents. We didn't long to be with them. In fact, we rather dreaded it. They didn't know us, and they didn't want to know us. We wouldn't have dreamed of going into the dining room when they were in there. We

wouldn't even have wanted to. I don't know why they had children, really.'

As Ann Fraser, daughter of the Raj, who spent her 1930s and
1940s summers in India, recalled, 'My mother couldn't speak
much Hindustani, but she could rattle off, "Ayah, can you bring
my children for an hour after tea?"'

*Ann Fraser's mother (second from right) attending a picnic
in Kashmir with her children, the Scottish governess
Miss Pearson, and quite a lot of help*

9

Fathers

'As for my father,' said Elaine Ashton, recalling her childhood in Wales, 'I don't actually remember speaking to him until I was sixteen. He never spoke on car journeys. He just sat in the front with Ricketts [the chauffeur], not talking. On summer evenings the farmer came to play bowls with him. Neither of them spoke. The farmer had his pipe in his mouth, and my father had his cigar in his, and after the bowls they just sat and enjoyed each other's company in silence.'

She continued, 'My parents didn't seem to have anything in common, except swimming. I think he was fond of us children, but he was very undemonstrative. He had a horse called Business. So when anyone called, we could say, "He's out on Business."'

Fathers could get away with being as antisocial and odd as that in the mid-twentieth century. While mothers oversaw the daily running of the summer holidays, fathers had their set-in-stone habits and their unshakable theories, and the whole family lived according to them. If a father needed his peace and quiet, he got it. Thus, marriages creaked along, some happier than others, mothers running the place but fathers running the whole situation in a deeper sense.

Here is a selection of fathers' unshakable theories I heard during my interviews:

'My father's theory was that you had to arrive at any restaurant by 12.30 because it got too crowded any later than that.'

'My father would only take us on our one Outing of the Summer – a day trip to St Cyrus, on the east coast of Scotland – on a day when the weather was good enough that when you came over the final hill there wouldn't be a haar [sea fog]. He would watch the forecast anxiously for days in advance. He had to align the weather with the tides, because he believed that the water was "warmer" if it was going over "warm" sand, so we were only allowed to swim on an incoming tide. In all our years of doing that day trip, he only got the alignment wrong once.'

'My father believed girls should not wear make-up. I arrived at lunch with powder on my nose and was sent straight back upstairs to wash it off.'

'My father planned our holiday abroad like a military operation. He commandeered the dining-room table for months in advance, planning every aspect of our travels, even finding out the precise hours when each Italian petrol station had its three-hour midday siesta.'

'Even though my father's factory actually made dishwashers, we didn't have one at home. He said, "I don't see the point in them."'

'My father's theory was that we must pitch our tent on a hummock. He believed the midges wouldn't get us if we were up a bit higher. [This was in Argyllshire.] Then he smoked his pipe *and* cooked kippers, both simultaneously, as he believed doing both would really keep the midges away.'

'My father was obsessed with avoiding the traffic. He made us leave home at 6 a.m. to get from Shenfield to Clacton – which meant we arrived far too early, so we had breakfast at a greasy spoon before the landlady of the boarding house opened up.'

'My father carried his Pevsners with him wherever he went. He had a compulsion to go into churches, when we were on our journeys. He wasn't religious. But sometimes tears would roll down his cheeks at the beauty of it. It had an incredible effect on him. I hated it. Sometimes I refused to go in.'

'When we were in France my father refused to do the driving, because, he said, "the French drive on the wrong side of the road". So my mother had to drive.'

Why were fathers like that? I think it was because most of them had spent time in the army, navy or air force, where they had acquired habits of discipline and theories about how things should, indeed must, be done, in a practical, sensible, military way. This rigidity had spread into their civilian life. Having lived under military orders, they now relished being the colonel in their own family: the one giving the orders and the one with the specialist knowledge. For many fathers there was a bit of one-upmanship going on: a belief that if you used your nuggets of hard-won wisdom, you could 'get ahead' of everyone else: arrive at places first, beat the weather, miss the traffic, avoid insects and so on.

Rather unfairly, while mothers were loved but often taken for granted, fathers were adored and revered. There was a glamour and mystique about them, from the children's point of view, because they were above domesticity, in the way that a monarch is above politics. They did pitch the tent, load the roof rack and switch off heaters if anyone tried to switch one on, which just about counted as domesticity, but that was as far as it went. Their preferences were indulged, and the very fact that they were often physically undemonstrative made their children all the keener to win their approval by doing things in the required fashion.

The mystique of fathers was summed up in the 1965 Ladybird Book *Telling the Time*, which described, with illustrations, a typical school-holidays day at home. It began 'we have our breakfast' (all together, round a laid table, cooked by Mummy) and 'we go shopping' (with Mummy, who carries the basket). It then came to 'Mummy cooks the lunch' (and you see the smiling mother in her brown dress and yellow apron putting a lidded dish into the oven); then 'we have our lunch' (stew, in the dining room), followed by 'we sail our boats' (for which the mother has changed into her pink afternoon dress for the walk to the municipal pond). Then, teatime (sandwiches and cake made by Mummy). But the highlight of the day is: 'Six o'clock. Daddy comes home.' The illustration shows the children running excitedly along the garden path as their briefcase-carrying father walks towards them, evening paper tucked under his arm. That's the apogee of the day. Daddy gets off lightly: an hour later, by 7 p.m., Mummy is policing the pillow fight, shaking her finger crossly. Daddy is nowhere to be seen until at 7.30 both parents look in on the children as they sleep.

Behind the benign paternal bedtime smile, there was often an edge of bracing terrifyingness about fathers. Although many of them didn't believe in an academic education for their daughters, they still expected them to know certain facts (such as the names of birds, trees, constellations and capital cities, and the laws of cricket) and to acquire certain skills (such as how to tie a reef knot, cast a fishing line and do military drill), and summers were a time to stuff some of that knowledge into them. At picnics, a father would suddenly inculcate the children into his own army-acquired skill of spotting an item in the landscape via the information that it was 'at five o'clock from the bushy-topped tree'. Quickfire general-knowledge questions, and sudden mental arithmetic problems, flew across dining-room tables, making the children quake. 'My father would always ask me who'd been imprisoned on Loch Leven,' said Rachel Meddowes, 'and I could never remember. When he started fining me, I did remember.' No one did ever forget the general knowledge drummed into them by their fathers.

'Our father wanted us to learn to be observant,' said Elfrida Eden. 'I'd be walking down a street in London and he'd suddenly turn me round and say, "Now describe the scene that was in front of you." Her father (who was Sir Anthony Eden's brother) does sound terrifying. 'He was a very Victorian father, born in 1893. We were meant to stand up when he came into the room. No trousers in the dining room: we had to change into a skirt, for lunch and supper, and he inspected our hands.' It was this father who sent his daughter upstairs to take her make-up off before lunch. 'He loved parlour games and playing the piano. He had a moustache and a bristly kiss. We all loved him.'

Always, there was a longing for fatherly attention, even if it came with a dose of terror. So when Julie Welch queued at the fish and chip shop during her 1950s Sheringham holidays, with her slightly scary father having a week off from his busy job, she was in bliss. 'The fish and chip shop was in a side road off the seafront, with turquoise tiled walls with smiley cod and grinning starfish,' she said. 'I loved queuing there with my father. It was my time to be with him, on my own. It was getting dark, and the lights were twinkling, and there was a fantastic smell of vinegar. My father was terribly approving of me. I was a greedy child and so was he. He liked it that I ate every last limp, greasy chip.'

As time went on and 'my parents' marriage got a bit iffy,' said Julie, 'my mother was more the one who claimed his attention. Once he'd started making his pile of money and rising up in the world, I don't think he found family life interesting any more. But I always knew I was loved by him.' (He was later to become such a heavy drinker that he once 'plumped up' the dog, thinking it was a sofa cushion.)

'I didn't mind at all being an only child,' said Ruth Deech. 'It meant I had lovely excursions with my father. Although he did tend the garden, he didn't like fresh air: it brought him out in a rash. He took me to the British Museum every Saturday morning, and parked me in front of the Egyptian mummies while he went off to the library for an hour or two. I roamed freely round the British Museum, aged seven, eight and nine. Then we went across the road to the jewellery shop Cameo Corner, run by Moshe Oved, a jeweller and poet from Central Europe, who wore a long purple gown. My father and he sat in the back of the shop discussing Yiddish poetry and Zionism. Then my father and I prowled Soho together for continental bakeries and delicatessens.'

Ruth Deech with her father Josef Fraenkel
enjoying a rare dose of fresh air, Folkestone, 1947

It made her feel grown up and special, and it certainly beat going to the Clapham shops and Harley Street dentist with her mother in gloves, who was nobly keeping the family household and oral hygiene ticking over. Note that Ruth's father was not taking Ruth to places a young girl might have chosen to go to. Fathers did what *they* wanted to do, and their children tagged along, being educated as a side effect. My father took me to cavernous second-hand bookshops where we stayed for hours. The only way to get through it was to develop a collecting urge, so I found myself accumulating the antiquated Shown to the Children series (*Bees Shown to the Children*; *Birds Shown to the Children*; *Butterflies Shown to the Children* etc.). 'My father used to take us to look round churches,' said the psychiatrist Harriet Mullan. 'Well, *he* went into the church, and we played around in the churchyard. We read the tombstones and you won the game if you found the child who'd died at the youngest age.'

Fathers were revered for their practicality and their belief that what was possible should be tried. The Tools Generation, they had carpentry workshops which were either a total mess or obsessively tidy, rarely anything in between. Some were practical out of necessity. 'My father,' said Dennis Skinner, 'mended all his children's shoes, with his iron hobbing foot.' 'Mine,' said Enid Hales, 'made us a cricket ball out of loads and loads of elastic bands.' Others did it out of a sense of fun. 'Our father,' said Katie Thomas, 'made wings for us out of cardboard, string and bamboo. He assured us that if we really concentrated, we'd be able to fly. He strapped us to our wings and told us to run down the big hill at Ashton Park near Clifton Suspension Bridge, flapping our wings, and to jump when he called. When we didn't soar upwards, he put it down to a lack of concentration.'

Who cared that they didn't actually fly? The attempt was heroic and their father seemed visionary for giving it a go.

It was also the boyish aspect of their fathers that children relished. 'Our father,' said the architect Timothy Makower, 'said, "let's all get onto the roof of the car and drive up the hill to look at the stars."' That was in Wiltshire in the 1970s, where they were camping in the garden of their aunt. 'It felt magical to be allowed to go to bed late, and to get onto the top of the Austin Maxi to go for a night-time drive.'

And children relished fathers' impulsive inventiveness. 'I grew up in a top-floor flat in Eaton Square in the 1960s,' said Mia Woodford, vintage equestrian clothes retailer. 'My father ran his own advertising and publicity company and we never had much money, but we did manage to rent that flat, though we spent the whole summer fending off the bailiffs. There was no outside space, so my father cut a hole in the ceiling and put a ladder up. He did barbecues up there on the roof. We were clinging to the rooftops. There were no balustrades. I don't know how we didn't die.'

The dark side of this impulsive stubbornness was that if a father didn't want to do something, he simply wouldn't.

'Please can you drive us to the sea?' Rachel Johnson and her siblings used to beg their father Stanley, when they were staying on Exmoor. To which he replied, 'Could easily.' '"Could easily" meant "no",' explained Rachel. 'A Johnson can't say "no". "Could easily" is actually a firm "no".'

That flat in Eaton Square with the hole in the ceiling was full of ashtrays heaped with cigarette ends, Mia Woodford said. 'My father smoked sixty to eighty a day, and my mother wasn't averse to the odd Gauloise, either.'

That glimpse gives a sense of how mid-twentieth-century summers involved a long spell of passive smoking for the resident offspring. To exist in a haze of cigarette smoke, stained wallpaper, yellow-fingernailed parents and cigarette boxes on every table seemed perfectly usual. 'We used to beg our parents to buy more cigarettes, so we could complete our set of cigarette cards,' said Walter Balmford of Birmingham.

*

Things were hard if your parents were divorced and thus the father had cut himself adrift and was on his own, living in some desolate faraway flat or hovel. In those days when children were more emotionally distant from their fathers already ('fathers weren't quite so chummy in those days', many reminded me), divorce could make them catastrophically distant, and visits to them could be painful.

'My parents divorced in 1947, when I was four,' said Sue Sabbagh. 'I remember my sister crying during the holidays. She pretended her daddy had died. She couldn't bear to say "divorced". It sounded worse than death. We saw him once a year. He visited us and took us to a hotel, and we'd really lost touch with him. He still referred to us by the nicknames we'd had as babies.'

'My parents' marriage fell apart when I was ten,' said Virginia Radcliffe (b. 1939). 'My father was a womaniser through the marriage. Then my mother met someone else, an artist, and she ran off with him. Daddy was livid that she'd left; and he didn't see why he should pay the school fees when we were living with Mummy. I was always terrified of him.'

Every weekend Virginia and her brother had to go and visit their father, taking the 27 bus to Devonshire Place (he was a doctor in Wimpole Street). 'His housekeeper cooked the lunch, and then our father took us to the cinema. On the way there he'd say things to us like, "I'll pay the school fees for next term if your mother gives me back the mink coat I gave her." We never knew whether we were going to be going back to school in September.'

That weekly outing was traumatic for Virginia. 'On the way back home to Kensington I was terrified we were going to miss the bus stop. I was a very anxious child.'

Caroline Wyatt's widowed father tried very hard to be as good a father as her mother had been a mother. This is how Caroline remembers the summer of 1978. 'I was so excited to be going home from Woldingham [her convent boarding school, nicknamed 'Wolditz'], knowing I was going to be at home for two months of the summer. We were living in Stockholm by then. I knew something was wrong when my mother didn't come and meet me and my brothers at the airport. Dad was there, and on the way home he explained that Mum was ill. When we got home we saw the curtains of her bedroom were closed. She was usually the life and soul of the house. We spent a lot of time in her room reading to her, or torturing her by playing the flute. She couldn't get up and do things. By the end of July, she was too weak to cook. My brothers knew she was dying, I think, but I didn't. She went to hospital, and I used to think, Oh, good, we're going to hospital to see Mum, so I can have an ice cream. It really didn't occur to me that she was going to die.' She did die, aged fifty-two.

'That,' said Caroline, 'was the summer when everything

changed. We moved back to Northern Ireland in 1979. My father sweetly labelled my drawers "Jumpers" and "Socks" – he was trying to be like my mother, but he just wasn't built for it. We lived on early boil-in-the-bag meals, which were terrible and actually made school food seem good by comparison.' A newly widowed father could be at sea in his own kitchen, scalding his fingers as he tried to hoik out the bags from the boiling saucepan.

*

The delineations of parental roles described in this chapter seem a bit shocking now, as does the fact that parents passed those delineations down to their offspring. Those long weeks of summer did reinforce and rehash parental stereotypes: mothers in the kitchen, directing the domestic chores; daughters helpful in the house, sons more helpful in the carpentry shed; fathers the glamorous returners. Victoria Peterkin, who spent her summers in Scotland, said that for her generation of siblings and cousins, 'by going out shooting with our fathers in the morning, we avoided helping our mothers prepare the lunch'. It was as simple as that. Out on the shoot, she said, 'the boys all had guns from the age of about twelve. The girls had game bags and were expected to carry the odd brace of partridges or a hare.'

Thanks a bunch. No one complained. There was no taboo about sexual stereotypes. In its unforgivable way, that absence of taboo did make the days run smoothly.

10

Grandparents, Aunts and Uncles

For many children, going to stay with the grandparents was the sole experience of Going Somewhere Else in the summer holidays. It was a matter of luck whether your grandparents were kind, welcoming people who loved you as much as or more than your own parents did, so going to visit them was a treat, or dried-up old sticks who weren't remotely interested in you, so going to visit them was an ordeal.

Luckily, there were two sets, so a child might be unlucky with the paternals but luckier with the maternals, or vice versa.

If you thought fathers had odd habits and weird theories, just wait for the grandparents, who'd been born in the nineteenth or early twentieth century and carried the rituals and beliefs of the olden days deep into the modern era. 'My grandmother, who lived in a house called Miramar [Sea View] in Porthcawl,' said Peter Susman, 'did not let me swim in the sea till two days after I'd arrived there. Two days! She said, "your body needs to adjust". I thought, "Adjust? Adjust to what?" She put raw onion onto my chilblains. She bathed my eyes in cold tea. If I was sucking my thumb, she made me dip it into *boiling* water. She was a nasty person, actually. She would go round the shops and pick fights with the shopkeepers.'

'My grandmother, Constance Jarvis,' said Caroline Cranbrook (b. 1935), 'used to eat our pets. Our nanny, Diddy, got us a rabbit, house-trained Sarah, from the keeper – and when we came back from staying with our other grandparents in Wales, we found that Granny had eaten our rabbit. This happened two summers running. We then had Donald Duck, and he too was eaten by Granny.'

'My maternal grandmother, whom I went to stay with in Northumberland in the 1950s,' said the television producer Angela Holdsworth, 'always wore a corset. She couldn't walk without one. She hadn't got the stomach muscles for it. I had chickenpox and called out for her in the middle of the night. The only way she could come and see me in the night was by strapping her stays over her pink nightgown. That just about held her up.'

We'll meet more such alarming grandparents; but the majority verdict, among the hundreds of people I spoke to, was that grandparents were a miraculous extra dimension of kindness and love in their lives, their houses welcoming havens with their own distinctive sounds, scents and daily rituals. Going to stay with them in the summer brought a vital layer of stability and reassurance to childhood.

Henrietta Petit (with whom I shared a dormitory aged eleven) and her sister the artist Annabel Fairfax told me that going to stay with their maternal grandparents at Archway House, near Kirklington in Nottinghamshire, in the 1960s and 1970s was a lifeline, not just for them but also for their mother, who had been widowed at thirty-two and found it hard to cope with her three children on her own during the holidays. All of them longed to be enfolded in the framework of a loving, bustling household run by the generation above. 'Our grandparents were absolute gatherers of us all,' said Annabel. That was what those grandparents were: gatherers.

As Henrietta described her grandparents' house, she said, 'I can go there now – I *am* there – I'm more there than here. In my mind, my grandparents are still there, and that life is still going on.' She was spot-on about grandparental-house recall. Even if our grandparents are long dead, we still inhabit their dwellings. Because their houses weren't our own, they combined the solace of the known with the unforgettableness of the strange. I can pour out the contents of my Austrian grandmother's button box, and describe each of the buttons inside, from red velvet to bulbous metal. I can hear her saying to me, as she put me to bed in the little spare bedroom of their ground-floor flat in Bickley, Kent, "I'll say goodnight now, but you'll hear me clattering the dishes in the kitchen."' That seemed a deeply comforting and kind way of saying 'goodnight'.

Children, who crave the stability of going back to the same place and seeing things done in exactly the same way they were done last time, treasured the unchangingness of the older generation's daily timetable. The older we get, it seems, the more we fall into the habit of doing exactly the same small actions in precisely the same way at the same time each day. Without meaning to, we provide amusement and reassurance for the generations beneath.

*

I'll start by recapturing three grandparental cocoons: that one in Nottinghamshire, one in Kent and one in the Republic of Ireland, all places of rescue and reassurance for the grandchildren. I think these descriptions prove that 'Granny' and 'Granny's house' are fused, almost one and the same thing, in the memory.

On arriving at that maternal grandparents' house in Nottinghamshire in their packed Mini, Henrietta and Annabel could breathe freely at last, knowing they would be there for a month. Archway House was a thriving household and it ran like clockwork. You might think that after a year at a terrifyingly regimented, bell-ringing boarding school, Henrietta would have had enough of places that ran like clockwork. But a grandparental house like this proved that an ordered household could be benign, its firm daily timetable providing a framework for liberty. 'I can't emphasise enough what rocks of stability our grandparents represented to us,' said Annabel. 'They were almost Victorian in their ways. They believed in fresh air in all weathers and they were strict about eating between meals, that is, you never did.' So, as strict as boarding school in some ways but with none of the cruelty.

'Granny was very thin,' Henrietta said, 'and always on the go. She carried a scythe and chopped down the nettles ahead of us on our daily afternoon walk. She kept masses of chickens, all with their own names, and we went to collect the eggs with her. She weighed each egg on her special egg-weighing machine and put them into old egg-boxes.' 'She wore navy trousers and a navy jersey and Dr Scholl shoes,' said Annabel, 'and had a 1950s hairstyle with two combs in her hair. She'd lived through the war so she didn't throw anything away. She'd kept all our mother's and her sisters' old skates, their old clothes and their coming-out dresses, in old leather trunks in the attic. The house smelled deliciously of mothballs. Nothing was ever redecorated. It never occurred to her to change anything. We loved sleeping in the bed our mother had slept in as a child, and reading the books she'd read: *Milly-Molly-Mandy* and *What Katy Did.*'

By contrast, Henrietta said, 'Grandfather was quieter. He had run a coalmine. He spent most of the day in his study.'

('Quieter' grandfathers were a running theme throughout my interviews. There was an element of 'don't mention the war' – the First World War. Nick Weeks, a Somerset farming contractor, told me that his grandfather had been gassed at Passchendaele, not once but twice, and 'he needed to be on his own after lunch in the study listening to his favourite music'. Humphrey Boyle was told by his grandmother Ethel, 'Your grandfather was at Passchendaele. Never mention the Great War to Grandpapa, or Passchendaele.')

Each day at Archway House began with breakfast in the dining room, 'with starched napkins, and boiled eggs wrapped up inside a huge brown china hen, with slices of ham carved by Grandfather.

By the end of breakfast, the cleaner Mrs Izzard had arrived and was starting to cluck around the place. 'The gardeners came in for elevenses, which they had with the cleaners in the long kitchen with the Aga. You reached the kitchen by going through a green-baize door into the part of the house with the scullery, the pantry, the silver-polishing room.' It was clear that Henrietta was smelling each room as she went through them in her mind, and even I could smell them.

After the afternoon walk with the scything granny, children's tea was upstairs in the day nursery, which had an out-of-tune piano in it as well as all the old toys. 'Tea was set up like a proper meal, round a big, round table: brown bread, butter and raspberry jam followed by Fuller's walnut cake. Grandfather always came up to the nursery to join us for tea. We heard his footsteps: "Grandfather's coming!" He had his own chair: "Grandfather's chair".'

Then, Alan, a Kentish man who has moved away from his native Ashford, told me how much he treasured his visits to his grandparents in the 1950s.

'I was born in 1947 in in Willesborough, Kent. I started off in a pre-fab and we graduated up to a council house. Every Wednesday evening in the term-time and all through the holidays, my two sisters and I walked the mile over the fields to Granny and Grandad's, and we sometimes stayed the night. Even now, I can smell the smell of Palmolive soap that greeted us as we walked in.'

The house was called Crow Corner. It was just by the railway line, and trains rocked the house. 'I loved it there,' Alan said. 'I slept on a feather mattress. Their whole life was based round a big kitchen table. There was a kettle on a swivel that went over the open fire. No indoor lavatory – just a tin hut in the garden. Granny kept chickens [another chicken-keeping granny – clearly the hall-mark of a sound grandmother], and everything we ate came out of the garden. Grandfather was a steam-engine engineer at the Ashford works. He cycled to work, came home for lunch, had his forty winks in his chair, and then cycled back to work. Granny

made the most wonderful meat pies, with thick pastry. She boiled
up all the feed for the chickens with the potato peelings and leftovers, all mashed up. After meals I helped her clear up and wash
up: "helping Granny" was what we did. I also helped Grandad
in the shed. He taught me how to sharpen a saw and cut wood.'

The house was later demolished to build the new high-
speed line.

*Aerial photo of Alan's grandparents' house
in Kent, very close to the railway line*

'Going to stay with my grandmother in Ireland rescued me,'
said Derren Gilhooley (the Catholic boy from Blacon in Cheshire
whose form teacher had blotted out the windows with Fablon).
It was partly a rescue from spending his summers on the Blacon
council estate trying to avoid the boys who bullied him at school.
'I was an effeminate boy, and I was horribly bullied.' But it was

also a rescue from a too-clean-and-tidy home. 'We lived in a flat in a three-storey block on Treborth Road in Blacon. It was lacking in charm and character. My mum was a single mother. She liked everything to be spick and span, and she always seemed to be busy cleaning something.'

By contrast, his grandmother's house in Mullingar felt like an earthier home; and on the day the summer holidays began that was where Derren went. Getting there was not easy. 'There was a lot of seasickness on the boat from Holyhead to Dún Laoghaire, and the crossing could take six hours on a rough sea, so I'd be in a terrible state when the boat docked. It took ages to couple up with the gantries: sometimes forty minutes or an hour. I was desperate to get off.'

As soon as he did, it was the softness of everything in Ireland that struck him and warmed his heart, as well as the delicious smell of peat and wood fires, after the stark, white, centrally heated tidiness of home. 'Granny lived in a two-up, two-down terraced house with a fireplace in every room, a house full of dusty corners and old furniture. It was a patchwork of wallpapers and curtains, and pictures of Jesus pointing to his breast, where his heart lay exposed. If you said something naughty, Granny would say, "In front of the Sacred Heart of Jesus!" Every picture had other pictures stuck into the frame – photobooth photos, or cards, or newspaper cuttings.'

'Granny was a such warm, humorous person,' said Derren. He loved settling into her gentle but regular routine. 'Toast for breakfast, and lunch was the main meal, cooked by Granny in her thick black frying pan – boiled bacon ribs, liver, or a chop, or plaice with a baked potato, and I'd leave the leathery skin on the side of my plate and just eat the white fluff with butter. She would say, "this is a lovely *floury* potato".'

She sent Derren out to the newsagent, from the age of six, to buy the *Evening Press* for her, and a packet of Murray Mints, and they did the crossword together.

Having no innate desire to roam the countryside, but a longing to mooch around the local shops, Derren was allowed to do exactly that. 'I was an indoor child. The newsagent was my library. I just stood there reading all the comics. I liked any shop that sold gifts, stationery and fancy goods. If it was raining, I'd think, Hooray! We're going to stay in. I'll be at the kitchen table all day and it'll be the most exciting day of my life.'

To spend the summer holidays in that little house, with albums and *Famous Five* books spilling out from under the sofa, was heaven – and it didn't matter a jot that the house had 'no running hot water till 1986'.

*

Grandparents were so bound up with the houses they lived in that their very furniture seemed redolent of them. Whether the house was a stately home or a back-to-back in a cul-de-sac, what mattered was that it was a place with unchanging rituals and a place where you felt loved, even if it was quite a fierce love, such as that of Maud Russell, chatelaine of Mottisfont in Hampshire, for her grandchildren. Emily Russell recalled, 'Our grandmother took one look at us when we arrived to stay with her, and said, "they look like little waifs". She invited us to play croquet with her and she was much better than all of us, even in her eighties. She would whack the ball hard and hit ours far out of the way. And in the evening she beat us at Scrabble.'

As long as children are enfolded in daily love, it doesn't matter so much who gives the love. Sheffield barrister Sally Terris and her sister were virtually brought up by their grandmother (a naval officer's widow) in the Sheffield suburb of Walkley through the 1960s and 1970s, as their mother was a chronic alcoholic. Their grandmother's kindness enveloped, nurtured and strengthened them, in every action and every daily ritual. 'Our staple of summer,' said Sally, 'was to be at home, in her two-up-two-down house – a house low on essentials – no car, no washing machine, no fridge, no central heating – but full of love. Our grandmother did all the washing – including the sheets – by hand in the kitchen sink.'

Then, one day in the late 1960s, a launderette came to Walkley. Now their week contained an in-built family outing. 'Our grandmother was in a high good humour on launderette day. She loaded up the wicker trolley and wheeled it down South Road, and we went along with her and bought comics and sweets at the newsagents on the way, and she bought the *Daily Express*, and off we all went to the launderette. We sat there reading and watching the washing going round and round, having a lovely, warm sort of time: it was a sort of holiday outing. It's why I like doing washing now.'

Who even needed Bridlington, let alone Spain, when the launderette afforded such pleasures? Every day the family had a traditional Yorkshire high tea at home: 'a boiled egg, or beans on toast, and then cake, and tea to drink. It was a real routine. That's what I realise is such a great thing – it helps children to flourish.' It was Sally who mentioned the 'fingers of green' coming in to Sheffield: for outings, they would take a bus to another district of Sheffield and go out for a walk to Stanage Edge, or the Rivelin Valley, and have a picnic of egg sandwiches wrapped in greaseproof paper.

In far-flung families, where parents were abroad because the father was in the army or navy or working for a firm in a distant colonial country, it often happened that the grandparents in Britain acted as the family linchpin or hub, holding everything together for the grandchildren in the holidays. Angela Holdsworth's paternal grandmother moved to Camberley in the 1950s especially so she could be near Heathrow to pick up the grandchildren and take them to and from their boarding schools and to and from the airport. She had three families of grandchildren, and her being there made the whole complicated operation possible. The only alarming aspect was that 'she was the world's worst back-seat driver. She had set up house with a gentleman friend called Chrissie, who did the driving, and she bossed him about terribly: "Put your right-hand indicator out NOW! Slow down, there's a corner coming! Don't get so near that car! Traffic lights coming!" and so on. Chrissie did tapestry.'

Lucinda Sims, whose father was an agronomist working for British Overseas Aid, also described the 'grandparents as linchpins' phenomenon: 'mine lived at Andover, and Grandfather – a retired colonel – did all the to-ing and fro-ing from boarding school (Eton and Lewiston) to Heathrow. Granny sorted out all our paper tickets and counterfoils in small envelopes, collecting them from the travel agents.'

'My grandmother's Edwardian house in Newquay,' said the retired surveyor Jennifer McGrandle, 'was called Lehenver, but within the family it was known as "The Anchorage", because it was an anchorage for us all – a place of stability and refuge for a family scattered across the globe.' Her father was away in the navy, and her mother sent Jennifer by train to stay with her grandmother, 'Granny Lean', every summer holiday. The summer she remembers most vividly was the summer of 1949, when she was twelve. 'Basically I ran wild. That was the last summer before reality hit me – the reality of having to work at school. It was my last summer of unadulterated childhood.'

Again, the character of the house and the character of the granny were intertwined. 'The house had a real family feel – full of photographs and presents given to her by her siblings who were in India – ivory jars, highly decorated toothpicks, furniture inlaid with ivory. She rarely travelled herself. She was always formally dressed in a skirt and blouse, and she stayed at home as head of the family, often playing bridge all afternoon with her friends. Everything was done on a set day: Monday was washing day, in the copper in an outhouse, Tuesday ironing day. Mrs Williams came in from the countryside on three days a week to do more laundry and the vegetables for the weekend, and on Wednesday and Thursday we had Ruby to help as well . . . ' The food was plain: Spam was accompanied by a salad of lettuce, tomato, hard-boiled egg, with beetroot served separately. 'The only lunch I looked forward to was boiling fowl with parsley sauce. In the evening my grandmother and I had scrambled eggs on toast and the luxury of a peach.'

(Peaches were considered a luxury, as well as decadent and dangerously juicy, in those austere post-war days. 'No peaches in the nursery' was the rule in upper-class grandparental country houses.')

The odd thing was that Jennifer had never learned to swim. She went surfing on her own four times a day in the dangerous Atlantic waves, in the days before lifeguards, and no one worried. 'There *were* drownings,' she said. 'But I knew the rules: never swim within an hour of a meal, and never surf at low tide.'

Jennifer McGrandle's 'Granny Lean', whose house
in Newquay was known by the family as 'The Anchorage'.
(Baby Jennifer on her knee, 1937)

*

The benignity is never forgotten. 'On the last day of staying with my grandparents, who lived three miles away up the road,' said Jean Parfrey of Newton-le-Willows (b. 1937), 'my grandfather put a shilling in each of my shoes.' 'On the day we left,' said Annabel Fairfax, 'our grandmother gave us a bag each for the journey, containing five little toys.'

More eccentric grandparents? Rachel Johnson's Exmoor one, known as 'Granny Butter', was kindness itself and the opposite of a health-and-safety granny, 'never cross,' said Rachel, 'and she encouraged us in whatever we were doing. If we were climbing a tree, she would say "Wonderful! Climb higher!"' But she did hurl wet tea leaves onto the kitchen floor: that was her method for sweeping everything up.

Rachel Johnson's 'Granny Butter'. © Johnson family archive

'My grandfather,' said Notting Hill-based author Tom Stacey, 'was a curmudgeonly old man. There was always some black cloud over a negligible problem, for example if the gardener had stripped creeper off a wall where he wanted creeper, of if a horse had been allowed to graze in the wrong field.' This was at the grandparental house, Castle Fields in Buckinghamshire, in the 1930s. 'I look back on him with pity. It was an essentially unhappy marriage, and an unhappy household. My grandfather lived in one wing, his wife in another and his widowed sister in another, and they all had their own dogs. The gong would go for lunch, rung by Dingle the liveried butler, and all of us hungry children were keen to get into the dining room. From different quarters of the house we could hear each of these elderly people summoning their dogs in their different voices: my grandmother calling her Pekingese, my great-aunt Busy calling her poodle and Grandfather roaring at the top of his voice for his corgi: "Come here, Taffy!"'

'My grandmother, "Granny Oaks", said George Oaks (the farmer's son in 1930s Suffolk), 'washed pigs' intestines, boiled them for twenty-four hours, put them in vinegar, and cut them into pieces, and we ate them: they were called "chitterlings". She made all her own faggots, with oatmeal and heart and lungs, and she put those into the intestine walls. She had a strong Suffolk accent and wore long black frocks.'

'My grandfather, Reg Hall,' said Edward Hall, 'had worked as a stationmaster in Kessingland, Suffolk, all his life, and had never travelled outside Britain. He really had time for us. I spent hours playing pontoon with him: he kept a big jar of old pennies for that. And I used to watch the wrestling with him: Big Daddy and Mick McManus. [This was the mid-1970s.] Every day at about midday, he would say, "I'm off for an hour or so." "Where?" I asked. "I'm going to see a man about a dog." Actually he was going to the White Horse pub for a pint and a go on the one-arm bandit. I only discovered that much later, when he took me with him. I had a shandy.'

Reg Hall

*

One question was: did these old people make you feel young, because you were so much younger than they were; or did they in fact make you feel old, because when you were with them you had to live in their old, slow ways, and spend time with their old, slow friends, and push their tea trollies about for them at the appointed hour? Old people had after-lunch naps: Caroline Chichester-Clark, going to stay with her grandmother at Camber Sands in the 1950s (which she was so excited about that she felt sick on the journey), had to tiptoe around the garden with her sister, not making a sound, for two hours after lunch while her grandmother had her nap. Then, refreshed, the grandmother took the grandchildren for a walk and a picnic tea, during which another grandparental theory was voiced: 'It doesn't matter if your plimsolls get wet, as long as you keep *moving*.'

It could be hard work if the grandparents were the type who made you feel old, as well as scared. 'My Jarvis grandmother could be terrifying to the staff,' said Caroline Cranbrook. 'When her chauffeur asked her "Where to, Madam?" she replied, infuriated, "I'll tell you when I get there."'

'I started to play with the pendulum on the clock in my grandparents' hall,' said Ben Thomas, 'and my grandmother caught me and barked, "Don't you touch the pendulum."' Like many adults, Ben is also haunted by a getting-stuck-in-a-locked-bathroom memory, which occurred in that house. "I couldn't reach the door handle. I screamed and screamed.'

*

Let us leave the snoozing grandparents in their dark dining rooms with their dark furniture, and turn briefly to the aunts. Aunts, too, came out of the woodwork in summer. Or they stayed in their own woodwork and their nephews and nieces went to stay with them. I've classed them among the grandparents here because, although they might be a generation beneath, they seemed fascinatingly old. And often, you didn't even know exactly who they were. They just appeared at the front door for tea, or came at you from round a corner while you were out shopping, and you were told they were your Aunt Someone, or Auntie Someone. And sometimes they weren't even your real aunt or auntie but just a close friend of your parents. 'We went to stay with our "Auntie Iris" and "Uncle Leslie" in Reading in the 1960s, said Jamaican immigrant Charmaine Alder, 'but they weren't our real relations.' Luckily they were nice and 'lived near a park'.

Rowan Williams remembers this multiple-aunt phenomenon in the little village in Wales, Ystradgynlais, where he started his life. 'I'd be walking along and my mother would say, "That's your Auntie Gertie." "That's your Auntie Betty." "That's your Uncle Tom." He grew up among a large group of elderly spinster aunts, some of them in long crêpe dresses, and 'it was fairly likely that anyone you bumped into was some kind of relation'. His first ever holiday was going in a taxi with three of the aunts to Swansea Bay, before his family bought their first car, a Singer called 'Bing', when he was five.

Aunts seemed more visible than uncles – perhaps because, like mothers, they were often around in the daytime, helping the beleaguered mothers with the housework. In my hundreds of conversations, uncles rarely cropped up, although Sabine Durrant did recall a great-uncle who, on a long journey, stopped at his club for an hour to play a game of squash, and left her in the car with the instruction, 'If anyone comes, just say your dad popped into the lav.' 'Also,' said Sabine, 'he would take me into M&S and get me to try on underwear and then come into the fitting room to have a look.' Tom Stacey mentioned his rather hopeless Uncle Cyril, who lived at Temple Guiting and was 'one of life's inadequates. He had no children and I was quite a focus of his elderly affection. He paid for my years at Eton. [So, not as inadequate as all that.] He told the same stories twice, and dribbled rather.'

It was the aunts who made their presences felt. They, too, had their weird ways and strange theories. 'Our Auntie Betty,' said Henrietta Moyle, 'used to say, "Wash behind your ears or cabbages will grow." On the bleak Kentish beach at Westgate she used to tell us, "Look for the treasure!"' The freezing cold girls searched among the pebbles in vain. 'One of my ancient Jersey aunts,' said Jackie King, 'had cut round holes in the sides of her shoes to let her bunions "breathe".' 'Our aunt,' said Vicky Peterkin, 'made us read the *Radio Times* aloud to her every morning so she could plan her whole day of listening to the Third Programme.' Sue Sabbagh is haunted by the frenzied way her aunt sliced a loaf of bread on a mountain. 'Our aunt and uncle were dragging me and my sister, aged eleven and seven, up Scafell Pike on a freezing summer's day in the 1950s. They told us there would be "a wonderful view" when we reached the top. We could hardly see our own hands. We were ready to cry. Then our aunt said it was time to stop for our picnic. She took a loaf of bread out of her knapsack, and some margarine, and she started cutting slices off the loaf against her chest, slicing towards her body so it looked as if the knife was slicing into her breasts.'

There was a doughtiness about these aunts. The most thoughtful aunt I heard about was the one who made everything all right for little Bubble Carew-Pole in that tricky 5 p.m. drawing-room situation at Antony House in Cornwall, when, dressed up in her frilly dress with a sash, she prayed that one kind person in the crowd of snooty grown-ups would take notice of her and play with her. Her sprightly married aunt, Victory Du Cane, was that kind person. 'She would say, "Now, I'm going to be Black Billy, and you've got to try and find me", and she went and hid behind the curtains and made funny noises. The best thing of all was that at the end of the hour, still being "Black Billy", she darted out of the drawing room and we chased after her, following her up the stairs, and in this way she steered us nearly all the way back to the nursery.'

Although journalist Hazel Wood spent three weeks of each summer of her post-war childhood staying with her two very old-seeming spinster great-aunts, Auntie Gert and Auntie Evie, at their house, Torre House in Washford, Somerset, they actually made her feel young. Her parental home in Devon was not a relaxing place: her father had been disabled by polio and was in a wheelchair, and her parents' marriage was not happy. Staying with these aunts, she said, 'was the only time I could be a child'.

This was another astonishingly ordered household in this chapter of ordered households. Even the handover of the great-niece was organised to perfection. The two great-aunts, dressed in their sage-blue knitted skirts and knitted tops, would be driven by their chauffeur to collect Hazel at the agreed handing-over spot on Dartmoor. When they arrived back at Torre House, 'Lucy would be waiting for us, her red hair going a bit grey.' Lucy was the aunts' live-in servant, whom they had taken out of an orphanage at the age of thirteen, and she'd lived with them ever since. 'She was quite complaining, understandably. She'd had a best friend at the orphanage, who'd been taken to live a glamorous life in Canada and had married her boss – whereas Lucy was stuck with my great-aunts.'

All three spinster women – Auntie Gert, Auntie Evie and Lucy – doted on Hazel. Again, Hazel's house-recall was razor-sharp: she was *there* as she took me on a tour from bottom to top: the black coke-filled boiler in the cellar, the big staircase and hall, the morning room with original William Morris curtains, the dining room where they had lunch . . . and, upstairs, Lucy's sewing and ironing room with its sewing machine and wooden ironing board, and, along the landing, her own 'special' bedroom that smelled of lavender, with a high single bed with crisp white sheets and an oak window seat, and the attic where the apples were stored. 'The house smelled wonderful, a slightly damp smell of old stone and woodsmoke – although no fires were lit until November: we just put on lots of jerseys.' Auntie Evie, had been one of the first women to climb the Matterhorn, and she didn't feel the cold.

The great-aunts came from a prosperous Victorian family in Liverpool, and there was no shortage of money, 'but they were so frugal that Lucy complained that they refused to buy new vests, because they wanted to keep their capital intact. We went glean-ing – picking up the corn from round the edges of the field. That was another instance of their frugality. It was to feed the geese and chickens.'

Living with these Victorians, Hazel said, 'it felt so safe and settled – everything I didn't feel at home. My aunts read Dickens aloud to me. I had lunch in the dining room with them, and supper in the kitchen with Lucy. When I came down to breakfast, she said, "We're going to have a cuddle until the toast burns."'

Then, after the three weeks, the end-handover happened at exactly the same spot on Dartmoor, with a picnic. And back Hazel went to her strained home life, in which she felt more like an adult than a child.

Like many children, her life was profoundly enhanced by those summer sojourns with the elderly. The miraculous rapport between relatives at the two ends of the human lifespan had a chance to take root during those long, empty weeks.

PART III

WHERE YOU HAPPENED TO BE

II

Industrial Summers

We *will* go on the summer holiday inside the summer holidays, I promise. Not long now. It's coming round the corner. Woollen swimming costumes are being knitted in readiness. Mothers are starting to sort out the towels. Fathers are beginning to fret about the strength and elasticity of the roof-rack octopus. But first, one more section of staying put.

This book is about the whole summer holidays, remember, and Factory Fortnight, or whatever it was called in the different places, when all the factories closed down so everyone could go on a simultaneous holiday, only happened for a week or fortnight. Sometimes even then, as we'll see, families still didn't go anywhere, as money was too tight. So it's important to keep emphasising the stasis. Here are some 'situational' summers.

Children's summers in coal-mining towns and villages were lived completely in the shadow, and to the timetable, of the fathers' working days. Off the men cycled at dawn; back they came, black with dirt and exhausted, at dusk, and the children larked about in the streets all day, the boys knowing that this would soon be their timetable, too.

'Bobbies didn't come down Wheldale Lane on their own. They had to come in't busload.'

So said Maurice Tonks, life and soul of the Pontefract Coal Industry Social Welfare Organisation, where I spent a day and had lunch (scampi and chips with vinegar, with a triangle of white bread and butter draped over the top) and sat in on the bingo.

'You had to make your own pleasure, and all the lot,' said Maurice, summing up the universal British childhood summer in those days of benign neglect.

Maurice was born in 1929 in Castleford, and had six sisters (Florrie, Edith, Elsie, Evelyn, Marjorie and Sylvia) and five brothers (George, Matthew, Johnny, Dennis and Enoch), of whom he was the youngest. His father was a miner and his mother 'worked on't farm', driving the shire horses. All the brothers started working at Wheldale Colliery when they were thirteen, so childhood was short. 'I wanted to work as an apprentice fitter or mechanic, but I had to do what my father told me to do. I left school at thirteen and went down't pit.'

His father was strict. 'He kept a big leather belt by the fireplace. He used to say, "if you don't behave yourself, you'll have a bit of that." He checked our clothes when we came home. We used to play on the pit-heaps, and we weren't allowed. If he spotted a spot of ash on you, that's when you were in trouble with him. When he'd had a drink of beer or two, and came home for Sunday dinnertime, my mother picked him up and hung him up by his braces onto the front door. She said, "I'll hang you up and you'll stop there till you calm down, and then you'll have your dinner."' That makes her sound terrifying, too, but she 'would help anybody', said Maurice, and she kept the vast family fed with an everlasting big round brown pot into which everything went, from rabbits to potatoes: 'all the lot went in.'

It wasn't just the trespassing on the pit-heaps that made the bobbies need to come down in busloads rather than singly. Brick-throwing was another favoured pastime: it was part of the game of duck-stone, which involved standing a house brick on end and throwing half-bricks to try and knock it over; but if you got too close, which you always did, other boys' bricks hit you, and it then turned into a brick fight.

That, plus 'spit-out' (an ambush game where if you were caught you were corralled in a den, and to get one of your team out you had to spit into the den), plus peggy long-stick (swiping a small stone as far as you could with a long stick and putting people's eyes out in the process), plus bendy-back (three boys bending over and the others having to land on their backs and if their feet touched the ground they were out), plus football with a bundle of old cloth full of rubbish as the ball, plus hopscotch and skipping for the girls, kept the children of Castleford occupied when they weren't going anywhere in the summers of the 1930s and 1940s.

It's the astonishing fitness of the miners' sons that impresses, reminding me of young Dennis Skinner training to be an athlete in Clay Cross. 'I was a good runner,' said Maurice. 'Me and Jim Bettridge were running races against the big grammar-school boys and we beat the lot of them.'

Meanwhile, the fathers went to work and the mothers kept the fires going on top of their work: 'the fire was there for the lads when they went out to the colliery,' said Maurice, 'and there when they got home, and there was a tin tub of water for them to get into.' And, he said, hand on chest, 'I used to do errands for people – not for money but out of the goodness of my own heart. I charged my brothers interest, though, on any money I lent them. They used to call me "the little Jew".'

It was a wet day in Pontefract, but the centre for retired miners was full of warmth and chat. 'What were you doing all day in your summers?' I asked everyone. Always a tricky question to answer, because summers blur in the memory, unlike term-time. We humans have a tendency to forget the details of the non-traumatic bits of our childhoods.

'Swimming in't dykes,' said Dave Coupland, in his broad Yorkshire accent. His father worked on the land, and his mother, too, but they lived in a pit house in Higham. 'My father got conscripted into the mines instead of the army. After the war he went back onto the land, but they let him stop in the house. But he couldn't claim for coal so we had to go coal picking on the soil heaps. You weren't allowed to play on the heaps – you were trespassing.'

The eternal allure of the out-of-bounds meant that everyone played on the pit heaps.

'Potato-stealing,' said David Hartshorne, whose father had had an accident underground, so had had to come out of the pit and worked twelve-hour shifts seven days a week in the steel foundry on the edge of Leeds, and his mother worked in the Burton's clothing factory. 'There were fields all around our house and we stole peas, too, and apples from the orchards.' David made one bid for freedom. 'I had my first holiday when I was fifteen – a week's holiday in Redcar staying with a friend of my parents, Mrs Robinson. I came back home, and cycled the seventy miles straight back to Redcar, and Mrs Robinson put me up again.'

'Hopscotch on the road,' said Violet Child, miner's daughter, whose mother worked in a sweet factory and then a munitions factory during the war. 'You felt safe.' Violet did go and stay with her grandparents on their farm at Kirkbymoorside for one week of every summer, though: a lovely week, and 'my sister and I took ginger beer and sandwiches to the fields to give to the workers, and we sat with them and rode back up to the farm with them at night-time when they'd finished work.' Her father 'used to have a little bet on a Saturday – 6d. on the horses', but he was careful with money: 'he put two shillings aside every Friday out of his wages, to pay for our shoes.'

I asked the same question to a roomful of women gathered together for tea and a raffle in the parish room behind the church in Newton-le-Willows, all of whom had been brought up in nearby industrial towns.

'Making a whole circus,' said Susan Gardham (the one we met a while back, who'd been sent to the shop to buy sugar at the age of two and a half). Her father worked down the mine and came home 'as black as the ace of spades, and my mother washed his clothes in a tub outside and rubbed them on a glass washing board – it was a bit posh to have one of those'. She and her friends put on a circus in their village (Hemsworth) 'with old stepladders for clowning, and crates from the shops to use as seating. We sold tickets for it. Once, we just sold three.'

The profound localness of her childhood was reinforced when she recalled the traumatic day the family moved to a new house across the road. 'It felt like moving to the other side of the world. I lost my old friends. There were washing lines hanging across the road from house to house, and grass in the middle. We played out all the time. But I lost my standing in the community.'

'Sitting in the gutters popping tar-bubbles,' said Noreen Rimmer. 'Our mothers had to rub our hands with lard to get the tar off. If you rubbed and rubbed, it did come off. Or we played skilly [hide-and-seek], or relievo ['It'], or we went down to the Flash [canal] to swim.'

'At the end of each day,' said Val, 'the mothers would stand at the end of the street shouting their child's name – or six names if they had six children – and someone else's child would answer, "I'm coming, Mum!"'

Trespassing on the slag heaps? Father arriving home filthy? Police on the lookout? The same happened in the coal-mining village of Wallyford in East Lothian, where Johann Dickson was brought up: the family moved into a new prefab in 1916, when she was six. Here, it was not only the children who were up on the slag heaps, or 'bings' as they were called in Scotland. On Saturdays the fathers were up there, too. They went up there to do tossing (coins). 'Tossing was an addiction for men,' said Johann, 'and it was illegal because it was gambling, so we children were posted halfway up, on the lookout for the village's one and only policeman.'

Her father's addiction to gambling made life difficult for the rest of the family. Her mother worked at the brickworks to make up the weekly loss, and the children worked in the fields. Johann did most of the housework from the age of eight, 'washing the bathroom, scrubbing the kitchen floor, scrubbing the outside step'. The family lived on a staple diet of soup made from the turnips and leeks they picked up round the fields' edges. In her free time, as well as the illegal bliss of sliding down the bings, Johann went down to the North Berwick road with her friends to do car-spotting, 'and we wrote down every registration number we saw'. There were few enough cars to make that feasible.

'Dad would go and spend his money on stupid things. His weekday life was tough. "I've been right out at the Forth today," he'd say, meaning he'd hacked his way right down to the shore-line, underground. He cycled home from work in his heavy pit boots and knee pads and Mum took off his stuff in the kitchen, stripped him down to the waist and scrubbed his back.' He'd had a traumatic childhood – he'd been 'shipped off to Canada by the church' at the age of nine, and had worked his own passage home. Weekend gambling on the bings was his outlet in a life of hardships.

Johann's outlet was going to stay with her grandparents for three weeks of every summer. They lived in a tenement house in Stockbridge in Edinburgh: another grandparental refuge. 'The whole family lived round one big table: they did everything there – sewing, telling stories, eating meals.'

There was something deeply comforting, for children, about those grandparents who lived their lives round one big table. The gradual trend, since those days, towards 'living in the kitchen' has brought this warm-hearted habit into the middle and upper classes.

What did Johann do all day, while staying with the grandparents in Edinburgh? 'We spent hours fishing for minnows in the pond in Inverleith Park while my grandfather was on his allotment.' In the afternoons 'the women all came downstairs to sit on the ground on the pavements, knitting, sewing and chatting, to get out of their dark tenements. It was so dark on the stairwells that you had to feel your way up and down the stairs.'

So, everyone, grown-ups and children alike, was downstairs and outside, soaking up what sunshine there was.

'We didn't know any people who went away on holidays,' Johann said. 'I didn't go abroad till I went on my honeymoon.'

*

We call it 'work experience' now. In those days it wasn't called that. But it was more useful work experience than today's sort, where both parties have to sign forms beforehand, so it can't happen casually, and it lasts precisely a week, and no one really wants you around, and you're not given much to do, and you're supposed to write up the experience afterwards to show to the life skills co-ordinator at school. In those days it was wandering into industrial areas, chatting to the workers and somehow finding yourself being allowed to have a go.

'When I became a shipyard manager in Aberdeen at the age of thirty-one,' said Fred Walker, born in 1936 by the banks of the Clyde, 'it was such a benefit having had that experience. Now the kids at university aren't getting any of this ...'

Fred's whole summers were spent cycling all over the Clyde. 'I could go into warehouses on the river and talk to the watchmen, and if I was courteous they would let me walk around the smaller shipyards. My parents trusted me. I used to spend days and days on the riverside with my bike. I locked it and went on board ship and asked to see the duty officer. They were usually bored out of their minds and happy to let you look around. They were there loading and unloading freighters or cargo ships. They let me look around the engine rooms. The most exciting thing for me was going out on the tugs that pulled the big ships in and out of the harbour. I went into the towing offices and got to know the towing managers. They would say, "Tomorrow we're taking an American aircraft carrier down the river. You can come, too. You might have to get a bus home." There were twenty-five tugs on the Clyde and the operators got to know me. This would *not* be allowed nowadays. It made me very aware of ship operation.'

Fred Walker, aged sixteen in 1952, on a Clyde tug

It was through these casual 'yeses', workman giving a friendly nod to anoraky child, that wisdom was passed down to the next generation and absorbed. Like taking other people's babies out in prams, this activity was beneficial to both parties. The grown-ups were flattered that the young found their boring jobs so fascinating.

It was the same for one man I spoke to who grew up near the Coal Board's network of railways in Newcastle in the late 1960s and early 1970s. 'It was a little colliery railway system, still with steam trains. I cycled to these places and started talking to the man in the shed. I was allowed to hitch rides with the Geordie men who were keeping their tea hot in billycans near the fire. I rode in the cab with them, and they showed me how it worked and even let me drive it. If you had a friendly driver you could spend a whole day with him. You might have to keep your head down if there was an inspector around.'

I call this 'deep formation': gradual mastery through fascination and absorption: by watching what others do and then starting to do it yourself. It could happen in those summers when there was enough time and fewer regulations.

Deep formation also happened when boys stood next to their fathers in their workshops or sheds for whole weekends, watching them make a wooden object and then making one themselves, which was what Richard Worsley (among many others I spoke to) did in his father's workshop in Northamptonshire in the early 1950s, 'and now,' he said, 'I *have* to be making something all the time'. It was the same with children watching their mothers or grandmothers baking, and absorbing the art. Dugald Cameron (b. 1939), a shipyard worker's son also on the Clyde, said, 'My father taught me to take my whole bike apart. I could take it apart completely and build it up again, from the age of eight.'

Dugald was a Meccano addict. The country was divided into the arty Lego children, the sporty Subbuteo ones and the sciency Meccano ones. (What was it about brand names ending in 'o'? It made things sound exotic and pacy, as with 'relievo' for the game of 'It' and 'Bromo' for lavatory paper.) From my chats, I discovered that boys who grew up near shipyards preferred Meccano.

'The world isn't made of bits of metal with little holes in them,' Dugald admitted to me, 'but Meccano taught me most of what I know about how to build real steam engines and cranes.' He would grow up to become an industrial designer, after a spell at the Glasgow School of Art.

'I started at the 'o' set, then went up to 1, then to 1 A. I lusted after the Number 10 set. I did get the Number 7, in post-war red and green. I made a locomotive, lying on the ground in the garden, in the hot summer of 1947.' Unlike with his bike, which he took apart and rebuilt in exactly the same way, with Meccano he mastered the art of taking something apart and building a completely different thing out of the very same parts.

He said, 'I ascribe Britain's decline in manufacturing to the decline of Meccano.'

12

Summers in the Capital

In coal-mining villages you were forbidden to play on the slag heaps, but everybody did. In cities you were forbidden to play on the bombsites, but everybody did. Nowadays, councils make doing such things impossible, with the help of razor wire and CCTV. In the mid-twentieth century trespassing was forbidden but still possible. So, of course, everyone did it. The Lord's Prayer line 'Forgive us our trespasses' really resonated. Everyone thought trespassing was what 'trespasses' meant.

Bombsites had a similar allure for urban children to the allure that islands had for rural children: the allure of the lawless zone, tricky to reach, possibly containing treasure, where adult rules didn't apply. Shirley Cotter, born in Putney Bridge Road in 1937, described this typical bomb event: 'A baby in our street was fast asleep in his pram, and he was then found upside down on the roof, crying.' One advantage of the world being turned (literally) upside down was that the children whose end of the street happened not to have been blown to pieces had an instant new playground.

'Every house in my aunt's street was destroyed, up to number twenty,' said Shirley. 'After that day, we used to come out of her house and walk along the back wall to get down into the bombsite. We couldn't resist it. My cousin was playing there one day and she stood on a paving stone and it tipped up and she ended up in a coal cellar. My aunt said, "Where's Jane?" and I said, "Down the coal hole."'

When it came to London, there were three distinct strata of street life, as you went up through the social classes. First there were the working-class children whose whole existences were spent playing on the streets and bombsites, in a state of near-penniless total freedom. Then there were the aspiring middle-class children, who wanted to be allowed to play on the streets but weren't. They took buses to museums and gazed longingly out of the windows, while being drearily educated. They were sent to bed early and heard other children playing outside till dark. Then there was the posh social crowd, who lived near the King's Road or Kensington High Street and went to parties and mooched about in the shops together. These ones had money in their pockets, so they could afford to buy new sandals and pay to see the same film seven times over.

'We were just street urchins,' said Bill Carroll, retired hall porter, born in Stepney in 1954, son of a warehouseman. 'As soon as we got fed, we were out again. Every street had a bombsite at the end of it, and we entertained ourselves in those. We were down there all day, making camps and bricking up cellars. We found good stuff there: I found a nice green carpet, put it in the pram and brought it back to our place.'

Throughout his whole childhood, Bill shared a bedroom with his sister and parents, in cramped rooms in a series of tenement houses. As he grew older they moved from Stepney to Holborn to Battersea to Islington, always running out of money. The notices on the doors of these places said, 'No dogs, no blacks, no Irish.'

He wished his family had been the settled sort that stayed in the same house – the sort that went hop-picking every summer – but they were perpetually unsettled: 'My dad was a lovely man, but he did like the drink. My parents were forever arguing, and we were always skint by the middle of the week. My mum would send me round to Minnie's on Leman Street in Aldgate to buy a pair of American tan tights for her, and Minnie, the little Jewish lady who ran it, who had a heart of gold, let me take the tights and said I could pay her back on payday. All my clothes were from the jumble sale: we'd bring 'em home and boil 'em. When we ran out of money for the gas, we cut a piece of lino the size of a sixpence to turn the gas back on. When we ran out of money for coal, Dad would say, "Go and get some wood in", and we went off with the old pram and filled it up with wood.'

Prams, as we've already seen, played a prominent part in the summers of the mid-twentieth century – but they weren't just receptacles for babies. In car-less families their usefulness as trolleys gave them an afterlife long after the last baby had grown out of them. Bill emphasised, though, that a boy like him didn't want to be seen pushing a pram. It was considered effeminate. 'If my dad asked me to get some coke in twenty-eight-pound bags, I'd do two journeys rather than take the pram. My dad was a bit like that, too: he wouldn't be seen dead with an umbrella.'

Another use for old prams was to make them into a go-kart with the wheels. Bill did this, and his front teeth were knocked out while travelling on it. He longed for a bike. 'My dad promised me one, and we went round to the bike shop in Bethnal Green, but his HP cheque was declined, so he took me into the Army and Navy store and brought me a Bowie knife in a big leather sheaf as a consolation.'

There was vast scope for immersing yourself in places of dereliction. 'We loved exploring derelict old houses,' said Susan Baldwin, egg-seller at Ridley Road Market in Dalston, born in 1958. 'You could walk through old houses on the beams under the floorboards that had been removed. We found a cupboard and an old rug and a chair, and made our own little "house" – this was in Wood Street, Walthamstow – and we brought biscuits and drinks along. One day a policeman knocked on the door and said, "Can I come in, children?" We invited him in and showed him our house. He said, "What a good job you've all done. Very good! But unfortunately it's not safe for you to be in here, so you really shouldn't go in here again."' They didn't; but 'there were streets and streets of these empty houses, all around Victoria Park, and if they were fenced up,' said Peter Julian (Susan's cousin, and a market trader in the next-door stall), 'we just cut through the fence'.

'We sneaked into the Bug-'Utch through the side door,' said Joan Borg, born in Fulham in 1937, evacuated to a haunted house in Clitheroe during the war and back roaming the London streets by the age of eight. The Bug Hutch was their nickname for the local picture house on the Wandsworth Bridge Road, 'because when you were in there you were scratching yourself all over'. A synonym for a fleapit. (So, for our summer insect collection in this book so far, we have John Julius Norwich 'accustoming himself to wasps', fathers chain-smoking to keep the midges away in Scotland and the street children of London being bitten to bits in the Bug-'Utch.)

'You don't see 'em in the street like we was,' said Joan, talking of children today. Her whole childhood world was her street and the local park round the corner. Again, it was the extreme localness of street life that struck me. I asked Shirley Cotter, brought up in a tiny flat in Fulham with a cooker in the bathroom and the kitchen table in the bedroom, whether she ever went into central London, or even as far as, say, South Kensington. 'I was scared of crossing over to Filmer Road,' she said. 'The rule was that you mustn't go out of your street unless you told your mum. There was a statue of Jesus on the cross looking down at me on the corner of Filmer Road, and I was told he was keeping an eye on me.'

The tiny cluster of streets on which she lived out her summers was watched over by a vast clan of aunts and cousins, 'and you could knock on any of their doors and ask to go to the toilet. Everything was lovely because of the freedom we had.' It was freedom within a very small radius. 'The lady upstairs would shout down to us, "Can you run over and get me some Oxos?" It was two Oxos per tuppence-farthing.'

Childminder Cathy Hawkins, who grew up in a London council

flat, said that each estate had its own porter in those days, whereas 'now one porter has to look over a dozen estates'. Not only was the porter keeping an eye on the children, so were Cathy's twelve aunts.

The localness affected the currency of what it meant to 'travel'. On one memorable day of her childhood, one of Shirley's uncles took her and her cousins on a long-promised outing to Burnham Beeches. The children never got over their disappointment that the place turned out to be woods rather than seaside.

A normal day out was a family trip down to the local park, half a mile away. In Fulham this was called 'Going down the Bishops', the park being Bishop's Park. Paddling pool, towels, sandpit, sandwiches: it was the warm-up to the major outing of the summer – the day trip to Southend-on-Sea in a charabanc. For East Enders the park was Victoria Park, and 'we used to spend hours playing a really simple game,' said Susan Baldwin: 'putting a lolly stick on the ground and lying down on the roundabout and going round and round really fast and you had to pick it up.' Those roundabouts were designed to go round almost frictionlessly fast.

The London children caught in the middle of the social classes had a more dismal time. 'My parents were quite hard up,' said Julia Little (b. 1949), 'but they had social aspirations. "Refugees from Romford," I called them. My mother was brought up in Gidea Park – the posh suburb with the show houses. My father was a bit socially lower, from Hornchurch. Their social aspirations meant that we moved to Earl's Court: a three-bedroom flat on the second floor of a mansion block, and I got into the French Lycée. There was no garden and I was totally isolated. I never learned to ride a bike. My parents wouldn't have thought it right for me to be allowed to play on the street unsupervised. The "playing-out"-type children were advantaged compared with me.'

That constricted existence made for summers of deep boredom, Julia said. 'Me and my mother used to traipse round the Kensington museums and Kensington Gardens together. I was an only child and my mother was my only companion. A lot of the time, I was doing nothing and being bored – and I think the boredom was bad for me. I didn't even like reading: I just associated it with school homework, and didn't discover the pleasure of reading till I was twenty-two.'

What everyone dreaded was being stuck with a parent, in a succession of enforced named activities to keep them busy. It did no good for the morale of parent or child.

Lots of families didn't have televisions until the Coronation, and 'what used to happen when I was very young,' Julia said, 'was that my mother and I would go and watch the children's programme *Watch with Mother* on the screen in the Science Museum after lunch every day. They did daily demonstrations of the black and white TV at 1.45 p.m. Lots of local mothers used to take their children into the museum for that. It was all about trying to find things to do that didn't cost money.'

It was the richness of freedom that children longed for, not the richness of a well-appointed des-res where you were stuck with a grown-up and cut off from other children. As with Nicholas Sagovsky stuck away in Ruislip, supposed residential paradises could be vacuums when it came to fun. 'I used to get onto a bus on my own,' said accountant Richard Hannigan, who grew up in Roehampton in the 1960s, 'and go into the West End, just to look at everything: the signs outside the theatres, the noticeboards outside the opera houses, the signs on the cinemas ... I couldn't afford to go to any of them, but just seeing the words inspired me: knowing what I *could* be going to.' 'Our mother just used to put us on the 74 bus,' said one woman I spoke to who grew up in 1970s Putney, 'and she told us to go all the way to the end of the route and back. So, Baker Street and home again. That kept us out of her way for the afternoon.'

What happened if you were a country-loving child who happened to be stuck in London for the summer? If you were lucky, you had Lilo Blum to help you. Mia Woodford (whom we last met in the Fathers chapter having a barbecue on the roof of the flat in Eaton Square, thanks to her father cutting a hole in the ceiling) spent her summers of the late 1960s and early 1970s at Lilo Blum's riding stables at Hyde Park Corner, behind where the Lanesborough Hotel now is. Lilo Blum came over from Germany as a refugee in 1937 and started her stables in 1943. 'She's still alive, in her nineties, but she looked about ninety *then*,' said Mia, 'a tiny old lady, shouty and very strict. Our mucking-out had to be just-so. The horses were living in a tiny urban space. I kept my own pony there – my father had bought me one during a flush time – and I belonged to the Hyde Park branch of the Pony Club. I went along to the stables every day: I lived in jodhpurs, and got up at six, and I was tacking up and walking there and back on my own from the age of eight. I came home to Eaton Square every evening to delicious toast and butter made by my father.'

When the Duke of Westminster converted St George's Hospital to the Lanesborough Hotel, he no longer wanted horses in the mews, so the stables closed down in 1988.

Mia Woodford (right) and her sister Sophie (left) riding with Lila Blum through the mews. Lilo's riding school is behind them, tel no. Belgravia 6840

*

You have to envy the Heathfield girls. They're the great exception here. While swathes of the country were sunk in unglamorous, day-dreamy fending-off of boredom, they were having fun, fun, fun.

Heathfield was the smart girls' boarding school at Ascot, not far from Eton, and it still strikes you, when you chat to Heathfield Old Girls, that their lives have been (a) extremely socially active since the age of ten and (b) mainly restricted to their own social class. (The other two girls' schools in this highly social bracket were Southover and West Heath.) The parents' instinct was to encourage this socially active bubble. They invited their daughters' friends to come and stay and arranged for them to be invited back, and it was absolutely expected that their children would spend their summers with their social equals, in a circle in which everyone knew everyone else.

'Southover was the school where everyone went on to marry one of their best friends' brothers,' the saying went; and for girls at those highly social schools those summers were the time for these relationships, as well as the girls' school friendships, to blossom and develop away from the tedium of the hopelessly unaspirational classroom. As the girls reached puberty, they started going gooey and putting exclamation marks in their diaries when they met their friends' good-looking older brothers. This was just what the parents hoped might happen. The reason they sent their daughters to these social boarding schools was not to give them a top-notch education; far from it. It was so they would meet the children of their own friends, and, through these girls, would start mingling with their handsome Etonian older brothers and friends of their older brothers, and they would thus make their way safely into a happy and suitable marriage.

The Heathfield girls didn't question this. They just thought this was what life was like. You arrived home for the summer holidays and, two days later, your best friend from school came to stay (hooray!) and you all went to a party in Kent or Sussex given by another school friend, and you played tennis on their tennis court with someone's brother, and you sat next to James Someone during dinner, and that was really exciting!!! and when you arrived home you were very tired, and you wrote a thank-you letter to the mother of the friend, whom you always addressed as 'Mrs', or 'Lady', never by her first name.

This is a vital aspect of the Great British childhood summer, and for a full picture we need to address it. It doesn't have the 'stasis' feel of the vast majority of Britain's summers. The girls were forever dashing from county to county to stay with another friend, or going to the social part of north Norfolk where all their other friends also were. It helped if you were good at tennis, because everywhere you went there was a tennis court, and there was usually a tournament going on in which you were expected to take part.

I've put this social aspect of summers in the London chapter, because one Heathfield Old Girl, Bolla Denehy (née Arabella Fordham), kindly lent me her large A4 diary for 1976, with two Pink Floyd stickers on the front, and she happened to be based in London, in a street off the King's Road, where her mother lived, having recently separated from her father. 'My mother would arrive home,' Bolla told me, 'and find twenty-five of my friends in the basement.'

It all kicked off on the last night of term, when Bolla and her friends put their beds into a star shape in the dormitory, pillow ends in the middle, and talked all night. School work, inasmuch as there had ever really been any, had been dying down towards the end of term ('We had ancient history first and we didn't do any work the whole day'), and when the end came, the girls moved seamlessly into an existence of best friends seeing each other on their home turf.

Heathfield girls warming up for the holidays with hours of happy idling at school. Rochelle Minson, Maryanne Herbert, Christian Forbes, and Bolla née Fordham in the dorm, 1977

This was the famously hot summer of 1976, but fourteen-year-old Bolla never remarks on the lovely weather. Again, it was what she expected: it was summer, so it should be boiling hot for months on end. Only the grown-ups noticed the plants dying and the grass going brown.

A French exchange girl called Natalie came to stay for weeks, and everyone was really nice to her and included her in everything. 'Natalie taught us rock 'n' roll! It was great fun.' The girls were all starting to smoke. Bolla mentions every incident of going out to 'have a fag', sometimes on the roof. 'We smoked outside my room and then went and had a gin and tonic!! We didn't quite put the fag out that we had dropped out of the window so we had to spit on it, it was so funny!'

Here we have that whole summer laid before us, including the fourteen-year-old girls not being able to make head or tail of what was going on in *All the President's Men.* ('Very difficult to understand. Not v. good.') Much better, 'Mummy, Louisa, Natalie and me went to see *The Sound of Music* (again, 7th time!). It was really brilliant, even better than I had remembered.' The next day she and Natalie went and saw it again ('8th time!'). This was the comfort of the repeat experience.

The highlight of the summer was going, in a group of friends with no grown-ups, to the Rolling Stones concert at Knebworth. 'At 6.30 10cc were due to come on but they came on late, 3 hours, everyone banging cans! 10cc were brilliant. After a wait the Rolling Stones came on. Oh I have never seen anything so brilliant. Mick Jagger was so funny, they played brilliant songs ... I think the Rolling Stones were so amazing and I love Mick Jagger.' The next day, 'we still couldn't get over the concert'.

There was a fair amount of restaurant-going among this cosmopolitan central London crowd – again, bucking the national trend. Non-spaghetti versions of pasta were the new trendy food items. 'We had lunch outside (ravioli and frozen cream cake!)'. At 'a lovely restaurant', Bolla had artichokes with butter, then cannelloni, then blackberries.

Typical week: Bolla goes to stay with her friend Christian in Berkshire for a night. 'We talked for ages when we woke up, then Christian insisted on showing me all the toys she had when she was little. After breakfast we mucked around and didn't do much. We went shopping etc. ... we were very stupid in Smith's!' Then, back to London. 'When I got up, I didn't do much, I just mucked around and read a *Cosmopolitan* story! I went to buy a silver cross for Lucinda C. G. After lunch Louisa [her sister], Natalie and I went to Madame Tussauds, it was fun except we lost Natalie.' Then, off she went to Norfolk.

It was another world, at that Sloane Square end of the King's Road. These girls were paying good money to go and see the new Hitchcock film, and *The Sound of Music* again and again. And they were going to Oxford Street to buy clothes. Bolla did cut holes in the toes of her espadrilles to make them into sandals, though, and, like all teenagers across the social spectrum, her days were punctuated with that mysterious occupation 'mucking about'.

We need to wrack our brains to remember exactly what 'mucking about' entailed: the activity that filled those vast swathes of time that would now be spent browsing on social media. I think, for a Heathfield girl, it meant listening to a record while trying on clothes; experimenting with make-up; reading the Problem Page of *Cosmopolitan*; rereading ten-page letters from school friends; washing your hair (in the bath or basin, in the pre-shower age) and having another 'fag' out of the window.

Those girls' boarding schools were notoriously hopeless at organising activities for the weekends, so the girls were already adept at mucking about, having done so over the endless Saturday and Sunday afternoons holed up at school. This skill was enhanced over the long summers. In the summer, though, a party, or the fun of going to stay with a school friend, was always just around the corner.

13

Two Institutions

The total flopping you could do when you arrived at home for the holidays – at *real* home, where your family lived – was not possible for children who didn't go home to their parents, because they lived abroad and travel was too expensive, difficult or dangerous, so they had to stay in Britain for the whole summer, either with relations, with whom they could never completely relax, or in institutions. I got a whiff of these institutions while flicking through the Truman & Knightley boarding schools directory of 1932, where schools tried to attract potential customers by boasting of unique selling points such as 'Children may be kept for the holidays if desired, and the household is transferred for six weeks of the Summer holidays to a house at Bexhill-on-Sea.'

So, some children, when term ended and everyone else had gone home, just traipsed back indoors for yet another school lunch, this time in an echoing empty dining room. Then they either stayed put for eight weeks, with a moderate relaxation of the out-of-bounds rules, and were taken to the seaside for a fortnight by one of the two spinster headmistresses; or they went to a holiday institution run by another pair of spinster ladies who would look after them for the whole summer.

I was prepared to loathe these institutions of holiday incarceration – a very poor substitute for going home, I thought. One man I spoke to remembered a boy in his dormitory at his 1960s prep school crying himself to sleep on the last night of the summer term, knowing he wasn't going home for the holidays the next day, but to a 'holiday home' instead – not the same thing at all. No proper home-flopping was in store for him.

But when Sheila McGuirk and her sister Leila Moshire described The Yews at Curry Rivel in Somerset to me, I realised that these places could be homely paradises, just as boarding schools could, if they happened to be run by kind people. Children who stayed at institutions could in fact be less neglected than many children were at their parental home. If the regime was benign, they spent summers in places of beauty with lots of other children to play with: all the fun of home with added nightly pillow fights; all the fun of boarding school with none of the enforced lacrosse. In the two examples of institutional mid-twentieth-century Britain in this chapter (the second being summers spent at the Barnardo's village in Barkingside) we see once again that it doesn't always matter who loves you when you're a child, as long as someone does.

The Yews was run by two ladies, Mrs Barkway and Miss Cartwright, known as Barkie and Pi. ('Pi' was a play on Miss Cartwright's Christian name, Eileen, which had once been altered to 'Pileen' during a long-ago parlour game on a boat to India.) Barkie had a sister, Lilian, always known as 'Auntie' and her husband as 'Uncle'. In the holidays Barkie and Pi had to double up and sleep in the same bedroom to make way for the influx of waifs and strays, children of the Empire, whom they took under their wing. Barkie's mother, Granny Marshall, also lived in, and Nanny Foster, the matron from Barkie's old school, visited frequently.

Barkie had been the headmistress of The Dame School in North Molton, where Sheila (born in 1946 to an Iranian father and British mother) boarded from the age of five, along with her older sister Leila, their parents being abroad in the oil fields of Iran where her father worked. From the age of five to eight Sheila stayed at The Dame School for the whole summer. Then Barkie sold that business and 'took' (i.e. rented) another house, The Yews, to run as a holiday home. 'She was the official guardian of the children of a BP family, and she had to honour that,' Sheila explained – and because of that commitment-honouring, it seemed natural to open the house as a holiday home for other children of parents in the colonial service. For a typical summer there would be about ten children staying: quite a few pairs of siblings, but the siblings didn't share bedrooms.

The children kept their home clothes at The Yews all year round. 'We had no possessions anywhere else,' Sheila said, trying to hammer home to me that The Yews was not merely 'like' home: it *was* home to her and her sister Sheila who was three years older. Their school trunks arrived at the beginning of the holidays and were carted up to the box rooms by the boys. They each had a small box of their own toys that they kept in the billiard room.

The place was run on a shoestring: it was a business, but in order to make ends meet, Barkie and Pi sold fresh eggs and flowers to the local shops. All the fruit and vegetables were home-grown; the butcher, baker and milkman delivered the rest in their vans.

'Miss Cartwright did the cooking and gardening,' said Sheila, 'and she was the one you'd see up on the roof, fixing the cowl on a chimney. Barkie ran the business side. She was brilliant at organising quizzes and board games and games of racing demon in the evenings. Pi took us out for picnics, firing up the primus stove for cups of tea. On summer evenings we just lay in the garden listening to the tranny. We had a Labrador and cocker spaniels, cats, geese and ducks, and some of the children had rabbits. Pi also kept a goat to keep the tennis-court grass down.'

The whole aim was to try to make it all as much like being at home as possible. 'We felt we could relax as if we were at home – but Barkie would say, "Come on – out!" if she felt you'd been indoors for too long.' A small ration of pocket money was handed out on Saturdays so the children could go to the Post Office Stores to buy sweets. There was no designated 'lights-out' time: 'we lay in bed singing songs from the musicals till finally Barkie came along and read the riot act. It was as close as you could get to family. It really was an extended non-blood second family. Barkie and Pi never had any desire to usurp the affection of our real parents. But when you got your first period, whom did you tell? Your mother in a letter, or Mrs Barkway in person? I told Mrs Barkway. The way I expressed it was, "I think I need some pads."'

But it was an institution. You couldn't quite get away from that fact. Bells were rung for meals: 'first bell, followed by second bell,' said Sheila, 'and if you were late, you had to put a penny into the poor-box.' There was fish on Friday, and you had to eat everything on your plate, and be quiet after lunch while Barkie and Pi were having their rest. Proper Sunday roast was served – and 'Pi always rushed out of the house just as the one-minute bell was tolling for church'. After compulsory church in their designated pews, dressed in their jackets and skirts or jackets and trousers, the children had to write a weekly letter to their parents, just as they did at school. The children did have their own private 'territory', but it was just their own bed, chest of drawers, bookcase and mirror in a communal dorm. 'We had to share the bathtub, and the boiler often went wrong – but that was country houses in general in those days.' There were rotas for washing-up and clearing the table, and the children were paid 6d. for every pound of dandelion heads they picked: Pi liked to make dandelion wine.

Sometimes friends from school invited the children from The Yews to stay for a few days, and Barkie or Pi took them to the station and collected them, just as a parent would. 'It gave us a break from institutional life,' said Sheila.

'Did you feel a pang when you saw your friends with their parents, when you were apart from yours?'

'There was a bit of that,' she admitted. 'But The Yews was so much my home that when I went to visit my grandparents I said to them at the end, "I'm going home now" – meaning back to The Yews – and I think my grandmother was a bit upset. Barkie wasn't my real mother, but that didn't matter: she was *there*, while my mother was at the end of a letter.'

*

Linda Bowley, born in 1954 to an unmarried mother in Nottingham and brought into Barnardo's aged four weeks, was fortunate to be housed in Sweet Briar, rather than in some of the stricter cottages in the Barnardo's village in Barkingside, where the children had to call their house mother 'Matron'. Linda's two house mothers were Auntie Anne and Auntie Pearl. Auntie Pearl was an old Barnardo's girl herself. The aunties did the cooking and made the birthday cakes, and they knitted and sewed the children's dresses. 'Auntie Anne read to us every night,' Linda said, 'and I used to make her kiss all my animals goodnight in my bed.'

There were about a thousand children in sixty-four cottages in the Barnardo's village, but only eight in Sweet Briar (next door to Pink Clover), 'and we all got on well. Three of them, Mark, Maxwell and Rita, were small like me.' By 'small' Linda meant officially of small stature. Having worked full time for the Gas Board for twenty-four years, Linda now whizzes round Barkingside on her mobility scooter, humanising the place and waving thanks as drivers slow down at Belisha beacons. She took me for lunch at the café which used to be Derek's sweetshop when she was a child.

'Our cottage also had a dog, Meggie, who lived to be sixteen, and a pussycat, a budgie and a guinea pig called Snowy.' Adorer of animals, Linda walked Meggie every day and went round the other cottages to look after their animals, too. 'Sweet Briar was the cottage "for delicate children". But we were never ill.'

In term-time the children were picked up by bus and taken to school in Ilford, but in the holidays 'poor Auntie had us for a full day'. ('Auntie' was what Linda called both house mothers; the one she was referring to there was Auntie Anne.) Like the rest of Britain, the Barnardo's children were encouraged to go out of doors to play all day. 'There were swings and a sandpit on the green in the middle' (the village being a large circle of half-timbered cottages built in 1903), 'and I had to score for Mark and Maxwell when they played cricket.'

The green in front of the Barnardo's cottages at Barkingside, on which Linda Bowley spent a great deal of her summers playing

Kind families who supported Barnardo's invited a child to stay for a fortnight each summer. 'I used to go to Auntie Christine and Uncle Marc for two weeks in August.' (Again, that use of the word 'auntie' and 'uncle' to describe close friends. I've heard it described as 'the northern honorific', but it happened in the south, too.) 'Auntie Christine and Uncle Marc lived in Kenton, Middlesex: they belonged to the Kenton & Harrow Barnardo's

Helpers' League, raising money for Barnardo's, and I was their protégée child. They had three sons of their own, Richard, Frank and Stephen. Auntie used to come and pick me up in her big Vauxhall Cresta car. All the children in the village wanted to get in and have a ride.' Before any child first went to stay with a family, Barnardo's visited it to inspect it.

'The journey round the North Circular Road was terrible,' said Linda. 'It was so long. I screamed and screamed when Christine stopped to get petrol and a man started putting a long thing into the car. He waved to me, and that made it even worse.' But once in Kenton, Linda was subsumed into the family, and became so close to them that she later became godmother to Frank's first daughter. 'Auntie Christine took me to London Zoo and she took me camping at Littlehampton with the boys. One year Stephen had chickenpox so I couldn't go, but Auntie Christine's neighbours said, "we can't let Linda down – she can come and stay with us". So I did and I'm now godmother to one of their sons' children, too.'

Linda Bowley at London Zoo with 'Auntie Christine', 1962

Every summer also included an official Barnardo's holiday to the Kentish seaside. 'Thanet Council lent us their church halls,' said Linda, 'and we went in pairs of cottages, in a coachload, plus a lorry with all the cutlery, kettles and furniture. We always had the last two weeks of August at a church hall in Ramsgate. We slept on mattresses on the floor, and the Aunties slept on the stage. Proper sheets and blankets on the mattresses, and a chair between each one: we were very tidy children.'

She showed me an extract from Auntie Anne's logbook from August 1965. (Auntie Anne kept a year-round log of what the children in Sweet Briar did every day.)

Camp holiday with 'Joy Cottage' at Ramsgate. We had a lovely holiday again this year and were fortunate to have good weather. The children were very excited the day we went to Margate as they love going to Dreamland. We had lunch in a restaurant and the children were thrilled to choose from the menu. On Sunday afternoon we went for a boat trip which we all enjoyed. We saw two films while we were there. One was *Dr. Who and the Daleks* – this was the first time Stephen had been to the cinema and he liked it very much. The other film was called *Help!*, and Ringo, one of the Beatles, was the main star. The last evening we were there we saw the Carnival Procession and we all cheered loudly when Miss Milko and Miss Nivea came by, as we had seen them both on the beach earlier in the day. We all thoroughly enjoyed the holiday, the time went by quicker than ever this year. We are so glad that we were able to go with 'Joy Cottage' and hope that we shall be able to join them next year.

Auntie Anne's log was written in the 'postcard' style of bland, optimistic, non-critical, controversy-free enjoyment which the British perfected.

The only thing in Thanet that Linda didn't like was the circus, mainly because she couldn't bear to think of any cruelty being inflicted on animals, but also because the circus people were always trying to get her, Mark, Maxwell and Rita to go off with them and join the circus. 'I just walked off. The boys were a bit more tempted and talked about it for longer.' But they turned the offer down and always went back to Barkingside.

14

Summer Jobs

Could you really just walk into a restaurant, shop, ice-cream parlour or farm and say, 'Have you got a job?' and the manager would say 'yes' and you'd start the next day?

You could, it seems, and people did, from the age of ten, or eight if it was car-washing in a car park, or six if it was pea-picking. The absence of pocket money created the urge. If you needed coins in your pocket you had to go out and earn them. Make your own fun; make your own money. As with those boys begging rides on the Clyde, and as with all those gardens giving onto meadows, there was also a remarkable porousness between the world of work and the world of children and teenagers wanting work. Today's barriers – HR departments, security guards, office passes, DBS forms, CVs, proof of experience, etc. – just weren't there. The manager nodded and signed you up, no questions asked.

You didn't earn much, but those 'few bob in your pocket' made all the difference. The only other way of getting money (apart from theft), as many reminded me, was going round every phone kiosk in your town or city and pressing 'Button B' in the hope that a residual coin might drop out. 'I used to stuff a hanky up the refund chute in the morning, so the callers would not get their refunds all day,' said one Bradford man I spoke to, 'and then I came back in the evening and took the hanky out and the coins came tumbling out.' Everyone craved that metallic clatter that signalled a jackpot.

For a more reliable income you needed gainful employment. 'We had no pocket money at all from our mother,' said Abby Scott, who grew up in 1970s Essex, 'so we had to work. My brother was washing cars in a car park by the age of eight. Aged fourteen, I was washing up in a Spanish restaurant in Great Chesterford for an insane Spanish lady who screamed and shouted.' Abby showed me a photo of her in rubber gloves in what looks like a shabby domestic kitchen but was actually a restaurant kitchen. She was smiling among the soap suds under the dish rack. 'I started my shift at 6.30 and washed up non-stop for five hours – I loved it, actually. It was a lively place. There was no dishwasher, so it was all by hand. I walked home on my own at 11.30 p.m. along the country lanes. Then I did waitressing in a country club. Blokes were always asking to buy me drinks, but I always accepted just one. I also went into other people's houses to do their ironing.'

'How did you spend the money you'd earned?'

'I spent it on going to a coffee house in Saffron Walden.'

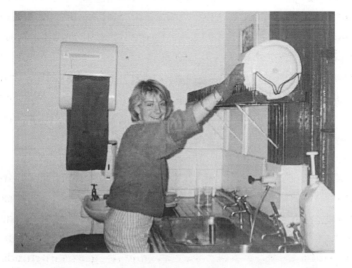

Abby Scott washing up in the Spanish restaurant in Great Chesterford

That was how it went: a succession of hop-on, hop-off jobs to keep coins in the pocket and to make treats such as coffee-house coffee (in a glass mug, with white-sugar spills to dip your moistened finger into on the Formica table) possible. Abby also spent her earnings on bus fares to visit her boyfriend. 'I did have a boyfriend by the age of fifteen or sixteen,' she said, 'but I only saw him once a week, as he lived nine miles away in Clavering. We wrote letters to each other. I think relationships developed more slowly in those days. It took a long time to get to know someone. You filled the vacuum with your imagination.'

When and if sex did take place in her social circle, I asked her, where did it happen? 'In cars,' she said, 'and at parties in a bedroom in someone else's house.' Sex, like hopscotch, seemed to work best away from home turf. From the age of fifteen onwards, Abby said, there were always at least two girls in her year who arrived back at school pregnant.

'We wouldn't have dreamed of asking our parents for extra money,' said writer Jane Corry, who grew up in 1960s Harrow and took a bus to Stanmore in her summer holidays to work in a school-uniform shop aged fourteen, learning on the job how to measure children's foot sizes. 'I started aged ten in an ice-cream shop in Walberswick,' said Libby Purves. 'Then I used to go and "mind the gallery" – the picture gallery – and I was told what to say. I did babysitting, and taught a child to read.' So, a portfolio of jobs to build up the skills set. The architect Timothy Makower worked as a maintenance man at his own school (St Paul's) in order to 'save up for a camera. It took three days to get the school pool clean. I was vaguely haunted by some reading list.'

All this helped with the learning-to-be-independent, discovering-that-money-doesn't-grow-on-trees aspect of Growing Up – something those Heathfield (and other posh) girls (as well as boys) weren't learning as they had enough pocket money already. The responsibilities and motivational pressures of adulthood would come as more of a shock to them. Well, that wasn't entirely true, about Heathfield girls not working: 'I sold ice creams on the King's Road when I was fifteen,' said Heathfield Old Girl Rochelle Madill, 'on the corner of Radnor Walk. I told Tony the ice-cream vendor I was looking for a job, and he said, "Well, do my job." He left me in charge of the Mr Whippy machine. One day a guy came up to me and offered me some dope. He said, "it's called Durban poison". I smoked it and was totally stoned and I pulled the lever to start a customer's ice cream but couldn't push the lever back, and the horrible white liquid was spilling out over the street.'

One of the pleasures of the ice-cream-vending job, Rochelle said, was 'playing "spot the Old Etonian". I could spot them by the way they walked, and by their stripy shirt.'

Meanwhile, in Kent, the Bateman triplets, Henrietta, Emma and Louisa, all of whom went to Heathfield in the 1970s, were made by their mother to pick strawberries on a local farm. 'But we weren't very focused,' admits Henrietta.

How did it work with paper rounds? Again, you walked into the newsagents and applied in the flesh. 'I was twelve,' said Douglas Addison, when I walked into Lyon's, the newsagent in Alva [Stirlingshire], and got my paper-round job. I started work at 5 a.m. so I could put all my papers in my round order. Alva's a small town, but when you deliver to most of the streets I dread to think how many miles I covered. The bag was huge, and the weather was irrelevant if I wanted to keep my job.'

There could be a bit of a Victorian-child-labour feel about all this. Dawn saw swathes of small boys in towns lugging back-breakingly heavy bags of papers, walking the streets in all weathers. Dennis Skinner was a ten-year-old Sunday-paper-round boy in Clay Cross. 'The biggest seller was the local *Empire News*. The papers were only four pages long during the war, so I could carry two hundred in a bag on my back. I used to go to the concrete houses. "I think there's a big turning-point today, Mr Parker," I said. "How d'you know?" asked Mr Parker. "Well, the

Germans have been stuck at Stalingrad on the other side of the river for three weeks."'

That politically aware little boy again. Depending on family finances, you could keep all the money yourself, or you gave most of it to your mother. 'I delivered newspapers three hundred and sixty-four days a year,' said Fred Walker (the boy who begged rides on the Clyde), 'every day except New Year's Day, from the age of fourteen. I got fifteen shillings a week, gave ten to my mother and kept five for myself.' 'I found an old bike in a bin,' said Douglas Addison, 'and with the money I'd earned on my paper round I bought some tyres and mudguards. I did up the bike, repainted it, sold it and gave the money to my mother.' Those colliery boys from Pontefract who started full-time jobs at thirteen had to give the money to their mother and they got a tiny fraction back. 'You were allowed to keep a bit of pocket money,' said Maurice Tonks. 'I had another job to make extra money – pushing a hand cart, knocking on doors and selling, sage, onions and carrots for the greengrocer's shop. Every shilling I made, I was allowed to keep threepence.' 'I earned £4 a week when I started mining aged fourteen,' said Dave Coupland. 'I gave it to my mother and she gave me ten bob pocket money. I spent 2d. on the bus fare, sixpence to go to the pictures, 6d. on fish and 3d. on chips.'

It all sounds jolly and satisfying in hindsight, but employers wanted their money's worth, and this could make for hellish working conditions. Take potato-picking, which took place in early September in Scotland. 'The hours were incredible,' said Douglas Addison. 'Up at 4 a.m. to get to the farm bus that took you to the field. Those late summer mornings could be freezing. The tractor would go up and down relentlessly, and if you didn't clear your marked section before it came back for the next plough, your money was deducted. In the colder weather, sticking your hands into the earth at speed to keep up with the tractor would break your nails and make your hands numb. The money was excellent, though, and you were allowed to take home enough potatoes to keep the family surviving on chips indefinitely.'

Tougher still was boulder-collecting. 'Alva is at the foot of a mountain, and all the rocks and boulders would roll down onto the field over the months. The job was to follow the tractor and trailer, lifting the rocks and boulders and loading them, always on a slope working towards the hills, and the farmer with his huge boots would give you a kick if you weren't working fast enough.' That's the thing with jobs: they're just about bearable for the first hour, but then they go on, and on and on.

Working alongside a parent, as mixture of helper and hindrance, was a kindergarten version of the summer job. 'I picked peas from the age of six,' said George Oaks (Suffolk boy in the 1940s). 'I was doing my mother's shift work with her. I picked a bag of peas as tall as I was, and they gave you a disc worth 1s. 6d., which you took to the farm to exchange it for money.' He spent what he was allowed to keep on 'a penny's worth of broken biscuits – they sold off the broken ones from the bottom of the tin'.

At least those children were getting paid something. If you were brought up on a farm where no one ever went on holiday, or if you just had parents with a strict work ethic, you were expected to work for your keep. Home slavery was part of life for many, at both ends of the social spectrum. Maurice Tonks: 'We had big bits of pig hanging from the ceiling, drying, and I had to shave the fine hair off them – I had to do that whether I liked it or not.' Children were endlessly being sent out into the garden to beat the dust out of the carpets. 'We had to do housework every day,' said Lucinda MacDougald, radiologist's daughter brought up in 1960s Surrey. 'I swept the kitchen floor three times a day, cleaned the basins and emptied the waste-paper baskets. It taught me how to run a house.' 'We were allowed to play out on the street as long as our chores were done,' said Charmaine Alder, daughter of a big Jamaican family in Birmingham in the 1960s and early 1970s. 'We all had our set chores: washing up, hoovering, cleaning.'

'Even your brother?' I asked, having heard too much about males having an easy time of things, where domestic duties were concerned.

'Yes! My brother's chore was to clean the living room and do the hoovering. My mother told us it was a life skill.' J. K. Rowling tapped into this inbuilt domestic work ethic for children in large, thrifty families with Ron Weasley being sent out to de-gnome the garden.

Luckier ones (such as Jenny Landreth in Sutton Coldfield) were 'paid to do the ironing'. 'We were paid 50p an hour to do this dreadful thing called "pulling fat hen", said Vanessa Buxton. 'Fat hen is a weed that grows in sugar beet, and pulling it out is really hard work.' 'We were made to do "wooding",' said Rachel Johnson. 'That was our penance for being alive. We tried to sneak back to bed after breakfast to read. But we had our chores – vacuuming, washing up, filling the Tilley lamp that took kerosene – or wooding. You heard the terrible sound of the Land Rover revving up, and our father shouting, "Come on, kids: wooding!" We had to gather in the yard. In rain, sleet or shine we had to drag branches into the back of the Land Rover, to be chopped into logs.'

If you lived on a farm, you were subsumed into a working life as soon as you could walk. Sitting high up, in the open air, in a typical early cableless combine harvester was not only the farmer but his small excited son or daughter, 'and I can still smell the dust and feel the itchiness,' said Jamie Blackett, now a Dumfriesshire landowner.

'What did you do all summer?' I asked the agricultural contractor and farmer's son Nick Weeks (brought up in Somerset in the 1950s and 1960s). 'Well, I worked, basically,' he said. 'I learned to drive a tractor when I was seven. I got up at six every day, and cooked breakfast for the family. After breakfast Mum and Dad said what jobs they needed us to do that day. I had to ask special permission if I wanted to go fishing or out with the lads. The day might start off with doing the milking, and cleaning up after the milking. I got a bit of pocket money. It wasn't till I was fourteen that I was given a wage.'

Nick's 'holidays' were going away from his parents' farm to work on another farm – his grandparents'. His grandparents were kind, gentle people and his grandmother made cheese. 'Tuesday was Market Day in Glastonbury, and my grandfather had his suit on and wore a blue flower in his buttonhole, and I could buy Dinky Toys and Airfix kits at Woolworths.' Nick's jobs at his grandparents' farm included cooking the breakfast, feeding the calves and picking snails off the dry stone walls to be sent to the London restaurants. 'I did that when I was quite little: it was a nice job, actually.'

The not-going-anywhere syndrome was especially acute with farmers who kept animals. The single weekly outing for the Weeks family was going for 'our Sunday-evening drive'. 'Mum and Dad went into the pub and had a drink and left me and my sister squabbling in the back of the car. They brought us out a packet of Smith's crisps.' Parents didn't think twice about leaving their children in the back of the car for an hour or so, with the window open an inch, as you would for a dog. It felt like pure abandonment, and was a stark reminder that a child's preferences were not a priority.

'There are no holidays for those who have stock if they don't have staff, and we didn't,' said Gillian Shephard (now Baroness Shephard) brought up in Knapton in Norfolk in the 1940s, a village with a population of 300 in which 'no child didn't have at least one parent involved in agriculture. So there were no family holidays in August. But we lived a mile from the beach and went there by bike every day – a group of us. Nobody felt deprived. Everyone was in the same boat.' If members of a family were going away to stay with their relatives, the whole village knew about it. 'My mother and I used to go to Sheffield for a few days to stay with my mother's mother. I loved it there, as I was an only child and the house there was full of cousins, aunts and friends going in and out. It was in central Sheffield, right next to the cutlery-finishing factory, which was open five and a half days a week and made a huge racket like the hammers of hell.'

Then it was back to Knapton and to the farm. 'We loved summers because they made our lives more interesting – the place became full of students who came to work in the pea-processing factories.'

'My parents started their own market-gardening business in 1962,' said the chartered engineer Simon Shimmin, born in Penrith in 1949, 'and it was quite a struggle for them. In term-time I did all my homework on the bus and then worked in the garden till dark. In the holidays I just helped my dad all day. I was training tomatoes, cutting lettuce, picking soft fruit. I learned to reverse tractors with trailers, so I've always been a good reverser. Our one family day out each summer was to go to the Southport Flower Show, a commercial show, where you could have a look at the latest machinery.'

It was a cramped household: 'We had an in-house grandfather, and there were eight of us living in a tiny house ideal for one. I was the eldest of five siblings and I slept downstairs in the living room on a bed that doubled up as a sofa during the day. I don't know how my mother did it. We lived on salad, boiled potatoes, pink meat out of a tin, and eggs. But we had long meals, and we talked about politics. It was an intellectual, talking household: a proper family, with regular meals.'

It sounded like a paradise of healthy eating, pulling together for the family business and intellectual stimulation, in spite of the sofa-sleeping and the constant work. Children like being helpful, as long as there's kindness and stability. This was emphasised by Pippa Allen from Chesterfield: 'I went to stay with my friend Carrie, whose parents lived on a farm. It was hell on earth at home – my parents were wrapped up in their own misery, and my mother didn't really like children. We were just a bloody inconvenience to her. Carrie and all her family were required to work on the farm, haymaking and helping to milk cows and move cows, and it gave me an idea of how a happy family could be – a family with parents who actually liked children.'

Fruit-picking was rife in Kent. 'It was a "supplementary job",' Alan (the Kentish man who loved staying with his grandparents) explained: 'done by the women. Families couldn't live without the extra money on top of the men's wages.' This was another young-children-helping-their-mothers job. 'It started with the cherries, in July. Then it was damsons and plums, then pears, then apples last of all. Me and my two sisters went to the orchards with our mother every day, on the back of an old Bedford lorry. All the children were there, helping with the picking. We were told off if we tried to climb the trees or larked about. If it rained, we still had to go.' Just one aspect of the job was done by men: 'the ladder-moving – moving the heavy wooden ladders round the trees – was done by old retired men, to supplement their pensions. The women sang all day, whatever was on the Forces Favourite or the Home Service. My mother had a really good voice.'

*

We're edging our way towards hop-picking here – or ''opping', the 'h' sound being absent in the voice of anyone who remembers doing it.

Taking the Tube to Canary Wharf, passing the pavement smokers in their suits, the distracted bankers on their phones and the cafés piled high with Parma ham and mozzarella paninis costing £9.50 each, I arrived seven minutes later at an adult day-care centre, a gentler place, where the activity of the day was peeling satsumas to make a large quantity of lumpy smoothie as a healthy afternoon novelty drink.

As near as that to the glassy financial district, old ladies in cardigans were sitting in a circle round a table singing their old hopping songs. Things like,

Our lovely 'ops, our lovely 'ops,
When the measurer 'e comes round,
Pick 'em up, pick 'em up pick 'em up off the ground.
When he starts to measure, he don't know where to stop.
So, oy, oy, get in the bin, he'll take the bloody lot.

And

Some say 'oppin's lousy,
I don't believe it's true.
We only go down 'oppin'
To earn a bob or two.

I saw how a song like that gets going, rather like at a football match. The self-appointed leader strikes up and the next thing you know, everyone's joining in in a slightly tuneless way. Suddenly we were not in Canary Wharf but in a hop garden in Kent in the summer rain, circa 1942.

The life and soul of the day-care centre was Kath – Kathleen Crawley – docker's daughter, born in Bow in 1932. 'It started in the last week of August. Five or six families got in the back of a lorry, all going to different farms. My family went to May's Farm at Paddock Wood, but later we changed to Yalding Farm. Once you got to the Bull at Swanley, you knew you was on your way. There was a pub sign hanging across the whole road. And we said, "we're nearly there!"'

She reminded me that the fathers didn't go hopping, just the mothers and children. The men carried on doing their London jobs and hitch-hiked down at the weekends. They went straight to the pub.

Bill Carroll (the boy who played in bombsites and avoided pram-pushing) had mentioned that he wished he'd come from a stable kind of family, the kind that went hop-picking, and I bore that in mind. Hopping did require a certain stability, because you were usually booked into the same farm and the same hut year after year, and you had to keep the palliasses (which you filled with straw when you arrived), and the cooking equipment, and the bit of carpet to put on the floor, and the curtain material to cover the unglazed windows.

It was a working month, but it was the highlight of the year. 'I loved it,' said Phyllis Reed, born in Poplar in 1932, whose father looked after the horses at a brewery in Whitechapel and left for work at 3 a.m. 'We planned it for months, putting everything aside to take with us. We stayed down in Kent for four weeks, and the money we earned went towards Christmas. And it meant we could afford little luxuries like soap and flannels. We were outside in the sunshine all day, singing, putting the hops in big bins made of sacking.'

'How did you do meals?'

'For lunch we ate big cheese sandwiches with our big dirty hands. In the evening we had a big stew cooked on a campfire – we took it in turns to go down to the village. We nicked a lot of the stuff off the farms – potatoes, mushrooms, onions, apples. We dug up the potatoes at night. All the kids done it. The pubs said, "Don't let the hoppers in, they'll nick all the glasses." And we did. 'They called us dirty thieving so-and-so's,' said Irene Protheroe, 'but they always asked us what it was like living in London.'

'The mothers pulled the binds off,' said Irene, 'and the children pulled the hops off the binds. That went on all day long, till the measurer came round shouting, "Pull no more binds."'

Everyone was nervous of the measurer. He was furious if he found too many hops dropped onto the ground.

The early Blitz years were horrible for Kath. 'I was evacuated to Chertsey and I was black and blue from the neck to the knees from where the woman of the house used to beat me with a stick. There were fourteen of us crammed into that small house – five of us girls in one bed. The boys were up in the loft and they didn't even have a bed, they just slept on the floor.' By 1942 she was back home and hopping again. Sundays were the best day of the week during the hopping time, as no one expected you to work on a Sunday.

But every gaggle of children comes with its Terrible Twins.

'I was told I could have a day swimming in the river, on a weekend,' Kath said. 'I was wearing my nice crepe dress – and I got slung into the Yalding River by them twins.'

'Which twins?'

'The Krays. Reggie and Ronnie. They were 'opping, too. They threw me head-first into the river. I told them I couldn't swim. They were boisterous kids. Handsome boys, though. You couldn't tell them apart. They used to say, "it wasn't' me, it was Ronnie." Or "it wasn't me, it was Reggie." Their mother, Violet, was a lovely gentle woman.'

Instantly I felt sorry for Violet, the gentle, hard-working mother of the twins from hell.

*

There's one last pram-related incident for this chapter and section, illustrating yet another use for an old pram. Evelyn Griffin, born in 1943 and brought up in Poplar, painted a similar picture of the journey to the hop farms: everyone piling into an open-backed lorry, taking their bedding, curtain material and cooking utensils in three tea chests, filling their palliasses with straw on arrival; and then the long working days: the big poles to pull the binds down, and the children picking the hops off the binds and putting them into hessian 'buckets'; and having to squat over the 'hole in the ground' toilets. 'That was our holiday. And we made sure we didn't forget the macs for rainy days. We could hear the rain bashing down on the tin roof of the hut. And we said, "It's going to be mud tomorrow. Wellington boots!"'

They also brought one other large item with them: the family pram. Evelyn explained that it was not just mothers and children who went hopping, but the extended family, too, on the female side: grandmothers, aunts and great-aunts. 'Sometimes my aunt came down – my dad's sister – and she was very ill and couldn't walk. But she needed her holiday just like the rest of us. It was a ten-minute walk from our hut to the field – so we pushed her there every day, in the big old Silver Cross pram. That wasn't easy if it had been a rainy night.'

We've ended this situational section with a modicum of actual travel: the journey from East London to West Kent (about thirty-four miles). Now it's time, at last, to turn our attention to proper travel, along A roads, motorways and country lanes, to holiday destinations.

PART IV

DOMESTIC DEPARTURES

15

Car Journeys in Britain

C an we reconcile these two facts, which I heard repeated often?
'There was hardly any traffic.'
'There was always a bottleneck in Honiton.'

They are reconcilable, if you think about it. There was so little traffic in Britain till the late 1960s that you could cycle down to the main road and wait five minutes for the next car, ready to scribble down its registration number for your collection. There was also so little traffic that no one had seen the need to build bypasses, so on the few Saturdays per year when large numbers of cars were passing through Honiton on their way to Cornwall, the small market town was unable to cope.

Inside those cars were children squished into the back, dying for the loo, unable even to look at the cover of their *I Spy* book for fear of vomiting yet again. In front of them were their parents, smoking away, stubbing out their cigarettes in the pull-out ashtray drawer, before passing round the travel sweets in a circular tin, stuck together from the heat of the car. Those sweets were meant to settle the stomach and produce saliva to help you swallow and clear the ears if you were going up- or downhill. They didn't really help. Nor did Kwells, the official anti-carsickness pills.

Nor did the chain hanging down from the back of the car.

The official name for this chain was the Anti-Static Ground Strap. 'There was a theory,' said Juliet Gardiner (who went from Hertfordshire to Paignton every year, feeling sick in the back of the car next to her horrible cousin), 'that if you attached a chain to the back bumper it would cure carsickness. The chain was supposed to act as a sort of lightning conductor with the road.' The theory (I've looked it up, and it sounds like another 'father's theory') was that these chains would cure the nausea caused by the body trying to protect itself from the effects of the high-voltage electrical charge accumulated on the metalwork of the car.

These contraptions generated an extra rattling noise to add to the din produced by the open windows, blowing everyone's hair about. Nothing could alleviate the core problems: the dreadful suspension of the low-slung cars, the constant lurching on the winding, bumpy roads, the pervasive smell of petrol from the spare can, the stink of dog breath, the animal odour of the leather seats, the stench of old vomit from journeys past, the hard-boiled-egg-and-banana smell coming from the picnic basket, and the poor interior design, which didn't allow enough boot space or seating space, so offspring and soft luggage were wedged into each other in the back.

And people took so much luggage. 'Everything but the kitchen sink' was literally true in the case of countless 1970s camping families who took an 'Osokool', the jauntily brand-named wireless fridge with a top made of chalk with an indentation in it, into which cold water was poured to keep the interior to a constant temperature. It was also the done thing to take the half-full milk bottle, which often spilled, creating a sour stench that lingered. Seaside boarding houses charged extra for the cruets, so you brought your own. 'My parents hated spending money,' said Catholic author Peter Stanford, 'so we always took our own deckchairs to Barmouth to avoid having to hire them on the beach.'

Peter Stanford with his parents on holiday at Barmouth, and the deckchairs they took with them on the journey

Resourceful mothers, again, helped. They were experts at stuffing luggage into every possible nook. 'My mother,' said piano teacher Anna Maxwell, 'sewed special huge soft travel bags tied with pyjama cords, that you could push and push into any cranny of the car, so our backs would be pushed right up against them.' 'My mother's trick with multiple Terylene sleeping bags,' said the broadcaster Eleanor Oldroyd, 'was to open them out and lay them on top of each other on the back seat, so we'd be sitting on top of five of them, all slithering about.'

No seat belts were worn in the back, which made inter-sibling punching, scratching and pinching all the easier – hence fathers turning half-round with arm outstretched for the 'random swipe', of which the child in the middle bore the brunt.

Despite the expectation of extended discomfort, and despite the fact that there was usually at least one member of the family in a foul mood before the whole adventure even started, there was also an air of high excitement: an enhanced version of the excitement Sally Terris and her sister felt as they set off with their grandmother in Sheffield on launderette day. Much as the not-going-anywhere existence had enriched everyone's souls and provided them with the inner resources to fend off boredom for life, the prospect of actually going somewhere else (somewhere where the air smelled different) was intoxicating.

Journeys, as mentioned in the Fathers chapter, often started at an ungodly hour in the morning, in accordance with fathers' theories about getting ahead of the traffic. This added to the atmosphere of unreality and thrill. Everyone was dazed and shivery from lack of sleep. The dawn preparation of the car picnics was the mother's job; a skilled one would ensure that picnic preparation and fridge emptying dovetailed perfectly, the last slice of ham and last dab of butter going into the last bread roll. 'My mother bypassed some of that picnic preparation altogether,' said psychotherapist and Oxford dons' daughter Catriona Howatson. 'She just stood by the open door of the fridge on the morning of departure and fed us directly from it: "Here, eat this up now."'

Note that it was preparation for picnics in the plural, bearing in mind that a journey from London to Tenby, or from the Midlands to Cornwall, would take twelve hours: 6 a.m. to 6 p.m. I have typed proof of this: my husband's eldest brother Peter Smith kept an annual schedule, throughout the early 1970s, in which he recorded (and later typed up) the precise times at which they passed hundreds of landmarks on the annual journey from Nottinghamshire to Treyarnon in Cornwall. It did take twelve hours, requiring an elevenses picnic, a lunch picnic and a tea picnic, all with their own designated thermos. 'We're LATE,' Peter would say, if they passed Wainhouse Corner five minutes later than they had the previous year. For some reason, they always stopped for the tea picnic on Wadebridge recreation ground, only twenty minutes from their final seaside destination. Why did they stop for tea so near the end of the journey? Why not wait till they arrived? 'But then we would have arrived too late for tea,' my husband explained. Meals had to be taken at the appointed hour, for everyone's peace of mind.

If you were doing a really long change-of-climate journey, such as from Kirkcaldy to Bournemouth, as author Harry Ritchie's family did in the 1960s, it took two days: early one morning till late the next evening. 'We always stopped for the night at a small hotel in Kendal,' said Harry. 'I passed the journey by memorising the whole *AA Handbook*, so I knew the populations of every British city in 1967. I was also very well up on car number plates. The two-letter sequence let you know which area the car came from – but it was confusing, because "XA" could mean either Fife *or* London.'

In everyone's mind was the dread that the car might break down. 'One did break down,' said John Julius Norwich, recalling his spontaneous 1930s driving holidays with his mother. 'My mother changed the wheel herself. If a nice man passed by, she might cajole him into helping her. Once she started cajoling, they didn't have a hope.' For all children in the backs of cars during the whole period of this book, the words 'fan belt' and 'carburettor' were dispiritingly familiar, as they seemed to be the parts that went wrong most often. Everyone had a breakdown story to tell: the car grinding to a halt on Spaghetti Junction or Bodmin Moor, and having to walk miles to the nearest phone box. (And breakdowns played havoc with the schedule.) You had to factor breakdowns into estimated journey times. 'Driving from Exmoor to Cornwall in the early 1970s took four hours, with the punctures,' said Rachel Johnson.

As for the job of loading the car, this was one in which fathers could shine. One father I heard of liked to do what he called a 'dummy run' on the eve of a journey. He packed the car to see how everything would fit in, then unpacked it in case someone drove off with the luggage in the night, and then repacked it at crack of dawn on the morning of departure, using his now tried-and-tested storage technique.

Right through to the end of the 1970s, the older generation retained the theory that it was necessary to 'warm up' a car before setting off. So, if you were travelling to a holiday destination in convoy with the grandparents, as sometimes happened, the grandfather would go out onto the drive ten minutes before departure time, and rev up the car, causing clouds of exhaust fumes, and then leave the engine idling. The father, meanwhile, was putting the finishing touches to his roof rack, pulling the octopus harder to make it grab hold of a further-away metal slat, for tautness's sake.

NB, also, 'annual journey', and NB the universal sentence opener, 'We always ...' The British are a nation of holiday-repeaters. Our once-great nation of Elizabethan merchant adventurers dwindled (mysteriously) into a nation of people who preferred to go back to the very same holiday spot every year.

'It was all about not having to deal with anything new,' said Julie Welch, when I asked her about this going-back-to-the-same-place syndrome. 'It was all about knowing the ropes.' Ah – so was it about fathers needing to be in control and, by repeating the holiday experience again and again, accumulating more and more travel wisdom each year, thereby eliminating all imperfections and getting ahead of everyone else in the country? It was partly that; but young people also crave repeats. For all the varieties of adventures on islands that you get in the *Famous Five* books, the chief question asked at the beginnings of the novels is 'Please can we go back to Polzeath this summer?' From that sameness, adventure follows: adventure against the backdrop of the known. 'All you wanted was to go back to the same place,' said Lizie de la Morinière, who travelled to the same shooting lodge in Scotland every year, 'and to find the things you remembered from last year.' Children are more nostalgic than you'd think. You'd expect them to be 'sick with excitement' about going somewhere new. Actually, they were sick with excitement about going back to exactly the same place they'd been last summer.

'We had an AA badge on the front of our car,' said Charles Fraser, describing his family's journeys up to Nairn in the 1930s, 'and near Grantown-on-Spey there was always an AA man on the side of the road, and he always saluted when he saw the badge. My sister and I thought it was us he was remembering. He had red hair, and we called him Ginger. "I wonder if Ginger will be there this year?" and he always was.' There was always, he always ... those 'always' incidents were a cause for annual delight and reassurance through all the changing scenes of childhood.

'Breaking the journey' was a key part of any road trip. 'When we drove from South Shields to the Norfolk Broads,' said Valerie Grove, 'we always broke the journey in Harrogate.' 'We always stopped for orange squash on the Hog's Back,' said Juliet Gardiner. Not only was it normal to do the same journey every year; it was also normal to stop at the exactly the same stopping places, year after year. Everyone liked it, and it prevented furious arguments in cars full of hungry people. It was all part of the great British tradition of 'knowing the ropes' and 'not having to do anything new'. A single unprepossessing lay-by could accumulate deeply sentimental associations, through years of stopping for tea from a flask and a leg stretch; even the dog was pleased to see the place again.

The Smith family (my future husband is on the left) enjoying coffee and biscuits at a bend in the road in Somerset on the journey to Cornwall, 1979. Photograph by Peter Smith

'Our annual stopping place on the journeys from Cheshire to the south of England was a paradise,' said the art dealer Philip Mould. 'It was down at the bottom of a farm track, and there was a pond, and every year we saw something special there – one year a duck and her ducklings, one year a grass snake swimming, one year a sparrowhawk: it was an unfailing tableau of nature, and it shaped my love of nature. I later became the president of a plant-life charity and now have three ponds of my own.'

Watford Gap Services opened in 1959, so from then on children were starting to fantasise about being allowed to break the journey at a motorway service station instead of a lay-by or field, but it wasn't yet happening in right-thinking families. Petrol stations were just places where a man filled the car up for you and then opened up the bonnet to check the oil. Sitting in a stationary car, unable to see ahead because the bonnet was open, was another dispiriting aspect of journeys.

In the 1960s I longed to stop at 'The Umbrellas', as I called the Rank services on the M2, whose official name was Farthing Corner (now Medway Services). There were coloured umbrellas on the bridge, offering seating with fine views over both carriageways, and they looked deeply enticing. Just once, we did stop there, but the greasy fish and chips were so revolting (the place was described by inspectors as 'particularly sleazy') that we never stopped there again. The Pavlovian response of automatic salivation at the mention of 'filling up with petrol', with its expectation of snacks, hadn't taken hold.

*

As for the moods of the passengers, were they dark or frivolous? 'Every year, we drove from Stirlingshire to our holiday in Dornoch [fifty miles north of Inverness],' said Ali O'Neale (the one who'd been made to play cathartic prisoner-of-war games in Stirlingshire). 'There were four of us children and our parents and the luggage squashed into the Ford Anglia. We were completely stuck and furious with each other from the start. My mother weighed twenty stone by then, as she had thyroid problems, so when she got in the whole car lurched down to the left.'

So, not much jollity in that car. Relief came at Dunkeld, where they met the grandparents who were travelling up from Fife in two Morris Minors. 'The great thing was you could escape from your family and get into another car with a much nicer person,' said Ali. She always hopped across to her grandfather's car at that moment. Also converging on Dunkeld were Ali's aunt and uncle from Kent, who'd put their Hillman Husky on a car sleeper as far as Stirling. From Dunkeld the four cars drove northwards 'in convoy' for the final 138 miles. 'I think "in convoy" was a wartime expression,' said Ali. 'My grandparents hadn't passed any tests, so they were terrible drivers. Grandfather (I called him "Pop") would get behind a slow tractor and start to overtake, with the flipper-indicator sticking out, and there was another car coming towards us, and he'd rock forwards and backwards, urging the car on as if he were on a horse. And I'd be rocking with him. He'd miss the oncoming car by a cigarette-paper's width.' Then, for the sake of maintaining the convoy formation, the three drivers behind felt obliged to do the same overtaking manoeuvre.

'My grandmother always brought a picnic that she had pre-ordered from Goodfellow & Stevens in Arbroath,' said Ali. 'Potted-meat and egg rolls, and cream buns. We had our picnic by the side of the road, on tartan rugs, everyone wearing winter clothes as it was always freezing, even in August.'

In other family cars, frivolity took hold soon after departure, brought on by the untethering from home, and by being forced to sit in close proximity to one's kin, in motion, all facing forward so no one had to look at anyone else's face, as you do in a house. 'Conversation unimpeded by the visage,' as Philip Mould put it, recalling his family car journeys along England's hypotenuses in the 1970s, where their mother set them all the challenge of making up limericks. 'In a car you can develop a level of contact that can take months in any other formation.'

Car-journey frivolity was a different sort of frivolity from the kind brought on at Christmas by the putting on of paper crowns, but the two were related, party hats and forward motion both being effective catalysts for de-inhibition.

It began tentatively, with someone saying, 'I'm thinking of something, and it's animal'. And everyone thought, Oh God, here we go: animal, vegetable, mineral. Must we? 'Has it got four legs?', someone else asked, with a sigh. 'No.' So the game slowly got going, everyone (apart from the sulky silent sibling) asking questions that must only be answered with 'yes' or 'no', till someone pinpointed the precise animal, or thing made from a part of an animal, that the person was thinking of. Then 'I'm thinking of something and it's mineral'. Here we go again. But gradually, the strange pleasures of family in-jokes started to be felt, and even the sulky silent sibling lightened up. The item made of mineral was something that only this particular group of people would find amusing or even know about. Everyone started to relax, even the tense mothers, exhausted from packing, even the fretful fathers, worried sick about the luggage on the roof.

Then, 'Coach and horses: sixteen!' This was 'pub cricket': points for the number of 'legs' in pub signs. It worked best in pre-motorway days when you drove through an endless succession of towns and villages. You got a 'wicket' if the pub was not legs but another part of the body, such as the King's Head. Observation games were good for alleviating carsickness, as they forced you to look out of the window. Families came up with their own systems of observational point-scoring. 'Our game was "Trickle, Trickle, Plop, Plop",' said Ali O'Neale. 'You had to be the first to shout "trickle, trickle" if you saw a petrol pump, "plop, plop" if you saw a pillar box, "oh what fun" for a caravan, "neigh, neigh" for a horse, "woof, woof" for a dog, "brrr, brrr" for a tractor, and "brrring, brrring" for a telephone box.'

So that was the road scenery of the 1950s. Time was passing, miles were being covered and the holiday mood was slowly but surely being got into.

Then the singing started. The bossy singing sibling made everyone start singing a round or canon. It could be something easy such as 'London's burning', or it could be a tricky eighteenth-century catch-song, and the less-musical siblings would find it very hard to hold their notes and not be drawn into singing what the person next to them was singing. This all kept everyone busy for a few more miles.

It got quite loud on those long journeys to the north of Scotland. 'My sister made a song-book,' said Olivia Fraser, 'called *Songs of the A9*, consisting of all the songs we sang all the way to Moniack every year. It was a compilation of Beatles songs, Joan Baez songs and old Scottish folk songs.' 'Our family had a whole repertoire of songs we sang in the car,' said Stephen Cottrell. '"Pack up your Troubles in Your Old Kitbag," "There Goes a Whizzbang', "The Man who Broke the Bank at Monte Carlo," "I'm Hen-e-ry the Eighth, I am" and "Daisy, Daisy".'

Compare and contrast today's travel silence, everyone locked into separate musical worlds with their earphones on.

The rot started to set in with the portable cassette machine, which revolutionised car journeys from the mid-1970s: 'We drove from Surrey to Norfolk listening to Philip's C90 tapes of T. Rex and *Thick as a Brick* by Jethro Tull,' said the photographer Harry Cory-Wright, 'and Mum and Dad stopped for a gin and tonic from the glove compartment.'

*

How slow were the roads? Nowadays, instead of factoring probable breakdowns into car journeys, you have to factor in the probability that the journey will include at least one soul-destroying patch of time when the exhilarating speed of motorway driving will slow to a glamourless crawl, or an even more glamourless standstill, during which you will be imprisoned in the situation, unable to go forwards or backwards or turn off. This will feel particularly painful, because motorways are supposed to be fast, so when they don't work, you feel it even more acutely, as you do when you're walking up a non-working escalator.

In the 1950s there wasn't such pressure for main roads to be fast, and when they slowed down you could get off them onto a side road or farm track, or just stop right there for a picnic by the side of the road. They certainly could be extremely slow, as Kate Grimond, daughter of Celia Johnson and Peter Fleming, recalled: she travelled up the Great North Road and back with her father, plus siblings, plus two Labradors, every summer in the 1950s to the family estate in Argyllshire.

'Driving was all about trying to avoid getting stuck behind a convoy,' she said; and by 'convoy' she meant the unintended kind: the cluster of vehicles that couldn't get away from each other on a single-carriageway road because there were too many of them in close formation and they were all very slow. 'You'd stop to fill up with petrol, and then find yourself rejoining the same "procession" you'd been stuck behind for hours. Typically, as my father described it, the convoy would consist of "one tiny old saloon car, three red lorries of Bristol Road Services in tight formation, an RAF trailer, a Rolls-Royce, an empty hearse, a Doncaster-bound horse box, and a gigantic elm-butt on a converted tank-transporter." And then the whole convoy would grind to a complete halt to let a herd of Friesians cross the road.'

The other dread, Kate said, was getting stuck behind a military convoy, of which there were many, consisting of twelve or more vehicles – 'great khaki snakes snaking along the Yorkshire road'.

These were more picturesque forms of slowness than today's sudden, random, slowness usually brought on by somebody else's tragedy. But the stuck-behind-a-convoy experience did cause Kate Grimond's brother to ask his father why on earth the road was ever called the 'Great' North Road.

*

Now for some specific annual car journeys. 'Our Austin Cambridge,' said Markie Robson-Scott, 'was looked after by a garage man round the corner from us in London, and he'd bring it round to us early in the morning on the day we left for Scotland.' This was in the 1950s and 1960s: Markie and her parents were setting off from Marylebone to the draughty holiday house in Roxburghshire, where they would stay for the whole summer. 'We left at 7 a.m. The car smelled of plasticky suitcases and leather seats and I'd start to feel sick straight away, saliva gathering in my mouth. As we drove past Finchley Road I just wished I could just get out and stay there all summer, with my aunt who lived there. I sat in the back, and Winkle, the dog, sat on my mother's lap in the front. My mother passed round the travel sweets. She'd say to my father, "Would you like a Jethart Snail, dear?"

'It was a huge relief to reach Stamford. We always stopped for lunch at the George Inn.' So, no roadside picnics on tartan rugs for this family: they stopped at hotels: her father's idea of how travelling should be done properly. The lack of luxury would come later, when they arrived at the house itself. 'I had *pâté maison* with curly toast, and peach melba,' said Markie. 'My father would get angry with the waiters. They spoke to him wrongly, or they weren't quite polite enough. We waited ages for the food to arrive, but at least I felt less sick. Then, on we went, taking detours if my father wanted to see a building mentioned in Pevsner.' (It was he who could be reduced to tears by the beauty of a church, even though he wasn't religious.) 'We always spent the night at Monk Fryston Hall, a hotel near Leeds. My parents left me alone in the room while they went down for dinner. I was scared of moths. If a moth got into the room, it was the end of everything. I started screaming.'

The next morning they drove on, and had the final lunch at the Otterburn Inn in Northumberland. 'The food was awful: wet fish in batter, or terrible meat with gravy, overcooked potatoes and soggy vegetables. But at least it wasn't the car, and it wasn't yet the house. I always had tomato juice as the first course. I loved tomato juice and I loved tomato soup.'

Then, 'my mother was convinced that Winkle knew when we were crossing the border into Scotland. She'd say, "He *knows* we're in the best country in the world", and I'd think, Oh, Jesus.'

As she grew older, Markie started appreciating breaking the journeys at hotels a bit more. 'There was always a TV in the lounge, and I'd sit there alone while my parents rested after the drive, watching *Z Cars* and *The Lucy Show* and all the other programmes everyone at school knew about, but I'd never seen because we didn't have a television at home. There were also piles of *Woman* magazine. Evelyn Home's problem page provided my sex education. Also, when I was fourteen, a travelling salesman tried to pick me up at a hotel in Ripon. He passed a note to me via a waiter, asking me out for a drink. My parents wouldn't let me go, although they did seem mildly impressed.'

'Got lost near Kingston and Ewell,' wrote Elizabeth Millman in her 1930s diaries. 'Got lost in Cornish lanes after St Austell.' Getting lost was part of the journey experience – worst of all during the war when the road signs were taken down. As a perk to its members, the AA would post you a customised print-out of the recommended route for your journey, if you wrote to them to ask. This was only necessary if you were going somewhere you hadn't been before, so not of much use to the vast constituency of holiday-repeaters, who prided themselves on knowing the route, but it was useful if you were trying 'a new inexpensive hotel in Swanage', as Nicholas Sagovsky (from Ruislip) remembers his family doing in the 1950s. 'I did the navigating,' he told me, 'sitting in the front while my mother sat in the back. The AA print-out looked like a small flip-chart, in reporter's-notebook format'. 'It was pages and pages long,' recalled Jonathon Green, whose family travelled from Lincoln to the Marks & Spencer holiday house for employees in Bosham, 'and I could never understand that Watford was nowhere near the Watford Gap.' 'Driving in our little 2CV from Suffolk to Wales to catch our ferry to Ireland,' said Libby Purves, 'we took a route through the Midlands, devised by our local solicitor, to avoid motorways. "Monty's Route" was on a carefully written notice on the dashboard. The little car wouldn't have coped with motorways, as you would know if you've ever driven a 2CV and felt its featherweight carcass shudder at the wind of a passing lorry.' At the ferry port at Fishguard, the cars were swung on board the ferry in a net: 'very entertaining for us: we once saw them drop a caravan onto a Bentley.'

Nicholas Sagovsky's glimpse of his mother sitting in the back reminds us of the family dynamics of car seating. The strongest-willed child – often the self-styled navigator – did somehow get to sit in the front, and the mother became the buffer between the warring siblings in the back: yet another example of maternal summer self-sacrifice. In Julie Welch's case, there were not one but two mother figures in the back: 'My father had a girlfriend, Jane, who lived with us all – surprisingly, it worked; she was a sort of leaven to the family, and she and my mother were rather fond of each other. We went to Widemouth Bay in 1959, and I sat in the front and had custody of the radio – a Motorola – and Jane and my mother sat in the back. My father said, "Fuck" when someone came out of a side road, and Jane said, "Your father said a rude word. Don't repeat it, ever."'

Parental swear words, like grandparents' acts of benignity, were never forgotten.

'I was a practised vomiter,' said Julie. 'On another journey down to Folkestone, sitting in the back this time, with my friend who lived in the same cul-de-sac as us in Buckhurst Hill, we were both being sick the whole time, and my mother kept saying, "Oh, Tim, stop the car, stop the car." She called him Tim, although his real name was Arthur, but she thought the name Arthur a bit downmarket. It was the sinky suspension that made us feel so ill, and the smell of the seats, and the cigarette smoke.'

In Annabel Heseltine's case, 'it was not only me being sick but the cat as well, and we begged to be allowed to go to Devon by train instead – but my father had actually opened the second section of the M4 when he was a junior minister in 1971.' So there was no hope of going by train.

The bottom line was that everyone – well, nearly everyone – was desperate to arrive. The most-asked question was 'Are we nearly there?' 'My father bribed us not to ask it,' said Rachel Meddowes, recalling interminable drives to Scotland. The bribe money made up for the fines for not remembering who had been imprisoned on Loch Leven.

Then, at last, a parent would say, 'Prize for the first person to see the sea!' Or, in Kevin Crossley-Holland's family's case, who'd been driving from the Chilterns to Norfolk at 29 mph in a Hillman Imp, 'Penny for the first person to see the windmill!' Or in Susan Brown from Bradford's family, 'Who's the first person to spot Blackpool Tower?' The first sight of the shimmering sea was an unforgettable Favourite Moment of the Year. There it still was, doing its dear old tidal thing, as if you'd never gone away for eleven and a half months.

16

The Day-long Holiday

We're going to dip our toes into the sea, first, with a short chapter about the shortest form of holiday known to man: the day-long one. This, for many I spoke to, was the only kind of holiday they had as children. They stayed at home all summer and then went, for a single, long-awaited day, usually to the coast, usually in a group, sometimes by train, sometimes in a charabanc. The short-form seaside holiday is possible in a country where no one lives very far from the sea (Coton in the Elms in Derbyshire being the village furthest from the coast in the UK – seventy miles).

So these children had the whole holiday experience – the dawn awakening on the great day, the journey, the communal singing, the longing to arrive, the arrival, the first moment of bare feet touching sand, the first paddle, the sandy sandwich, the ice cream, the frenetic ball game, the building of the sandcastle, the watching of its destruction, the cup of tea, the fish and chips, the packing up, the trudge back to the train or bus, the journey home, the arrival home, the unpacking, and the wistful sense of anticlimax – all within the space of fourteen hours.

It was the cheap way of doing a holiday, as you didn't have to worry about accommodation. No cruets necessary. Working men's clubs organised these family days out, for which tickets were required, and they always took place on a Sunday.

'My dad died when I was ten,' said miner's son Ian Oxley (the one who built his own bike), 'but I had a friend in the village whose dad was a member of two local working men's clubs, the Empire and the Moorthorpe, and he got me a ticket for the Empire club outing.' (This was in the early 1950s.) 'We went to Cleethorpes by train. It was a great day. The whole train was put on just for the club: four hundred passengers, mums, dads and kids, with single compartments for ten. As soon as we arrived at Cleethorpes, the mothers and children went down to the beach, with flasks of tea and sandwiches. The fathers went straight to the pub. I never saw dads on the beach.'

So it was the hop-picking-weekend segregation-scenario all over again. If you glimpsed a father it was on the promenade, with a knotted handkerchief over his bald head.

Everything about that day was a thrill for Ian – the train journey, the rides and slides ('my mother didn't come, but she gave me ten bob'), the exotic food: 'my mate always bought a crab on the seafront and let me have a bit of it' – and the sea. But 'I couldn't swim,' he said. 'If the water went above my knees, I were frightened of it.'

For Maurice Tonks, it was 'busloads' to Bridlington or Scarborough, with the Vicker Street Working Men's Club. 'Up early in't morning and put on your Sunday best, and go in six or seven buses, all full.'

'Our town, Hemsworth,' said Susan Gardham, 'had three working men's clubs, the Old Soldiers, the Albion and the Beeches, and they all ran day trips to Cleethorpes. My dad belonged to the Old Soldiers, and went there a lot. He didn't come on the trip, though. My mother and I went on a steam train to Cleethorpes, and just once to Blackpool. I wore my Whitsun dress – we always got a new dress at Whitsuntide, and a new cardigan, new shoes and new ankle socks. My mother wore a beautiful dress and her best

shoes, and a Juliet cap, like what a bride would wear. We brought
a flask and sandwiches in a basket.'

A brief digression on the lost British convention of dressing
up, rather than down, to go on holiday. I kept hearing about this:
excited children wearing ties to travel. 'When we travelled by boat
to see our grandparents in Jersey in the 1950s,' said Jackie King,
'my mother always wore her suit and hat, my father wore his tweed
jacket, my brother wore his prep-school grey shorts and jacket, and
I wore my purple coat with a velvet collar.' 'I wore my tie to go
Alpine walking,' said Kevin Crossley-Holland.

*Smart clothes for travel: Kevin Crossley-Holland wearing a tie to go
Alpine walking with his grandmother, 1947*

As those working men's club outings were on Sundays, there
were two reasons for dressing up: the innate grandeur of travel and
the fact that it was the Sabbath.

For London children, the day out to the local park a mile away
could contain all the elements of a seaside holiday, but in municipal form: sandpit instead of sand, paddling pool instead of sea,

but still the towels, the splashing, the picnic, the ice cream and the sense of adventure. If you rarely ventured beyond your tiny cluster of local streets, a mile felt like a proper journey. 'It was our family holiday,' said Dorothy Rice, descendant of the music-hall comedian Dan Leno, 'all organised by our mother and aunts, with a picnic and the luggage and all of us setting off on foot. We were tired out when we got home.'

More examples of day-long holidays: 'Our only holiday of the year was a once-a-year Sunday-school trip to Aberystwyth or Tenby,' said Grace McNulty, farmer's daughter in Lancashire. The same for George Oaks: one annual Sunday-school outing to the seaside. 'We went on day trips from Birmingham to Rhyl,' said Charmaine Alder, 'organised by the play scheme set up by our parents.' (That was a long round-trip, 240 miles, but possible if you left early enough.) 'Once a year, twelve charabancs set off to Southend from the Rifle pub in Fulham Palace Road,' said Cathy Hawkins. 'A day beside the Tower of London was our trip to the seaside,' said Shirley Cotter. 'There was lots of sand down there at low tide.'

That patch of the Thames by Tower Bridge was known as London's 'Riviera', and a proper beach was created in the 1930s when 1,500 barge loads of sand were tipped out onto the shore. 'Half the East End was down there,' said Bill Carroll, 'and I sometimes went. But my family holiday was a single day trip to Southend, by train, and we weren't allowed to eat on the train. Dad was itching to get us settled on the beach as soon as we arrived, so he could go for his pint. "I'll just be up there," he'd say, pointing at the pub.'

If anyone had a car, everyone else jumped into it. 'My sister had a boyfriend who had a car, and we all jumped in and went to Southend for the day,' said hop-picker Phyllis Reed. 'Dad liked his drink then – all the men did.' 'My grandad had a car,' said Kath Crawley, 'and he'd say, "Get in the car, and we'll go down Canvey." Just a day trip, and we had a stick of rock and went paddling in the sea.'

The three Herron boys from Sunderland didn't want to go anywhere else except Eastgate, forty-five minutes up the Wear Valley, for the day-long family holiday, all standing up in the back all the way. 'Turn off at the Cross Keys, down a track, park the car, and we'd be off – shirts off and straight into the peaty water of the river. Then get our fishing net out to catch minnows. The waste-water channel of the Blue Circle Cement Works came down into the river just there, and if we were cold we bathed in the waste water and got covered in white limescale. That was our working-class hot spa.'

This short-form holiday phenomenon reminds us that holidays are as much psychological as they are physical. You were back home tucked up in your own bed by midnight, but you were left with a sense of definitely having 'been away on holiday', and that was what mattered.

17

Not Going Abroad (Seaside)

'**A**bsolutely Baltic' was how Ali O'Neale described the temperature of the sea at Dornoch, north of Inverness.

The slow convoy of Austin, Hillman and two Morris Minors had arrived. (This was early August in the late 1950s.) Ali's grandfather was generously paying for the whole family to have this annual fortnight's holiday at the Castle Hotel. Fresh grapefruit was served as a first course for breakfast, which seemed extremely exotic, and Ali's grandmother asked the waiter to send back her portion of scrambled egg because it was slightly too large and she didn't want to waste any.

After breakfast on the first morning, 'the men went off to play golf, in their plus-fours. "I'm orf to play goff" was how they pronounced it. We children went down to the beach with our mothers and grandmother, and we put the tartan rug down by a sand-dune to provide a bit of shelter. The mothers made us change into our gathered swimsuits and put on tight yellow rubber swimming-caps with straps under our chins. Aunt Brora, Granny and Mummy then sat down cosily on the rug, in their thick tweed coats, with their thermos of coffee and their cigarettes. Then they said, "Go off and enjoy yourselves."'

Five minutes later, any possible 'enjoyment' of swimming in

the icy water, which 'never gets above 50° Fahrenheit, even in summer', was already over. 'It was numbingly cold and there were jellyfish everywhere. So we ran back to our parents, but they said, "Go back and stay a bit longer." The only way we could survive was by running along the beach to try to keep warm.'

After forty-five minutes of this ordeal the children came back to the rug, blue-lipped, shivering, imploring to be allowed to get dry. 'Our mothers handed out the towels and we dried our sandy legs. The towels felt like sandpaper. It was impossible to get the rubber swimming-caps off without pulling half your hair out.'

There were some rusty old swings by the beach so the siblings and cousins spent the next hour or so playing on those, and there was a pond known as the Witches' Pool, where one of the last witches had been drowned, so that gave everyone something to talk about.

Then, at last, it was time to go back to the hotel for a hot lunch in the dining room: mince and potatoes followed by syrup sponge. Beach time was done – but it would be repeated every morning for a fortnight, unless it was absolutely pouring, in which case 'my aunt would take us for a drive round the local airstrip, letting us have a go at the wheel. I could drive by the age of eleven. Aunt Brora smoked in the car, so the windows got smoked up and I could hardly see out with the smoke and the rain and being so small. My sister sat in the back screaming if it was my go, and I sat in the back screaming if it was hers.'

The afternoons were calm by comparison: paper games in Aunt Brora's annex, while the men all went off fishing. Then, afternoon tea in the hotel, followed by playing in the gardens, and then dinner.

A fortnight in Dornoch could seem like a very long time. 'I always made a day-chart at my school, St Leonards,' said Ali, 'to count down the days till the end of term. By my mid-teens I was making a chart on holiday to count down to the day when I could get away from Dornoch.'

*

A few syndromes emerge from that account, one of which I've already noted: the syndrome of the men going off to do exactly what they wanted all day, leaving mothers, aunts and grand-mothers in charge of the children, but they just said, 'run along'. It seemed horribly unfair that mothers on beaches were just as heartless as games mistresses at school, who always wore warmer clothes than their shivering, skimpily dressed pupils.

The Not Going Abroad syndrome was so ingrained that it didn't even feel like a decision; it was just a fact of life. It felt completely normal to shut your front door and turn northwards. Lots of people I spoke to didn't go abroad till adulthood. 'Of course, there were foreign currency restrictions in those days,' people kept reminding me; 'you weren't allowed to take more than £50 out of the country, right up to the end of the 1970s.' I think those restrictions were just an excuse to do what parents wanted to do anyway, which was to keep their children in their own English-speaking, non-rabies-infested country, than which they were certain (if the weather was good) no foreign place was any better. It went with their whole unflashy, lack-of-luxury philosophy. The seaside was the perfect venue for expressing and vindicating the philosophy of thrift, as its entertainments – sand, stones, shells and sea – were free of charge.

'Please can we go abroad this year?' the young John Mullan (now a professor of English at UCL) begged his mother in 1966, when he discovered that some boys at his state primary school in Sheffield were going on their first package holidays to Majorca, while his family was just going to shingly Suffolk as usual. 'My mother shook her head and said to me, "Darling, going abroad is vulgar." She thought going abroad was something people were starting to boast about, like having a new car or a new conserv-atory.' That seemed a bit tasteless to her.

Note also that the holiday in Dornoch lasted for a fortnight.

Today's out-of-office autoreplies (those dispiriting emails that ping back within seconds, making you hope at first that it's a wonderfully prompt reply) rarely announce that the person is away for a whole fortnight. 'I will be back at my desk on . . . ' they reassure you, and it's usually within a week and, what's more, they'll be checking their emails 'intermittently'. The only time people go abroad for a fortnight is if it's to another continent, or maybe three weeks if it's Australia.

In the period of this book, if you weren't doing the day-long beach holiday, you went to the other extreme and did at least a full fortnight. It took long enough to get there, so, once there, you stayed put. Fathers knew how to relax in those days, cutting themselves off entirely from their place of work. For children, a fortnight could seem either a paradise of free time in a glorious setting, or an extended period of even more boredom than usual: a new kind of pebble-based kinetic stasis. It depended on the company, the beach and the weather.

Note, too, that in spite of all the spartanness of the children's mornings on the freezing beach, Ali's grandfather was paying for the extended family to stay for a whole fortnight in a hotel. That must have been expensive. But hotel prices (like school fees) were not absurdly exorbitant in those days, and it was considered the right and done thing for a normally successful professional to afford to take his family to an unflashy but 'proper' hotel, to which you came back every day for a hot brown lunch in a brown dining room. A proper hotel   but no wasting of scrambled egg. Where you stayed was a quiet manifestation of your social status, and it mattered. Occasionally I found myself asking the wrong person, 'Where did you stay? In a hotel? Or a boarding house?' As I uttered the word 'boarding house' I regretted it. Mouths were turned down in Lady Bracknell-like disdain. 'No, we wouldn't have stayed in a boarding house.' A chief aspect of home table manners among the professional middle classes, I discovered, was teaching the children never, ever to reach across the table for anything they needed, such as the salt or the butter. That was known as 'the boarding-house reach'.

*

Britain has two kinds of beach surface, and it was just bad luck if your parents chose a pebbly one rather than a sandy one. If they weren't going to be on the beach themselves, they didn't bother to check. I chatted to a man (born in 1935) who asked to remain anonymous, so I'll refer to him as the Trumper's man, as he'd come up to London to have his hair cut at Trumper, the grand barber's in Mayfair. ('I've travelled through life incognito,' he said, and he was not about to change that.) He was a classic example of a beach loather, and you can see why. 'My parents took a house on the coast. It was my rotten luck that it should be on Cooden Beach, a dreary pebbly beach near Hastings. My parents liked going racing – to Folkestone, Brighton, Lewes, Lingfield and Goodwood – and they left us with the keeper – our nanny, a girl from Lancashire called Betty Smith. We were just left on the pebbly beach all day. I've never liked the sea, ever since. What was there to do except throw pebbles into the sea? I suppose one had an ice cream every now and then. The whole thing was utterly forgettable.'

So – once again – a whole holiday arranged around what the father wanted to do in a sporty way. Neither parent had thought to suggest, 'Maybe a sandy beach would be nicer for our children to play on every day for a month?' The Trumper's man's life was changed for ever one morning aged twelve, when his father suddenly asked him whether he'd like to join him at the Folkestone Races that day. 'I jumped at the chance. Anything to get away from the beach and my sisters. I loved trains. We took an electric train from Collington Halt to Hastings, a steam train to Ashford and we sat in a drawing-room car with armchairs on swivels, and then another train to Westenhanger for a wonderful day at the races. My eyes were out on stalks. That was the start of a lifelong love of horseracing.'

The British repeat-holiday instinct meant that whichever kind of beach it was, you went back to the same one again and again, year after year. As is still the case, the question to ask British people about their seaside holidays is not 'Where did you go in Cornwall?' but 'Where do you go in Cornwall?' Or 'Where do you go in Norfolk?' Children grew up with one particular vision of what the seaside was like. Only later in life did the pebbly-beach ones discover the delights of the more exciting kinds of beach on offer round our 7,700 miles of coastline (or 19,000 if you count the islands).

As the Trumper's man illustrated with that glimpse, going to the seaside with one's nanny was the done thing among upper-class children before the war. In his case, his parents were actually staying in the same rented house on Cooden Beach (there'll be more later on the upper-class British habit of 'taking' houses for the summer); but the parents and children lived separate lives, the children's centred entirely on nursery, nanny and beach.

Often, in those cases, the parents did go abroad, on their own, to glamorous hotels and villas on the French Riviera. They wouldn't have dreamed of bringing their children, who were sent with the nanny to a British seaside resort instead. Sometimes the nanny had a sister who lived in a genteel coastal town, so that was the chosen place. Nannies tended to prefer the tame, boring kind of sea to the dangerous, exciting kind you get on the north coast of Cornwall, where they really would have had to keep a close eye on their charges all day for fear of the rip currents. The nannies clacked away with their knitting needles on their deckchairs, and the children just amused themselves.

The modern habit you hear of, of the super-rich photo-shopping the nanny out of their family holiday snaps, has its 1960s precedent. One woman I spoke to (who also asked to remain anonymous) said, 'our parents drove us children and our nanny to Frinton, and as soon as we arrived we posed for a photograph on the beach with our parents, for the album, so it would look as if this was a family holiday. Five minutes later our parents left to go on a foreign holiday, leaving us with the nanny for a fortnight.' Cameras do lie for the sake of the photograph album; I heard another instance of camera-on-beach lying from Pat Doyne-Ditmas: 'My father was not a tactile man,' she said, 'and I never used to sit on his lap when I was a child. But my mother was taking a photograph on the beach and said to him, "Go on, put Pat on your lap, just for the photograph." So there he is in the album, immortalised in that tactile fatherly pose.' She showed me the photograph. He has a cigarette in his mouth and looks a bit uncomfortable with this alien two-year-old plonked on him. Of course, the chief lie about beach holidays in photograph albums is that they only show the good-weather days, not the moments when (as my husband recalls from his 1960s and 1970s Cornish holidays) 'we sat on the beach in the pouring rain, all holding up a big polythene rain-sheet above our heads, but it didn't keep the rain off – it doesn't, it just drips down the back of your neck, if you're holding the very edge of the sheet, which you have to.'

On the subject of seaside-holiday weather, Marnie Palmer painted a bleak picture, as memorable as any photograph, of her one and only seaside holiday, in the early 1960s, camping in St Ives, during which it rained incessantly: 'We sat on the beach with a big umbrella and windshields, eating our sandwiches. Wind and rain. Sat in the car, eating our sandwiches. Rain on the roof of the car. Our tent let the rain in. I woke up soaked. In my stripy top, bell-bottoms, patent plastic mac and flat white winkle-pickers, I walked on the dunes in the rain – just dreaming.'

Marnie Palmer on Paignton Beach, dreaming of being carried away by a handsome prince on his white steed. To play with, she had a much younger cousin and a rubber horse

*

It seemed that there was a belief among 'educated' and upper-class parents (and nannies) that the fewer official activities there were laid on, on a beach, the better it was for you. It was a similar belief to the one that inspired upper-class parents never to take their children to the zoo: the philosophy that children should be brought up to use their imagination and not have treats laid on. The main aim of parents in those days seemed to be to ensure that their children had not so much a happy life as an appropriate life. It was the lower classes who were allowed to go on beaches with entertainments like donkey rides, slides, swings, ice-cream parlours, games arcades, Punch and Judy shows and so on. Upper- and upper-middle-class children had to make do with pebbles, a bit of sand at low tide, a bucket and spade and a shrimping net. 'I went to Frinton with my nanny in the 1930s,' said the architectural historian Mark Girouard. 'No parents – I think they were having a good time far away – no beach hut, and no donkeys. I can only remember sand and nannies. Making elaborate sandcastles probably encouraged my interest in architecture.' Sandcastle-building was definitely considered a worthy occupation, prop-free and therefore good for the imagination. Castle-shaped buckets – the kind that Juliet Gardiner longed to have but wasn't allowed to – were seen as vulgarly imagination-sapping. Collecting shells, fossils and amber was also considered worthy: making the most of what nature herself provided. Walter Balmford summed the experience up in the simple sentence, 'There wasn't much to do at Sutton-on-Sea.'

Juliet Gardiner and her adoptive mother (who wouldn't allow her to have a castle-shaped bucket) at Paignton

Hence – amid all this lack of laid-on entertainment – the real sense of excitement, and the nannies' sense of relief, when a Christian beach mission arrived on the beach, taking the children off the nannies' hands and giving them a mission – not so much the spiritual kind of mission as the practical kind that would keep them busy for a few hours.

At Borth, on the Welsh coast north of Aberystwyth in the 1930s, where Henry Villiers and his brothers went every summer, not just for a fortnight but for a whole month, with their nanny, while their parents were on holiday in Italy, the banner of the Children's Special Service Mission was on the beach each morning when they came down from their boarding house, Glendower. 'We'd all assemble in front of the minister,' said Henry, 'twenty-five boys and girls aged from five to thirteen, and the first thing we had to do was to build an enormous sandcastle to be his pulpit. We worked away at it, dressed in our shorts and Aertex shirts with our bathing suits underneath. Then the minister went up into the pulpit to preach his sermon to us, and we sang hymns. Nanny could relax – she knew we were in good hands.'

Those missions were on beaches all over the place through the period of this book, except during the war when southern beaches were out of bounds and barbed wired. Teams of Church Army recruits spent their summers doing what was called 'Seaside and Trek': travelling southwards from beach to beach and rounding up as many young malleable souls as they could before moving on.

This was supposed to be a social leveller, but it was rare to get the two extremes of the social classes onto the same beach in the first place, to make any such levelling possible. The Frinton-ites wouldn't go near Clacton; the Broadstairs-ites wouldn't go near Margate; the Filey-ites wouldn't go near Bridlington; the Barmouth-ites wouldn't go near Rhyl. 'Clacton was seen as sin city,' said Giles Fraser, who spent his summer holidays at the more genteel Frinton, seven miles away. Diana Holderness told me that, in the 1930s, beach photographers at Bembridge on the Isle of Wight used to go around taking snaps of beautiful upper-class little girls like her and then made them into postcards to sell to the lower orders further down the coast. 'I didn't think that particularly odd,' she said.

The British are experts at nicely and politely avoiding each other. The level crossing barriers at Frinton are known as 'the pearly gates': passing through them you enter the elite seaside heaven. But even on arrival at the beach suited to your social standing, there were still more subtle gradations. The less discerning plonked themselves down the moment they arrived on the sand; the more discerning walked a long way before plonking themselves down.

So it was not just that the British went to the same beach every year; they went back to exactly the same spot on the same beach; and the less paraphernalia they brought with them, the more superior they felt: no windshield, tent, sunshade and rubber rings for the nannied crowd: just a deckchair for the nanny and a rug for the children.

*

Meanwhile, further up or down the coast, the rest of the world was having an unashamedly entertaining time. 'Just once we went to Bridlington,' said Les Ranson, born in 1946, son of a steelworker, 'but the magical place was Blackpool. You went on a steam train to get there, through the Pennines. Blackpool had everything: the Tower with a lift to the top, a circus, a zoo, aquariums, three piers with shows on each, trams, a theatre where I saw the Beverley Sisters, a pleasure beach, and a massive promenade.' 'Donkey rides, oysters for sale, Blackpool rock: I loved it,' said shipyard worker's son Dugald Cameron. Frinton would have seemed unbelievably dreary by comparison.

Not only that, but these families went to the seaside in a big song-singing crowd: three generations, all together. The whole holiday was based on communality. Neighbour went on holiday with neighbour: 'we went to Blackpool with the Colemans who lived next door,' said Alan Brown, a textile designer's son from Bradford. 'We called them "Mr and Mrs Coleman", and even our parents called them "Mr and Mrs Coleman", even though they were close friends and had a gate into each other's gardens.'

Everyone I talked to who lived in places that had scheduled factory holidays – the unpaid week or fortnight, staggered among local towns, during which all the factories closed – recalled the unforgettable excitement of the first morning of the holiday: the girls dressed in their Whitsun dresses, ankle socks and sandals, the boys in shorts, shirts and ties, fathers and grandfathers in smart trousers, ties and hats, mothers and grannies in their Sunday best, all queuing up with their heavy non-pull-along suitcases.

'There was a queue half a mile long up the Leeds Road, to get to the trains,' recalled Susan Brown of Bradford. 'A stream of people walking down Market Street to Earlestown station,' said Jean Parfrey (b. 1937, whose father worked at T. and T. Vicars' biscuit-machinery factory in Earlestown, but they changed to making parts for guns when the war started). 'They laid on special trains twelve coaches long, but we still couldn't find seats and I sat on my case in the corridor.' This was the best day of the year for train-obsessed boys. 'My brother thought it was wonderful,' said Dorothy Matthews, born in 1939, daughter of a worker at Courtauld's fabric factory who paid for the whole works to go to Blackpool. 'You were given your allotted train time, the eight, nine, or ten o'clock, and we carried our buckets and spades to Leigh & Bedford station. Courtauld's paid for the special trains to be laid on. My father wore slacks, an open-necked shirt and a trilby. I wore a pretty dress and sandals – my Easter dress.' 'They put on extra carriages and had to have two engines to pull the train out of Bradford to get it up the hill, there were that many people going,' said Susan Brown. 'When it got to Low Moor they took one of the engines off.'

'In the shipyard where my father was chairman and managing director,' said Sandy Stephen, born in 1927, 'everybody from the managing director downwards, except a few security staff and maintenance men, went on holiday as soon as the Glasgow Fair started. Glasgow fell silent, with skeleton services on the trams and underground, some shops closing completely. Black smoke usually belched into the atmosphere, winter and summer, but suddenly that stopped, and the result was that from the hill above our house in Lanarkshire sixteen miles away, the whole of Glasgow was laid out like a map and you could pick out the university and the cathedral.'

The only spanner in the works was the Scottish weather: 'It was traditional that it rained during the Glasgow Fair, the storm clouds gathering on Fair Friday and remaining in situ for the next two weeks.'

The posher classes would rather have died than be corralled in this way, forced to travel on public transport, with thousands of other people, on the same day, to the same place, to have a communal, jolly time. Well, the grown-ups would rather have died. Their children would probably have loved it. But it wasn't an option. And I must note here that by no means everybody went away during these holiday fortnights. 'Lots didn't go,' said Dennis Skinner. 'Cliff Alan's family went away for a week.' (The fact that he could remember the name of the boy whose family did go away emphasises how rare it was in Clay Cross.) 'We didn't go. Six of us went to Blackpool in the pit holidays when I got my first job aged sixteen. My friends said, "Dennis, it's this way to 7 Albert Road" – that was the hotel we were staying in. But I said, "I've never seen the sea. I'll have a look at it first."'

For those who could afford to save up to go away, the moment of arrival at the seaside town was thrilling. 'Local Blackpool children were waiting at the station with carts, ready to pull your luggage along to your boarding house for 2d.,' said Susan Brown. 'We always sent a tin trunk ahead of us, full of tins of food: you were expected to contribute to the catering.'

The fathers didn't all go straight to the pub, as the hop-picking husbands did. But nor did most of them actually swim. The grown-ups sat in hired deckchairs on the sand (a man came round with a bus-conductor-style ticket dispenser), the mothers and grandmothers still in their dresses, the fathers and grandfathers still in their suits with ties and tie-pins, and their hats on. 'My dad paddled,' said Jean Parfrey, 'but he just turned his trousers up to the knees. Even I didn't learn to swim till I went to college.' She showed me a photograph of her grown-up cousin helping her to build a sandcastle, in his suit.

Jean Parfrey's cousin building a sandcastle in a suit, her suited father behind him, and Jean wearing her smart 'Sunday coat'

*

Children wore woollen swimming costumes, often lovingly knitted by their mother or grandmother. 'Mine even had seahorses knitted into the pattern,' said Ann Lindsay. No one could accuse the mothers, grandmothers and nannies of not trying their hardest with eye-catching knitting patterns. Wool seemed a sensible material in principle, as it would cling to the children's bodies like jerseys, but no one had solved the problem of what happened to wool when it got wet. Jane Adams particularly hated those costumes, as they forced her to dress identically to her detested sister: 'My grandmother was an exceptionally gifted knitter, and she knitted me and my sister matching pink woollen bathing costumes. As soon as we got wet they sagged down to our knees. My main feeling was, What a disaster. They even had smart little knitted belts, but they were completely unfit for purpose.' The other form of swimming costume for girls was the 'ruched' or seersucker swimming dress made of cotton. That, too, sagged dreadfully when it got wet. 'And those rubber swimming-caps didn't work,' said collector Angela Lynne, who went to Bridlington every summer of her early childhood. 'They were always full of water when you pulled them off.'

Nor were you allowed to show an inch of your private parts to the world or even to the other members of your family, while changing, even when you were pre-pubescent. Hence the invention of the gathered, cylindrical, closed towelling-cloak or 'poncho' under which children hunkered in the dark to take off their clothes and put on the costume, and, harder still, to do the reverse after the swim. 'Ours were white with red blanket-stitch round the top,' said Ann Lindsay. Again, lovingly sewn. In families where everyone swam, you would see them all hopping around inside these gathered cylinders as they groped with their clothes. 'My father wore a black woollen bathing costume that went right up to his neck,' said Angela Lynne. 'I never once saw his bare chest.'

It was partly to avoid this public embarrassment that families shelled out for a beach hut. Inside a beach hut they changed in exactly the same way, but at least it was only the rest of the family who was not seeing them naked, rather than the rest of the world. Beach huts answered to other deep British needs, such as the longing for a neat and tidy nest, the longing for somewhere to dry wet towels, the longing to be able to brew your own cup of tea, and the longing to have somewhere to hide when it rained. 'The beach huts in Sheringham all had names on their doors,' said Julie Welch. 'Our favourite was Nickel Coin, who was a Grand National winner. My father and I always tried to get Nickel Coin. You really needed a beach hut as it often poured. The hut smelled of damp towels and butane gas. It came with a card table and we brought our cards for Snap and patience in the pouring rain. I remember being in the beach hut quite a lot.'

*Julie Welch outside the beach hut
in Sheringham, aged nine, 1957*

That was the danger with beach huts. They became preferable to being outside. 'Our parents spent most of the day in the beach hut,' said Walter Balmford, recalling his trips to Sutton-on-Sea in the 1930s. 'Neither of them was enthusiastic about helping us to build sandcastles. I think they just read the newspapers in there.'

As for the exposing of flesh, I heard just two exceptions to the anti-nakedness rule. Sabine Durrant went on holiday in the early 1970s with her friend Jessica, while her own widowed mother was holding down her office job on Charing Cross Road. 'Jessica's family stopped to spend a night camping by a lake in the Brecon Beacons, on our way to Wales. Her mother was very earthy. She stripped all her clothes off and said, "A-h-h-h!" as she got into the lake.' Phoebe Fortescue's father, the Anglican vicar of St Andrew's, Ham Common, did change into his swimming trunks in the normal modest way, but as soon as he plunged into the sea, early each morning during their vicarage-swapping holidays in Thanet in the 1960s, he took the trunks straight off. 'We all liked skinny-dipping,' said Phoebe. 'My father would then put his trunks on his head, or throw them around.' This naked swim was a liberating, bonding, frivolous start to the family's day. 'We were always on the beach by 7 a.m. so we could have it to ourselves. After the bathe we had breakfast on the beach, sausages and bacon cooked by my mother on the Calor gas stove. Then we had iced buns at 10 a.m., and then we were off the beach for the rest of the day. Off we'd drive to look round a local church with our Arthur Mee's guide to Kent. Always on our minds was trying to find a replacement for something we'd broken in the borrowed vicarage – the lid of a butter dish or something. We scoured the shops.'

*Phoebe (right), her sister Emily and their parents,
the Revd John and Marion Burridge, having breakfast on the
beach at Herne bay after the early-morning dip, 1967*

... and then off to look round a church

Shop-scouring was going on all over the place in seaside towns, but the lack-of-luxury philosophy meant that not much buying was going on among the 'educated' classes who were supposed to have more taste than money. As well as longing for a castle-shaped bucket in Paignton, 'I longed for a Muffin the Mule, but I wasn't allowed one of those either,' said Juliet Gardiner. 'I spent all my pocket money on a pair of flippers from a shop on the promenade,' said Honor Mottram (daughter of a radial arm driller in Lancashire, who went to Lytham in the late 1940s), 'but my mother made me take them straight back.'

18

Not Going Abroad (Seaside) continued

The 'we always' syndrome – British families doing exactly the same thing at the same time each day on holiday – was particularly in evidence at the seaside. Perhaps it was that the crazy, unpredictable wildness of the sea made parents all the more determined to keep a firm hold on tameness by punctuating the day with a rigid timetable. You could set your watch by families' rituals. They arrived at the beach at exactly the same time each morning and set up camp in the time-honoured chosen spot. Neat queues formed at one minute to the hour, for the single permitted ice cream, 'in a cone, without a flake', as many recalled from their 1950s summers. (The 99 had been invented in 1922, named after an Italian ice-cream shop at 99 Portobello High Street in Edinburgh, but the flake at a jaunty angle was shunned as a superfluous extra by the paying parents.) Treats were acceptable only if they were written into the schedule. Mr Coleman, the Browns' next-door neighbour in Bradford with whom they always went on holiday to Blackpool, 'always had his knickerbocker glory immediately *before* going back to lunch in the boarding house.' That was his holiday indulgence.

'Our two-swims-a-day, whatever-the-weather holidays,' was how Angela Lynne described her typical middle-class 1950s timetabled holidays in Bridlington, emphasising that she did not go to Filey with her nanny (as the upper-class Yorkshire children did), but to

Bridlington, or 'Brid', twelve miles down the coast, with her parents, and they stayed in a hotel, which was the right thing for her middle-class family's status, but in order to save money she had to share a bed with her sister, sleeping head-to-toe, 'so we could at least scratch each other's itchy shoulders with our toes' – the itchiness caused by the peeling skin.

'The ritual was, always a bathe before lunch, then we were dragged back to the hotel for lunch, usually something like roast mutton, cabbage and potatoes, followed by jelly and custard – we had to go back to the hotel for lunch, as our stay was all-inclusive, so we could never just have a sandwich on the beach as we would have preferred to; and then we had to wait an hour before our afternoon bathe. The theory was, "you'll get cramp if you swim too soon after lunch". If it was raining, my mother told us, "It's warmer in the water when it's raining."' (Those were two more adult theories peddled to children, to add to the collection of theories in this book.) 'We had no choice but to get in for our second bathe, and we came out freezing and shivering, and our mother dried us vigorously with a rough towel, and then we put on our Fair Isle jerseys and felt warm and could dig again.'

Angela Lynne (right) with her sister and their mother,
whose rule was 'two swims a day, whatever the weather'

Every ritual had its own mantra spelled out to the children. The bathing mantra was 'don't go out of your depth'. The digging mantra was 'dig until you get to water'. The ice-cream mantra was 'never eat an ice cream unless you're sitting down', so you had to carry it back to your beach spot before having the first lick.

'Dig until you get to water'. Angela Lynne at Bridlington

Note the word 'bathe' rather than 'swim'. 'Going for a bathe' is still considered, by the older generation, the correct verb for what you do in the sea. '"Swim" is what you do in a pool, with chlorine,' people told me, holding the word 'swim' with tweezers rather as they did 'boarding house'. The verb 'bathe' does make sense in places like the north coast of Cornwall, where you don't actually swim with strokes, but surf instead: the typical mid-twentieth-century sight of two people 'going for a bathe' in north Cornwall was to see them vanishing off seawards in their unflattering costumes, with wooden surfboards tucked under their arms, and they'd return twenty minutes later with bits of seaweed in their hair, in a state of exhilaration.

Because – never forget – being by the sea does make everyone feel extraordinarily well. Those lack-of-luxury parents were on to something. Not only were nature's seaside entertainments free but they were also, somehow, a shortcut to happiness, even of the Sulkiest Member. A big beach at low tide on which to play a home-invented variation of cricket or rounders; rock pools to dam, or to search for crabs in; the communal building of a huge sand-castle, father reverting to boyhood as he commandeers the design of the moat and pier to be slowly destroyed while the imaginary pier show is going on inside; a thermos of hot coffee and a tin of digestives to come back to after the first 'bathe'; the daily drama of the tides ... It's hard to nurse a bad mood for long by the sea, and parents knew it.

Pure, undiluted seaside contentment:
Celia Burns at Morecambe Bay, 1968

'Swimming was *central*,' said Libby Purves, of her childhood summers, summing up those watery weeks. 'I believe in the theory of the aquatic ape – that our ancestors went into the water and were habitual swimmers.' For Ian Skelly it was the colours of the seaside village of Branscombe in Devon that changed his life for three weeks every year, during the brief escape from the flat grey coldness of Lytham St Annes where he spent the other forty-nine weeks. 'Branscombe seemed absolutely beautiful by contrast. It had everything: sun, hills, sea you could actually swim in without being swept away by a rip tide. It has the longest village street of any village in the country. Every morning I walked the whole length of the village to the thatched baker's, and the smell of their fresh bread wafted down the valley. I just wandered off and walked for miles into the countryside. Wildlife was abundant: swallows, swifts, yellowhammers, farm animals. Apart from gulls, you never saw any wildlife in Lytham St Annes. Those summers blew all the doors open for me. I lived for those three weeks.' This was the boy who gazed at the sign 'To Kirkham and beyond' on Lytham station. 'Those times in that other landscape "beyond" really were my salvation,' he said.

We need to dent the seaside bliss slightly with the matter of sunburn, in the days before Piz Buin. (Water-resistant sunscreens were invented in 1977.) By the 1960s, mothers had discovered the new-fangled substance called olive oil, bought in small bottles from the chemist's, which they smeared onto children's shoulders, so the shoulders fried like bacon. Some families, at the same time, were experimenting with Nivea as sunscreen: a disaster. Before that, the whole seaside skin cycle was based on peeling. '"Have you started peeling yet?" was what everyone asked each other, two days into the fortnight's holiday,' Angela Lynne said. 'You dabbed the peeling shoulders with calamine lotion. By the start of the second week, the top layer of skin had peeled off and the new, tougher skin came through, and that was when you got your tan.'

Not much fretting about sunbathing causing skin cancer, throughout the period of this book: in 1976 Evelyn Armstrong and her grandmother were still having a 'who can get the brownest?' competition on their Butlin's holiday.

*

Before we go to Butlin's to see what other entertainments people got up to at seaside holiday camps, a brief word on the difference between Cornwall and East Anglia. Cornwall is cliffs, coves, surfboards, waves, high-up walks with the sun setting over the sea. Norfolk is creeks, mud, islands, boats, vast beaches, birds, skies, early-morning walks with the sun rising over the sea. The kind of seaside you went to as a child dictated your lifelong view of what the seaside meant. For the Cornwallers, there was a boundary between land and water. You were either in the sea or you weren't. For the Norfolkers, there was a blurred boundary: you wallowed in the mud of a creek, or pottered about in a boat and sailed to an island across from the creek at high tide. 'It was all about the island,' said Kevin Crossley-Holland, who longed to tear off to the creek as soon as he arrived at his grandparents' cottage after the interminable drive, 'but to begin with we had to observe the routine and the niceties – my grandfather saying to my mother, "Joan, have a gin and tonic."'

Norfolk was more social than Cornwall, as depicted by fourteen-year-old Bolla Denehy in her diary entry describing a typical Norfolk day, 6 August 1976:

> Cinda and I went down to the quay where we mucked around and then we went and had drinks with Giles Catchpole. We then came back and had lunch at the quay. After lunch Annabel Green and me sailed to the island and (slightly funny!) I sailed back from the island with Cinda and Giles Catchpole. Giles came home with me and we smoked on the way home. When we got back we made some supper for James, and then Laura Kennedy came. After our supper Cinda and I went to post our p.c.'s and to buy some fags and went on a spin round the village.

'You gravitate towards each other here,' said Harry Cory-Wright, of Norfolk, as we sat under a vast sky at Burnham Ovary Staithe.

Thorpeness, in Suffolk, was another social seaside place where people gravitated towards each other – and by 'people' I mean mainly the privately educated young, exalting in their seaside freedom. Life was centred around the country club, for which you could buy a week's or a fortnight's membership while you were there.

How to sum up Thorpeness? 'It was the complete freedom,' said the journalist Mary Ann Sieghart. ('Freedom' again: the overriding theme.) 'Everyone rented houses – we were there for three weeks of every summer – and our parents turfed us out after breakfast and we didn't have to come back till dark. Our parents were playing golf and sailing. I had two brothers and a sister, and we just hurtled round on our bikes all day. We'd go to the club after breakfast and see who was hanging around there, and that was our posse for the day. Aldeburgh's only a mile away, and we cycled there, no locks on our bikes. We rented funny 1930s clinker wooden boats from Albert the old boatman and took them out on the recreational lake. I remember deciding not to wear shoes for a whole summer, priding myself on how hard the soles of my feet could get. No one was supervising us: we were drinking Dubonnet and lemonade by the age of thirteen.'

Thorpeness freedom: Mary Ann Sieghart (second from right) with her sister and brothers Matilda, William and Alister, 1965. Photograph by Paul Sieghart

In the evening the country club laid on activities: general knowledge quizzes, bingo (known as 'housey-housey'), and a fancy-dress competition. 'It was bliss,' said Mary Ann – such bliss that one year, when she was thirteen and her parents decided not to go to Thorpeness that summer, she begged to be allowed to go on her own. 'My parents rented a room for me in the country club, and I tagged along with seventeen- and eighteen-year-olds for the whole week. One of them spotted a cheque book on the back seat of someone's car, stole it and took a whole group of friends out to an expensive lunch, with lobster. He was caught and went to jail.' It was all getting quite racy by then. Mary Ann did slow dances with boys at the club dances, 'and I recall the feeling of pebbles digging into my back as I groped with a boy on the beach'.

Similar things were happening in Bembridge on the Isle of Wight after the Bembridge Dinghy Club Ball. This seaside exist-ence, based around sporting clubs, with tennis tournaments, was like boarding school but without rules.

*

I wasn't sure whether to include Butlin's here, as, although the holiday camps were all at seaside towns – Minehead, Bognor Regis, Skegness, Clacton, Ayr, Pwllheli and Filey among others – the campers were expected to stay within the perimeter fence of the camp for the duration of their all-inclusive stay, and the camps were near but not opening onto the actual sea, so this was defi-nitely a 'swimming' holiday rather than a 'bathing' one: gigantic rectangular concrete chlorinated pools rather than seawater. But the seaside air, and the frivolous seaside mood, were so strongly present at Butlin's camps that I think they are allowed to be in this seaside chapter.

In the same way as I found it hard to gauge exactly who stayed in boarding houses, I also found it difficult to pinpoint the pre-cise social class of people who went to Butlin's as children. Either people said to me, 'No! We couldn't have afforded Butlin's.' Or

'Butlin's? No! We were a bit more upmarket than that.' So, who exactly were the 65,000 people a year who went to a typical Butlin's camp? They were by no means all working class. In 1937, at one Butlin's camp, an emergency call for a doctor was put out over the loudspeakers, and it was answered by twenty-three physicians. Paul Hansford told me his father was the managing director of a herring-canning operation that moved from Norfolk to Aberdeen, and they were occasional Butlin's-goers. Paul found the tropically themed restaurant with a fake stream and a bridge 'very exotic'.

'My dad was a postman till I was nine, and then worked for the Co-op insurance company,' said Evelyn Armstrong, born in 1955, who grew up in Saltcoats in Ayrshire, and spent most of her summers swimming in the Saltcoats lido and in the local harbour, unsupervised, 'my brother diving off the rocks', and 'the most glamorous boutique in Saltcoats was one called Chelsea Girl'. But once a year the family did the forty-minute drive to Butlin's in Ayr for the family holiday. 'It felt as if we were going on a real journey,' she said. 'Nearly everyone on my street went to Butlin's. The holiday was pure, unembarrassed, primary-coloured fun. 'The Redcoats took us off to play all day – there was an outdoor pool, an indoor pool, a games room, a boating lake, trampolines, and a fairground with a ghost train.'

Who cared that there was no running water in the chalets? What mattered to tired-out mothers was that the family had their own private chalet – the very word seemed exotic, Swiss, cosy and luxurious – and even a chalet maid to make the beds. And what's more, three large hot meals per day were served without your having to touch a saucepan.

Evelyn happened to marry a man, Peter Witchlow (now a social services worker) who had also been on Butlin's holidays as a child – his were at Minehead and Bognor. He showed me a photograph of himself as a young freckly faced boy smiling from ear to ear at the treat of sitting at a long table in a vast packed dining room, with his parents and grandparents, all about to tuck into platefuls of cooked tea: sausages, mashed potato, baked beans, and cups of steaming tea among the ketchup and HP sauce. 'First sitting for tea' was announced over the Tannoy. In fact, the Tannoy announced everything, from the cheerful 'Good morning, campers!' to, in the evenings, 'Baby crying in Chalet Number 50'. 'Once,' said Evelyn, 'that baby was ours. My brother's cot base had collapsed and he was on the floor, screaming his head off.'

Teatime at Butlin's, Clacton, 1963.
Peter Witchlow bottom-right, thrilled by it all

The removal of inhibitions, always brought on by seaside air, went further than ever inside the perimeter fence of Butlin's. Entertainments among strangers, which would have made the upper classes curl up and die with embarrassment, because they were mainly based on the human physique – glamorous granny competitions, bonny baby competitions ('I came second!' said Evelyn), knobbly knees competitions, and beauty pageants with young mothers lining up in swimsuits – were lapped up here. Sonia Malcolm, who'd arrived in England from Jamaica aged thirteen in 1965 and was brought up in Handsworth, Birmingham, was taken to Butlin's by a white family who lived in her street. 'Not a lot of West Indians at Butlin's,' she recalled, 'and sometimes I did feel odd and I was stared at'; but the children, social pollinators as ever, took no notice of her colour and everyone just jumped into the vast swimming pool.

Parents whisked each other round the ballroom in the evenings, 'and we were allowed to watch,' said Evelyn. Even the interior design was loaded with in-built entertainment, to justify the motto in huge lettering on the front of some of the camps: 'OUR TRUE INTENT IS ALL FOR YOUR DELIGHT'. 'The Beachcomber Bar,' said Peter, 'was trying to be tropical: there was a scene of palm trees and a volcano, and the volcano "erupted" every now and then and light rain would fall. We were fascinated by that.'

Somehow the most poignant thing Peter told me about his whole Butlin's experience was how excited he was on the last day, when 'Butlin's in Minehead gave us a packed lunch to take away with us when we left. I was so excited about that packed lunch. It had sandwiches and cakes . . . it felt like you'd been given this big present of food.'

How very different, I thought, from my children's reaction on being given a school packed lunch to take with them on a trip. One glimpse into the bag at the ham sandwich, the ready-salted crisps and the Granny Smith, and into the nearest litter bin it all goes. They might, just, keep the crisps.

*

Seaside accommodation was strictly socially stratified.

Caravans, for the slightly hard-up, were fine as long as your parents were happily married or at least happily single. If they were unhappy, as one person said to me, 'the holiday was just a worse version of being at home, with the added strain of all the parental rows happening cooped up in the pressure cooker of a caravan. I remember thinking, as we arrived at the stationary caravan at the far end of a field in Cornwall, Maybe this will be the year when it's going to be exciting or exotic.' It never was. 'Pressure cooker' was an apt metaphor, because caravans got as hot as saucepans in hot weather. When it rained they were chilly and the noise was deafening.

The concept of the caravan is always exciting for children, most of whom have a raggle-taggle-gypsy streak. The line 'What care I for a goose-feather bed?', with its impertinent emphasis on the first syllable, sang through the heads of all brought up on *The Oxford Song Book*; and most children relished the idea of sleeping on the edge of the land and having a little kitchen next to a cosy seating area where you could play cards after a supper of tinned chunky chicken followed by tinned fruit salad with fresh clotted cream. Pippa Allen was thrilled, in the late 1960s, 'when my dad had buggered off' and her siblings and mother were invited on a caravan holiday in Pembrokeshire by kind cousins. 'But the problem was that my mother, who now had no money, was beside herself with anger and misery', and being stuck in that caravan just summed up her dreadful comedown in social status. We children loved it. We loved piling out into a field every morning, and Uncle Bill and Auntie Joy were in a big tent next to us, and it was lovely. All my mother did was bemoan her lot. She shouted at us all the time and made us all go home early.'

As for the next step up – boarding houses – they always sound a bit disappointing. Again and again I was told, 'the boarding house we stayed in was not actually on the seafront. It was two or three streets back from the seafront.' This somehow seemed to sum up boarding houses. They were just shy of the sea – in Nelson Street, or Wellington Street, or Victoria Street, or Albert Street, without a sea view – and many of their landladies didn't seem actually to like the sea. The nearest boarding house to the sea I heard about was the one in Frinton where Nicholas Soames and his four siblings stayed with their nanny for three weeks every summer in the 1950s. That was 'within spitting distance of the sea, run by a widow whose husband had been an officer in the Indian Army'. I think by 'spitting distance' Sir Nicholas meant that you could actually see the sea from it. 'Our mother came down to visit us,' he added, so they weren't totally abandoned with the beloved nanny who was 'with the family for fifty years'.

Normally boarding houses were well beyond spitting distance of the sea. 'We stayed at Mrs Pollard's boarding house in Paignton, a few streets back from the sea,' said Juliet Gardiner. 'Mrs Pollard was not welcoming. It was a job for her, I suppose. There was no sign of Mr Pollard. He was probably in his shed. You had to pay extra for the cruets – the salt, pepper and mustard. Mrs Pollard made us sandwiches every day, wrapped in greaseproof paper, and we had to clear out after breakfast and not come back till the evening, but we weren't allowed to be late for supper. "Don't be late," Mrs Pollard said. "It's chicken for supper this evening." Chicken was a special treat.' 'The landlady at the boarding house where we stayed at Weston-super-Mare,' said Peggy Thomas, brought up in Small Heath in Birmingham in the 1930s, 'didn't start serving till everybody was there in the dining room, so if someone was late you all had to wait and the food got cold.'

So, a bit like school, with the rules. 'We had to be out all day even if it was raining,' said Enid Hales, who stayed in a boarding house in Scarborough in the 1940s.' 'We were sent out all day with corned-beef sandwiches made by the landlady,' said Peggy Thomas. 'If it was raining, all you could do was go to the cinema. They changed the films twice a week.' Butlin's camps were started precisely to rescue boarding-house waifs and strays from tramping the wet streets in search of something to do that didn't cost extra money. 'We weren't actually allowed to leave our boarding house in Blackpool after breakfast,' said Susan Brown, 'until we'd podded all the peas for supper. Then we had to go out all day.' Enforced pea-podding was a common theme. The most dispiriting boarding-house rule I heard was at one in Scarborough where Sue Sabbagh stayed in the 1950s. The rule was 'no sand to be brought into the bedrooms'. Every shoe and towel had to be nervously rechecked and reshaken on the pavement before entry. What was wrong with these landladies? If they showed a jot of kindness, it was hugely appreciated. 'Brunswick Lodge in Scarborough had illusions of grandeur,' said Susan Brown, 'but I called it a boarding house because you weren't allowed to stay in during the day. When we came back in the evening there was always a tray with a plate of Marie biscuits and glasses of orange juice on a doily in the dining room. I thought that was a lovely touch.'

Susan Brown (second from right) between her two sisters, lined up with fellow guests outside Brunswick Lodge, Scarborough, 1949

The next grade up from boarding houses were small seaside hotels of the crenellated variety. Whereas crenellated buckets were frowned on by parents, crenellated seaside hotels seemed to be popular with them. The crenellations added just the right amount of grandeur to announce 'this is not a boarding house', as well as 'you will be safe here'. 'It wouldn't have done at all for our family to go to a boarding house,' said gallery owner Jane Adams, brought up in the 1960s, whose father was a specialist in community medicine – she was the girl who couldn't bear her sister.

'My father would say that so-and-so was "common" because they stayed in boarding houses. We stayed in a second-rate three-star hotel in Scarborough – I think it later fell down – and to me it looked like a massive castle.' As with boarding houses, crenellated hotels had a daunting atmosphere of rule-enforcement about them. 'It was dark inside,' said Jane, 'and we had to creep around, not making a sound. For me, the terrible trouble was the food. I was an instinctive vegetarian. I had a deep sense that meat wasn't food – I couldn't actually bear to put it into my mouth. But my parents had no intention of allowing me to be a vegetarian. The hotel served us great hunks of greasy lamb with watery boiled vegetables in the dining room. I hid the meat in my hotel napkin if I could. "Best manners!" our mother kept saying to us. My sister and I had to be on our very best behaviour. We were on show in our matching frocks.'

Nor, in that emotionally repressive family, was there much chance of Jane developing any relationships with boys on these holidays. 'My parents would say, disapprovingly, of any boy I liked, "he's a bit common". I was very inhibited and shy.'

Peter Stanford's family also stayed for a fortnight each year at a crenellated seaside hotel, in Barmouth, called Min-y-Mor (Welsh for 'by the sea'), and it really was by the sea. (This was in the 1960s and early 1970s.) 'Castellated, panelled, smelled of cabbage, full-board' was how he summed up Min-y-Mor. 'Both my parents came from poor backgrounds and they were desperate to be middle class. Dad was a sales manager for Hovis. Going away on holiday was a sign of affluence, and we needed go to the right place. Rhyl would have been a bit naff, a bit kiss-me-quick, and so would Prestatyn. Those places were not for aspiring people. We drove across the mountains from the Wirral to Barmouth. We had to come back to the hotel every day for a warm lunch in the dining room. That was considered the lap of luxury. There was a huge entertainment room downstairs, with Welsh dancing one night, bingo the next, ballroom dancing the next, a quiz the next, and a bridge evening. Sometimes I played bridge with spinster ladies in the upstairs lounge.'

For the top notch of seaside-hotel grandeur, we need to go back to the 1930s and to the hotels described to me by Elizabeth Millman, whose father, a doctor in Northamptonshire, died when she was nine, at which moment all the expensive holidays ended. But for the first nine years of her life the family went to grand seaside hotels for a fortnight every year.

'Holidays were a very class sort of thing,' said Elizabeth. 'Where the middle classes didn't go was to Clacton, Ramsgate or Margate. We went by train to Torbay, Broadstairs, Bexhill, Scarborough and Ventnor. We sent our luggage off two days in advance – two trunks and an enormous hat box for my mother. A horse and dray met us at the station. The hotels we stayed in were magnificent.'

They were vast piles on the seafront, with rows and rows of windows and enormous lettering across their whole façades: THE TORBAY HOTEL, THE GRAND HOTEL (in Broadstairs), THE NORMANHURST (in Bexhill), THE ROYAL MARINE HOTEL (in Ventnor). It was the palm trees in the palm court at the Royal Marine Hotel in Ventnor that most impressed the young Elizabeth. 'It was very, very smart, in its own grounds, with ornate staircases and beautiful gardens. The rooms were airy and spacious. Our luggage was there waiting for us when we arrived. Arthur and I had our own room; our parents dressed for dinner in the dining room and we had ours brought up to us.'

That was a glimpse of pre-war elegance before post-war tawdriness set in. 'My mother did try to get to know the other families staying in the hotel', which Elizabeth found slightly grating. It was the done thing to make conversation with other people in the lounge. In her teenage diary, written four years later, when they stayed at a less grand hotel in Cornwall, Elizabeth wrote, 'Sat in lounge. In bad mood. Deaf people.'

Elizabeth Millman at the seaside, 1935

Then it was home again, for more weeks of muted summer days, the backdrop for the whole national scenario of the uneventful British summer. The really important thing for Peter Stanford's parents was, on arriving home, to announce to the world where they'd been. 'We always drove back home across the heather, and we stopped to pick a sprig of heather that we wound round the chromium bars of the radiator of my father's company car, a green Ford Zephyr. That sprig of heather announced, "We've been on holiday, and not just on the coastal road: we've driven back on the discerning, scenic route across the mountains."'

Peter Stanford and his father's company Ford Zephyr

19

Not Going Abroad (Fields)

Parents had a thing about views. They liked to stop the car and sit there, gazing at the view, perhaps with a car door open. They liked to take the long and winding route to a place of historic interest, if the drive included a view. Having looked round the historic place, they then said, 'Let's go back a different way.' They liked to take the family for obligatory extended walks with views. In some cases they liked to camp for a fortnight in a place with a view. 'Stopped to look at view of Cotswolds,' writes Elizabeth Millman in her diary, sounding not pleased. 'Tea in a field on way home.'

If the previous chapter was about the blue, grey and yellow of Great Britain, this chapter is about the green: the vast rolling interior, which to young eyes just looked like a mass of fields.

'We'd rent a cottage,' said Daniel Finkelstein of his 1960s and early 1970s summers, 'normally in different places, but three times we went to the same farm in lowland Scotland. A bit of walking, loads of ruined castles. I never hated anything my parents did but it was totally not what I wanted to do. My definition of a holiday is a hotel with a pool.' A hotel with a pool was a million miles from what his family, and other families like his, were doing: renting a cottage on a farm with no pool and just lots and lots of fields.

Daniel Finkelstein (right) with his brother Anthony and sister Tamara, in the car park at Lindisfarne, 1978, and at a rented holiday cottage in Cumbria

This was what the non-complaining generation had to put up with. There was no question of hating any of it out loud. 'The only time I got slapped by my father, who was a lovely, lovely man,' said Jilly Cooper, 'was in the middle of a walk in the Lake District, when I kept nagging him, "Why aren't we boating?" He slapped me on my thigh.' The correct thing to do, on walks, was to keep walking, and to engage in mind-widening conversation, and if possible to point out the names of the wild flowers. 'My mother taught me all the names of the wild flowers,' said Jilly, 'and it's been an abiding love. 'If you teach your children about wild flowers, they'll never be bored on a walk.'

Well, that's an optimistic slant. Walks – another clever wheeze for passing hours of family time without spending any money – could go on and on for field after field, and lane after lane, as Julie Welch recalls from one inland walk in Norfolk in the late 1950s. 'The trouble was, we'd met another family, the Munros, who were staying at the same hotel as us – well, really a jumped-up boarding house – and competitiveness had set in. The Munros had to cap everything, and so did my mother. The Munros' house had four bedrooms, but ours had five. The Munros' children seemed to be extremely stupid, and I was the child prodigy. We went on an enforced walk with them along the Norfolk lanes, and it was so competitive, I thought we'd go on walking for ever and ever. My mother refused to be the first one to throw in the towel. I became poleaxed with exhaustion.'

That glimpse echoes the experience of those young sisters frozen half to death on Scafell Pike, watching their aunt slicing towards her breasts into a giant loaf. Children were brought up on the theory 'you'll like it when you get there'. Once they did get there and still didn't like it, it was too late. '"I've found where we're going today," my father used to say, when we were staying on working farms that did full-board,' said Jenny Landreth, 'and it was usually a long, torturous walk.'

For easy-going children who longed for nothing more than family harmony, walks did at least make everyone have a conversation rather than fight. You could just pair up with the other family member who found you least annoying, and put one foot in front of the other until someone gave you permission to stop.

Among the vast section of middle-class Britain with more taste than money, and with the deep sense that going abroad was indeed a bit vulgar and unnecessary, there was a great deal of staying in musty cottages in the Lake District or the Yorkshire Dales: places that smelled of damp paperbacks and were surrounded by fields. The cottages were usually so draughty and the weather so April-like that you had to light a log fire every evening. Peaceful daughters with a deep love of all things domestic, such as the young Debora Robertson (now a writer on domestic subjects), loved going on that kind of holiday: 'going to look round country houses open to the public, and wandering around imagining I lived there,' she said. 'And reading my way through Elizabeth Goudge and Jean Plaidy.

It was on those holidays that I really learned to love reading.' 'A friend of ours lent us her cottage in Gayle in Wensleydale,' said Celia Burns, 'and we went there every summer. Simple stuff: Middleham Castle, picnics overlooking the dales, historic buildings, markets.'

Those were the kind of muted holiday activities that proved that 'a change is as good as a rest'. Mothers still had to carry on running households here: British drudgery continued, but at least there was a different view from the window behind the sink.

Celia Burns's parents outside the borrowed cottage in Wensleydale; and at Middleham Castle. Photos taken by Celia

The general drift I picked up, asking people about these British outdoorsy holidays, was that it was the fathers who drove the whole enterprise – just as it was fathers in those days who were the main deciders of where their children would go to school. Fathers did wear the trousers more than they do now, when mothers seem to have seized control of the diary, the networking and the holiday-destination initiative.

And fathers tended to pull in the direction of even simpler

holiday living: camping in tents. Not all fathers, by any means, but some, especially ones who'd been in the army, and if they did, they inflicted their heartiness on the rest of the family, except on the few resolute mothers brave enough to put their foot down, for example Ann Lindsay's mother: 'My father wanted us to have a great outdoor life and took us camping in Argyllshire. My mother stayed in a nearby B&B.' But most mothers went along with camping, gritting their teeth, doing anything to keep their man happy.

In camping situations, fathers delighted in reliving their old military ways and attempting to pass on the wisdom and outdoor-survival skills to the next generation. 'We slept in ex-army-surplus sleeping bags made of camel hair – they were very scratchy but my mother made us gingham sleeping-bag liners,' said Ann. (That was the least she could do, from her B&B vantage point.) 'My father taught us to put tents up, and there was a huge to-do if one of the wooden pegs had got lost. We had to tramp down on the heather, trying to find a patch to pitch the tent on, and then we laid down an ex-army groundsheet.' It was her father whose theory it was that if you set up your tent on a high hummock, the midges won't get you; and her father who insisted on simultaneously smoking his pipe and cooking kippers, to deter the midges at breakfast time.

It was thought good for children to be brought up with these drills, and character-forming for them to endure a 'freezing' (as Ann put it) night or two on the heather. Nowhere did the 'expectation of discomfort' – which we've seen quite a lot of in this book so far – come more true than in a tent in a field without a pillow.

It was more than a night or two for Anna Maxwell, brought up in Sidcup in the 1960s and early 1970s. Her family's annual camping holiday lasted a full fortnight, and took place in various wet fields in the south-west of England. Her father had indeed been a captain in the army and was now a schoolteacher. So military was the whole camping operation that preparations began a full week before departure day.

'Daddy started packing up the Bedford van seven days before we left,' said Anna. 'In went the tins of corned beef, the Fray Bentos tinned stew and the packets of Smash. Then, four days before departure, we started our daily tent practice. Every morning we had to muster on the lawn and practise the drill. My father would say, "On the count of four, lift!", or "On the count of four, hammer!"'

'What was your mother doing to prepare for the holiday?' I asked.

'She was in the kitchen, making pastry cases and sponge cakes to take us through the holiday fortnight.' On the holiday itself she would stew apples to put inside the pastry cases.

The journey was long and wistful for Anna, as she braced herself for the fortnight ahead: 'five people facing forward, but I reserved the seat at the back, facing backwards, so I could gaze out of the window and dream as the landscape receded.' Their father also seemed to believe in training his children in bladder-control, 'because if one of us said, "please can we stop – I need to go to the loo", it would be miles and miles before he'd stop. I ended up resenting it.'

Then they arrived, at a no-frills campsite booked by their father, 'and we always found that our tent was somehow out of fashion. In Dorset in 1967, we still had a green ridge tent – the classical triangle shape – you could only stand up in it if you were directly under the ridge. By then, people were starting to have orange and blue tents with extensions. We did eventually get one of those, but by then everyone else had gone over to muted greens and browns, with lamps you could hang inside.'

Compartment tents were indeed the new excitement of the late 1960s. Neil Herron's family referred to their smart new tent with three separate bedrooms as 'a Continental tent'.

*The Herrons' 'Continental' tent, 1976, with Neil's mother,
and his sister Rachel doing a headstand*

Anna's family instantly got to work gathering bracken to put under the groundsheet, 'to be our pillows'. There was no room for real pillows in the Bedford van. 'My mother did make us sheet bags to put inside the sleeping bags, but she didn't anticipate the tangle you could get into with those.'

'It rained every time' was how Anna summed up the weather. Never, ever was there a rain-free fortnight. 'One night, my mother became almost hysterical with the rain. It was coming into the tent like a fine mist. We'd pitched it on clay so the water didn't drain. Daddy went out and dug a channel beneath the tent. On another night the groundsheet started heaving under us. A tree was rocking and we were sleeping on top of its roots. We had to move our tent in the middle of the night.'

Never mind hotel or boarding house: for Anna, even a caravan seemed the height of unattainable, watertight luxury. 'We wished we had one. Cousins of ours did stay in the field of someone their friends knew, and they slept in a caravan with an awning and beds.'

As usual in this deep stratum of unflashy Britain, there was absolutely no question of going to a warm indoor restaurant or café for lunch or supper, or even tea. The family lived purely on the food they'd brought with them, with added fresh fruit. 'Just once in my whole childhood,' Anna said, 'we had a small car crash and were allowed to go to a café for cheese on toast. That was the only time we ever ate out.'

'So, just sandwiches for your picnics?' I asked.

'Not even sandwiches. Usually just bread sliced off a loaf, with hunks of cheese.'

'Romantic breakfasts in the dewy dawn?'

'Just cornflakes with milk bought from the camping-site shop, eaten out of our melamine bowls. Nothing as romantic as "fresh milk from the farm", or anything.'

The fourteen daytimes of those camping holidays were as hearty as the fourteen night-times, and again they were mainly father-driven. 'We did a lot of walking, following behind him. The walks seemed to go on for ever. He always brought along a box of reference books: *The Butterflies of Britain*, *The Birds of Britain*, *The Concise British Flora in Colour*. We visited cathedrals and steam museums. He wanted to instil us with knowledge.' Fresh air, exercise and knowledge about nature: those were the things considered truly priceless for children by the older generation, and they (like the free entertainments on a blank bit of seaside) were literally price-less.

*

So the utter daydreamy freedom of the home weeks changed, on these British inland holidays, to a more rigid and rule-bound daily timetable. It was a holiday in terms of going somewhere different, but not in terms of leisure. Much of the day was spent watching the back of the person walking a few feet ahead of you. 'We all had to make our own sandwich and carry it with us all day on the ten-mile walks,' said Katie Thomas, of the Lake District holidays of her 1970s childhood. 'We got to a point in the middle – a place with a stream – and the entertainment for the next three hours was damming the stream, everyone carrying great clods of earth. Then, having built it, we watched it slowly break.'

The whole thing was based on the belief that fresh air was good for you – healthy for the lungs and made you sleep well – a belief that underpinned the whole of British life. I married a man whose mother's simple rule for the school holidays was that all three of her sons must be out in the garden between coffee time and lunchtime, and again between lunch and teatime, whatever the weather. If it was raining they huddled in the garage but had to keep garage door open so it counted as fresh air. If they wanted to watch the Test match they had to watch it from the garden with the doors open. Watching it indoors with the doors open did not fulfil the full fresh-air requirements.

The daily drill for rented- or borrowed-cottage life was to go on an all-day walk every day, with a map carried by the chief map-reader and contour-understander. The truly, deeply loved cottages, such as Common Hill Cottage in Underskiddaw in the Lake District, where Katie Thomas stayed, and where her father and grandfather had stayed before her (it belonged to close family friends), contained a dog-eared walk-book in which people recorded the walks they'd done, with tips about where best to scale a dry stone wall or how not to get lost, and the notebook contained drawings: 'sketches of people sitting on rocks', as Richard Worsley (Katie's father) recalled of his family holidays there in the 1950s. 'I could flick back and look back at my own parents' entries from years ago.' Reading about other people's walks and adding your own was a comforting pastime in the evening with aching legs, before the games of racing demon began. Cottages needed to contain at least fifteen full packs of cards for this evening activity.

20

August Retreats

This is the *Country Life* chapter: the mouth-watering one about Augusts spent in the kinds of houses and shooting and fishing lodges miles from anywhere, with vast amounts of land attached, that you drool over while flicking through the first few pages of *Country Life*. 'An impressive sporting estate. About 900 acres. Inverness 42 miles.'

It was to places like these that certain families – they would call themselves 'old' families, rather than 'posh' or 'wealthy' – vanished off for the whole of August. Sometimes they went to an old family house that was closed up for ten and a half months of the year (as it was too expensive to run) and just came to life in late July and August, during which time the whole family, who lived in the south, suddenly came over all Scottish; sometimes they just 'took a shooting lodge' or 'took a fishing lodge', but it was the same lodge every year so it still felt as if they owned the place, and the same loyal old Scottish-accented ghillie (who did live there all year round) was always there to greet them.

Not that these houses were particularly grand inside: 'in need of extensive refurbishment', the small print might now say. The 'upper-class taste for the threadbare', as I heard it frequently described, was very much in evidence here: carpets, curtains and sofas thin and drained of colour, mattresses lumpy, the whole place smelling of damp oilskins and woodsmoke. It was normal, at the end of a hard day of shooting, stalking or fishing, to have to take turns with baths, often with the rule (as we've already seen) of boys being given priority, so by the time a girl got into the water (which was already peaty-brown when it came out of the tap), it was black and covered with a film of sweat, hairs and heather.

These retreats were so remote, so cut off from the urban, sub-urban, Home Counties or even averagely busy rural world of the Cotswolds or Yorkshire, that to spend a month in them made you emerge as an even more changed person at the end, having been forced both out into the limitless wilds and, while there, into the deepest recesses of your own mind.

Getting to these places was half the fun, especially if it involved a night sleeper. You have to admire Anna Dalrymple's mother, who sacrificed the train journey. (This was in the 1960s and 1970s.) 'My mother passed her HGV licence so she could drive an eighteen-horse lorry from Hampshire to Perthshire,' said Anna. 'She took seven ponies, two dogs, the bantams, and one of the au pairs, plus the luggage and all the fishing rods, guns and Wellington boots. My father went out to dinner at his London club and met me and my brothers at the station, with the other au pair. We stayed at my grandfather's Highland home in Perthshire for six weeks: a lovely house, with a cook, where the gravel drive was raked each morning.'

As so often, the luxurious shell of that existence contained a marked lack of luxury beneath the surface: 'we were sent out every morning with a floury bacon bap for our picnic, and if it was raining we found a hut to eat it in.' Also, lumps of peat tumbled out of the bath taps, along with the brown water. Once, in 1970, the two seventeen-year-old au pairs took a gaggle of children including Anna up a Highland hill called Farragon and they got lost in the fog and had to dig holes in the peat to spend the night in, and they were all skimpily dressed in summer clothes, and they heard explosions, and it was the mountain rescue team looking for them, and at dawn the fog cleared and down they came, and the *Daily Mail* headline was 'Children Lost on Mountain All Safe'.

'First sitting for dinner' – the announcement that so inspired young Peter Witchlow at Butlin's, except that at Butlin's it was called 'first sitting for tea' – similarly thrilled children on night sleepers, if they were on a train that left London in the early evening rather than at eleven. Night sleepers contained every element of the romance of travel: compartments; a dining car (even more thrilling a word than 'restaurant') with lamps on the white tablecloths; brushing your teeth in your nightie or pyjamas while passing through Doncaster; drifting off to sleep in a bunk bed, lulled by the rhythm. 'It was the most magical thing, when you consider that our normal big outing was going to Ricemans [the local department store] in Canterbury,' said Lizie de la Morinière, who travelled every summer from Kent to a shooting lodge in Morayshire that belonged to an uncle. 'Waking up early in the morning and seeing the heather out of the train window was unbelievably exciting.' Then it was back to the dining car for the thrill of individual miniature jars of marmalade and your own wrapped-up pat of butter.

You woke up in another world, on the same land mass but unimaginably different. Nowadays the first shocking realisation on arriving at such a place is that the wifi doesn't work. In those days you were spared that sickening lurch in quality of life.

Then you were just there, for weeks on end. 'Summers were golden,' said Nicholas Soames, whose family travelled from Kent to Loch Stack Lodge in Sutherland for a month every summer. 'My parents took the same lodge every summer for years. It was paradise on earth. The sisters and mothers weren't great fishermen, but the beaches were heavenly. We fished and sometimes we stalked. We were out of doors from nine in the morning till late at night – till we came home with a stag, on the stalking days.'

'What did you think about while you were fishing all day on the fishing days?' I asked – perhaps expecting him to say something like, 'I was meditating on my grandfather Winston and on my own future in British politics.'

'What the hell d'you think I thought about?' he barked back at me. 'I thought about fishing.'

Ah, yes – the gift for concentrating entirely on the matter in hand. The non-butterfly mind.

'Were you ever bored?' I asked, bracing myself for another blow.

'Bored? Never for a moment bored. Never been bored in Scotland in my life. I never went abroad till I was a soldier. I might have been envious of friends who went to Majorca and learned to water ski, but they didn't have as much fun as we did, and they didn't have a salmon on the end of a line.'

That present-in-the-moment mentality sums up the total immersion of the August retreat, especially for the men and boys caught up in the field sport with which they were obsessed. These places were cut-off worlds to vanish into, and it was just you and (sometimes) the ghillie, and the wind, the heather, the wildlife, the water, the fish, the game and the midges.

'You *had* to go out all day,' said Kate Grimond, who spent a month of every summer in the great expanses of Rannoch Moor in Argyllshire with the extended Fleming family. 'There was no choice. You had thousands of acres to yourself.' Picture a small girl on her own in corduroy trousers in the middle of nowhere. 'Then back to the house for a delicious tea of freshly baked scones with homemade blackcurrant jam and cakes.' Kate enjoyed roaming around in the vast area of low-lying rough ground and peat hags that was Rannoch Moor, but her sister Lucy preferred their annual Cornish surfing holidays with their mother Celia Johnson in much busier Polzeath. 'My mother loved surfing. She didn't come to Scotland.'

Among the ones who 'took a lodge' rather than staying at a family house, I noticed that they never, ever said 'we rented' a lodge. The smart word was 'took'. I suppose it was used because it didn't hint at anything as grubby as money being exchanged, although money must have been. I had a blast of the verb 'took' from Diana Holderness (b. 1927), telling me about the houses she spent her summers in as a child. 'Almost everyone took a house,' she said. 'My parents took a house for a month. Some people would take a castle for twenty years. My parents lived in Leicestershire from September to Christmas, then they always took a house in London, then they took another house for Ascot, and then they took a house in the Isle of Wight for the summer. People in those days even took a house to have a baby. They wouldn't want to have a baby in their own house.'

*

In our minds, running alongside this portrait of months spent in the middle of nowhere, we should keep a vision of French family Augusts in '*la France profonde*': clans of cousins vanishing from Paris to stay in family country houses, where lunch for twenty-four on the terrace appears as if by magic, and the lid is kept firmly shut on seething family feuds by a fierce Catholic presiding grandmother, and the greengage tart is made from the overripe fruit dripping from the trees in the orchard: a world unforgettably captured by Rumer Godden in her novel of 1958, *The Greengage Summer*. I stumbled onto one of these French families one August recently, and came upon a laid tableful of plastic toy bowls of stagnating 'nature soup' in a far corner of the garden, made by a gang of French cousins for their dolls, out of nettles, berries, twigs and water, and the glassy-eyed dolls were all just sitting there at their *places à table*. I'd chanced upon the whole daydreaming world of the imagination going on among French *cousinage* in the middle of nowhere.

Britain, as these glimpses show us, has its own '*Grand Bretagne profonde*' into which families vanish, and the most *profonde* part is those wilds of Scotland, where it's possible to be far out of reach of the nearest shop or even human being, as Jo Ropner (now Lord-Lieutenant of North Yorkshire) described to me. To get to her family's shooting lodge on the Pait and Monar estate in Inverness-shire, which they went to every summer of her 1960s and 1970s childhood, 'you drove north-west from Inverness for an hour, through Beauly and Struy, and then you went through a padlocked gate into Glen Stathfarrar, then twelve more miles along a single-track road till you reached the east end of Loch Monar. Then you left the car and did the final ten miles to the other end of the loch in a boat, a big diesel Noah's Ark called the *Cleopatra*. Then we piled the luggage and supplies into an old Land Rover and the children had to walk the final mile to the lodge, whatever the weather.'

Having done all that, the family arrived, bursting with excitement, at a beloved house with no electricity, no telephone and no deep freezer. The venison and grouse were kept in a freezer at the nearest electricity point ten miles away at the other end of the loch. 'Hello, Monar, can you hear me? Over,' her mother said on the radio telephone each morning ('a sort of wall-mounted walkie-talkie', as Jo described it). 'Please can you take that leg of venison and a loaf of bread out of the freezer and send it up today? Thank you. Over and out.' Even a loaf of bread in a freezer seemed cosmopolitan, from the vantage point of this candlelit and gas-lit existence.

No sickening lurch on arrival here; quite the opposite. Having unloaded the Land Rover, everyone ran straight out into the wilds and picked up the sporting habit where they'd left it off last time. 'The first thing I did on arriving,' Jo said, 'was to turn up some stones, find some worms, find my rod and go down to the burn to catch trout.' Off she would go, in her kilt, taking one of the dogs, 'and I slotted the fish onto a rope tied round my waist, and I came back with a row of fish dangling from the rope, and I gutted them all on the bridge and put them in the smoker.'

Jo Ropner (right) with her sister (far left), sister's friend and brother, at Pait, Inverness-shire after a successful 1970s morning's fishing (yes, this is summer)

If you think children were free to roam on the edge of villages in Essex and Surrey, here the freedom was tenfold. Children became mere dots in a vast unpopulated heathery landscape. More than ever, parents had to trust their children to come home when they were hungry. 'When I was five,' said Jo, 'my mother found me all alone on a rock overhanging a huge burn in spate, dangling my rod, worm on hook.'

Even back at the house, they were truly cut off. If a child was ill there was no way they could get to a doctor in a hurry, especially if, as sometimes happened, the loch was too choppy for the boat to run. The medicine cupboard had to act as the local surgery: 'it contained Zam-Buk, a kind of green Vaseline that my mother put on everything – cuts, bruises, every kind of injury. She said she could have taken our appendix out if she'd needed to. I stuck a pitchfork through my foot and had septicaemia, and we couldn't get to a doctor. Helen the nanny put stitches into it. She put stitches into various children. She was known as 'the sergeant major. She was as hard as nails, from Aberdeen.' Even in the middle of nowhere the children still had to have extremely good table manners.

Children don't like things to change and they would have been horrified at any refurbishment or decluttering. Pait Lodge was full of lovingly hoarded items: Victorian biscuit tins labelled 'buttons', 'nearly new batteries', 'zips' and old board games and card games like Happy Families. There was always a jigsaw puzzle on the go, and 'a single game of Monopoly could go on for days,' said Jo, 'evening after evening'. A typical supper was 'once round the fridge': in other words, leftovers. (The fridge was a camping fridge that ran on gas.)

There needed to be a zestful and willing adult to drive this existence: to make sure food appeared on the table and that magical things happened, and Jo's mother was one such. She organised 'bonfire picnics' across the loch: everyone piling into a boat and sailing across, fishing for lunch on the way, frying the fish once they got to the other side, and lighting a bonfire to keep the 'walls of midges' at bay. She organised grouse-plucking operations, 'all of us standing on a bridge over the burn and plucking grouse into the wind'. 'My mother was seriously frugal,' said Jo, 'a Northern Irish war baby' – hence those tins of nearly new batteries. 'Our treat was a backlog of old comics.' The currency of non-materialism made it all the more special when one of the children was ill. 'There was a "get-better box". You could look at it if you were ill for one day, and you could keep one of the items if you were ill for more than one day. You almost wanted to be ill for more than a day so you could keep one of the items.'

'What kinds of things were inside?'

'Things like football cards and free gifts from cereal packets.'

*

These August retreats were quite fish-based. 'I remember endless days sitting round the kitchen table doing the crabs,' said Mary Miers, telling me about her 1970s childhood summers on South Uist in a great gathering of cousins and friends, twenty or thirty for each meal. Her family travelled from army postings around the world to spend holidays in their house on the shore of Loch Boisdale – a former merchant's house and shop at the centre of a Gaelic-speaking crofting community, with its own pier but no mains electricity. They stocked up the Volkswagen dormobile for the long journey north, bringing catering-size Nescafé jars of homemade marmalade and sacks of flour. The familiar smell of diesel and feeling slightly sick on the Caledonian MacBrayne ferry, the screaming seagulls and the sound of Gaelic being spoken all meant they were nearly there.

Morning kitchen scene: 'White meat in one bowl, brown meat in another, always taking care to extract the pale sliver of flesh from the black-tipped main pincer – a particular delicacy. We chatted away as we worked with our nutcrackers, hammers and needles.' The choice for meals was: baked crab, cold crab with mayonnaise, crab lasagne, fish pie, baked mackerel, smoked mackerel pâté or kedgeree. 'Neighbours gave us potatoes grown on the machair – slightly salty, fertilised with seaweed: the best ever.'

As so often in these family situations, it was the mother who worked hardest to kept it all afloat. Faced with the urgent need to feed thirty hungry people three times a day on a limited budget, Mary's mother rose at 5 a.m. to bake ten loaves of bread that would see everyone through breakfast and lunch for the day. Breakfast included porridge and fried trout. So fishy was the existence that the boys, who slept in dormitory formation on camp beds in the pier house, had fish boxes as bedside tables.

It might seem like drudgery to be 'doing the crabs' all morning, but Mary tended to choose it over the more hearty pastime of going out on the boat to check the lobster pots and put out the lines. 'You'd be cold if you stayed on deck, seasick if you took shelter in the cabin, and ordered about a lot: endless pulling on ropes, fending off, hooking buoys and hauling up creels.'

Most days there would be an expedition to a remote sea loch or beach, involving the boat and careful planning according to tides. There'd be fishing, cockling, shrimping and collecting mussels, as well as swimming and fire-making. Picnics consisted of bread with mackerel pâté or hunks of cheddar and chutney, followed by a slice of ginger cake and an apple. 'For some families,' said Mary, it was Tunnock's Teacakes, but, for us, Penguin and Club biscuits were the currency of our childhood; our parents distributed them like gold coins and found them useful for bribes.'

Much of the holiday was spent in gumboots, but the children went bare-legged when the weather was good. 'By the end of the summer,' said Mary, 'I had a healthy wind-tan and could walk along the gravelly road in bare feet without wincing.'

Always in remote Scottish places like these, there was endless free time induced by days of rain. Hours were spent playing the piano, reading, pressing wild flowers and sticking shells onto old matchboxes.

*

One more 'take me there right now' August retreat, before we turn our attention to organised fun – courses and camps – for the final chapter of this section on domestic departures. This retreat, in Northern Ireland in the 1930s, felt to the young Marianne More Gordon as much as if she was going back in time as going far away in place.

She was staying with her grandparents in a wonderful old house, and summers there contained (as I mentioned in the Grandparents chapter) the extra layer of reassurance and stability that staying with grandparents brought to so many children: the fact that it was not just them, but their mother, too, who was feeling protected in the cocoon where she herself had been brought up and where her own parents were still in charge. 'Having tea in the very same nursery where our mother had had her tea as a child gave us an astonishing connection to the past.'

But what impressed Marianne most was the oldness of everything in Northern Ireland: the remoteness in time. 'In England, ribbon development was going on, so you were having to look forward to new ways. Society was looking forwards. In Ireland I felt they were holding on to the past. I remember the absolute joy of arriving off the boat in Belfast – the noise of horses pulling drays with iron-rimmed wheels along the cobbles, the smell of ropes and sacking, the different words, and different accents. I lapped up the countryside: the small fields, the white thatched cottages, the intensity of the green.'

The grandmother who greeted them fitted nicely into this colour palette. 'She was tall and slim, with silver hair, and she dressed in mauves, purples and greys.' Marianne found deep comfort in her grandmother's favoured piece of advice for life: 'Be good, sweet maid, and let who *will* be clever.' There was a display of armaments on the wall of the outer hall in symmetrically circular patterns, and stuffed birds behind glass, and in the inner hall a dividing staircase. 'The sound of my grandmother clearing her throat echoed round the hall. The huge dining-room table had been polished for three generations by the same much-loved butler. I dug my fingers into its accumulated layers of beeswax.' Even that beeswax, laid down in layers, represented continuity, and therefore security.

Jimmy Meechan who lived on the estate arrived every morning with a yoke and two buckets of spring water which he poured into filters at the back of the house courtyard. That was the drinking water; the bathwater was peaty-brown, 'lovely and soft,' said Marianne. 'We rejoiced in anything that was particular to the place.' The lift-up key to the walled garden was kept in a drawer in the table in the inner hall. Nothing changed. The smell of apples in the apple storeroom was 'wonderful'.

How, *how* were people going to extract themselves from these retreats and re-enter the contemporary world's frenetic atmosphere, when September came?

Marianne and her brother Marcus with their grandmother Eileen McCausland, outside her house, Drenagh, in Northern Ireland, 1936

21

Courses and Camps

There sometimes came a moment, in the vast ocean of unscheduled time, when you found yourself experiencing a short burst of scheduled time. This was when you went away on a week-long course or camp, in order to get better at a hobby you liked or to have your character built or soul moulded in a team situation. This short, sharp, scheduled shock was a mere drop in the said ocean compared with the daily 'colouring in' of children's free time that diary-filling parents do these days, with the non-stop tennis camps, cricket camps, choral courses and sailing courses, but it was a foretaste of that.

Rather as the day-long holiday was a microcosm of the whole holiday experience, the course or camp was a week-long microcosm of the whole institutional experience. The full arc was there, from start to finish: packing and ticking off items on the clothes list; butterflies on the journey; the stomach lurch on arrival, at the sight of other people you didn't know arriving at the same time; registration at a trestle table by a man in shorts; the first sight of your dorm or tent and finding the best bed or sleeping patch already bagged by someone else; the pang of loneliness; the communal gathering on the first evening when you thought, 'perhaps this won't be quite so bad after all'; the militaristic fire drill; the first fit of helpless giggles after the first lights out; the gradual realisation over the next three days that this might in fact be the best week of your life to date; getting so caught up in the scheduled tasks and occupations that by Wednesday you couldn't remember any other kind of life; the accumulation of in-jokes and specialised vocabulary; the shock on Friday when you realised the end was approaching; the culmination of all you'd learned and achieved with a final-day competition, service or performance; the staying up all night on the final night, someone buying cider and someone else setting fire to something; the goodbyes and see-you-next-years; the total exhaustion on arrival home.

These camps and courses, coming as they did in the middle of a seemingly infinite spell of daydreaming, were shocking in their seven-day intensity (or sometimes fourteen-day: some of the Christian camps lasted ten days or a fortnight). The instant friendships, self-improvement and character formation were distilled. The camps often happened towards the end of August, so there was a slight nip in the air, and the first blackberries were ripening, vital sour thirst-quenchers on the organised scavenger hunts. The camps inspired profound loyalty: it was normal to go back to the same one every summer for eight to twelve consecutive years, and then to become a member of staff on them.

Of all areas in which you might have expected the social classes to be integrated and rubbing along happily together, Christian summer camps would surely be at the top of your list, inspired as they were by the archetypal non-snob, Jesus. But it was not so. In fact, the world of Christian summer camps was divided up into social strata just as seaside accommodation was, if not more so.

At the top of the tree were the VPS camps – the Varsity and Public School ones, run by E. J. H. Nash, known by the nickname 'Bash'. A grammar-school boy himself, born in 1898, he was having tea in D. H. Evans in Oxford Street one day as a young adult, when he 'fully acknowledged Christ as his master and his Lord', as his Wikipedia entry puts it. That was a proper

Evangelical-style Damascene conversion: an overwhelming sensation, coming upon a person suddenly and in a mundane venue. Bash's vision from that moment on was to evangelise the males at the top of society and thereby Christianise the government of the nation. His prayer was 'Lord, we claim the leading public schools for your kingdom'.

For over three decades from 1932 he ran his Evangelical boys-only summer camps held at Claysmore School at Iwerne Minster in Dorset – a place whose reputation was blackened recently by revelations that a later chairman of the Iwerne Trust after Bash's time, John Smyth, befriended boys at the camp in the 1970s and 1980s and then caned them in his garden shed at home.

In accordance with the Evangelical belief in male headship, the only women present at Iwerne were 'the lady-helpers', i.e. the kitchen staff doing the cooking and washing-up. A parallel camp for girls from top girls' schools did later open up in the Lake District.

Seven thousand boys from Britain's top public schools passed through the Iwerne camps during Bash's time. Attendance was by invitation only. The staff were known by military nicknames: Commy, Adj., Docko for the doctor and 'Q' for the quartermaster. Bash was clearly a genius when it came to evangelising young teenagers, drowsy, receptive and spiritually malleable during the 'heavy' session in the evening after a day of hearty outdoor activity. He liked his acronyms: ABC stood for 'Admit your need of Christ; Believe that Christ died for you; Come to him.' He also liked his Tube analogy: 'the only way to Mansion House is via King's Cross' – strangely memorable, even if not strictly accurate in the Tube sense.

'We never played normal sports,' one man who was there in the 1960s told me. 'There were specialised camp games, such as "Ragger" – throwing a tennis ball through a hoop – and "Crocker" – baseball-cum-rounders – and "Tenni-hock-la" – a combination of tennis, hockey and lacrosse, played with old tennis racquets and hockey goals.' These games bonded everyone with a sense of being part of an exclusive club.

From that top tier there was a gradual descent, through the non-top-public-school camps, to the grammar-school ones (the Crusader camps), to the state-school ones, such as the Devon Christian Youth Camps held from 1946 in fields rented out by Christian farmers. These camps only cost fifteen shillings per camper, giving children from working-class homes a chance to have a week away during the summer. The staff gathered a few days before camp started and prayed individually for each child who was coming. They dug latrines to the required measurements of 8 feet by 2 feet 6, and placed a gospel hall bench across, with round holes cut into it.

'As I child I didn't realise how class-ridden Evangelism was,' said the Revd Andrew Davey, a vicar in south London, who went on the camps every summer – his parents helped to run them from 1948 to 1974. Nor did it seem at all odd to him that a clothes list should say 'sleeping-bag, Bible'. It was all just part of the life of a young boy growing up in the Evangelical tradition. Every morning began with breakfast and Bible study, before the 100 boys from the ten tents were sent out in all weathers to play volleyball or rounders, followed by a trip to the beach. 'The canoeing lessons were supervised by grown-ups who'd never done a canoeing course, but they had all done National Service so they knew how to do a tourniquet.'

Every evening there were talks to the sleepy boys given by a padre who adapted the RAF emblem as his favoured acronym: 'Redeemed, Active, Fighters'. Then, young people came forward for the evening conversions, which the staff had prayed for, because the main point was to get as many conversions as possible during the ten days. 'It was a sort of head-hunting,' said Andrew. 'The idea was that the younger boys would be inspired by seeing the older ones taking Christianity seriously.' Converts then spoke about their conversions at testimony meetings, known as 'say-so' meetings, from the quote from Psalm 107: 'let the redeemed of the Lord say so'.

A girls' camp was started in 1947, at a nearby school rather than in tents, and sometimes the staff ran out of things for the girls to do in the day time, so they just sent them off to look for as many breeds of dog as they could find and write them down.

It was all very hearty. Pony Club camp was similarly hearty, as Lucinda Sims recalled from her 1960s and 1970s days, first with the Royal Artillery Pony Club in Hampshire and then with the Cattistock Pony Club in Dorset when she moved there: two of the 345 branches in Britain.

The junior club was non-residential, but the fortnight-long senior club, from the age of eleven, was residential, in tents, boys and girls at the same camp on a field at the Bath & West Showground. 'It was wild,' said Lucinda. 'There was a late-night round to hoof the boys out of the girls' tents, after massive water fights with the hose. Boys were dunking each other in the water trough and throwing them into the muck heap. They were letting down the guy ropes in the middle of the night.' It was a wilder version of end-of-summer-term madness.

It was not only children but ponies, too, who were loyal to these camps: 'a good pony,' Lucinda said, 'will go on for twenty-five years doing the junior camp: they'll do all the children of one family and then all the children of another'.

The wildness was reined in with borstal-style strictness when it came to how you were turned out. 'You were assessed every morning on your turn-out, your pony's turn-out, the tidiness of your tent, and the tidiness of your stable. Marks out of ten for each one, and if you hadn't done your pony properly you were made to do it again there and then. I got pocket money from boys for plaiting their ponies' manes for them – we all did that for the boys.'

Lucinda Sims (hatless) and her friend, on Lucinda's pony
in pre-health-and-safety days, 1968

Again, the specialised language made everyone feel part of an enclosed society. 'You were put in rides according to your ability,' said Lucinda: 'Foxhound, Deerhound, Staghound, Otterhound, Harrier and Beagle, in descending order. When I came out of Beagles I felt I'd arrived: I'd finally made it to Harriers. Every morning you did a ride with your group, and we all had to do drilled bareback rides: jumping with no reins or stirrups, sometimes with your hands on your head or out sideways. That taught us balance and horsemanship. That's all gone from the training, and British riding standards have been diminishing – in fact, all the old-fashioned training has vanished entirely due to health and safety and fear of litigation.'

There was not a moment for self-pity. The instilling of the rule that you must 'get straight back onto your horse when you fall off' began here, and became a metaphor for what action to take immediately after adulthood's failures and falls. 'I was winded when my horse fell on me,' said Miranda Johnston, recalling her North Cotswold Pony Club camps of the 1970s. 'They were run by good worthy women in huge breeches. One of them just barked at me to "get up, get back on your horse and stop crying".'

The week was always rounded off with a gruelling end-of-camp competition watched by the parents who had arrived to watch their insta-matured children's new accomplishments. The competition consisted of gymkhana events, such as (according to Lucinda Sims) 'canter to the finishing line, leap off your pony, dunk your head in a bucket, bite into an apple in the bucket, hold it in your mouth, leap back on, and canter back to the starting line'. There was also an egg-and-spoon race on horseback; if you dropped the (hard-boiled) egg you had to leap off, pick it up and leap on again. 'The whole thing was very competitive.'

Boy Scout and Girl Guide camps provided further possibilities for camping on grass for a week, as if more were needed. 'I was a member of the 7th Hendon,' said Daniel Finkelstein, referring to his Scout group in the 1970s. It didn't sound to me like seventh heaven, but in fact Daniel said, 'I really grew up through those camps and they were an annual highlight. We rented a field and went on camp for ten days. It was in the middle of nowhere, as far as I was concerned. We learned how to cook and make fires. We were given a small amount of money and you had to buy and make a meal for your team. Then we were dropped off somewhere even more remote and had to find our way back to the field.' That sums up the Scout-camp experience. It was another big dose of 'not going abroad (fields)'. 'For me, Scout camps were the real deal,' said Alan Brown, who belonged to the 22nd Bradford East group in the late 1940s. 'It was getting out into the country, up Wharfedale to Appletreewick, being out with your mates in the open air. Our Scoutmaster was great. He had two tin legs and went about in a cart – the mobility scooter of the time.'

It sounded quite military, with a strict four-day cycle of duties.

'You were on cooking, or fatigues [washing up the utensils and porridge pan], or wood-collecting, or day off. I liked day off best.'

This was all lovely if it was sunny, which it always was, according to Alan; but a rainy Scout camp, or any kind of camp, could be hard. During the wash-out summer of 1966, a tent officer at the Devon Christian Youth Camp was found crying in a tent in a state of midweek despair. 'We got washed out at our Scout camp at Ravenstonedale in the Pennines in 1962 when I was twelve,' said Simon Shimmin. 'Two boys were bullying me mercilessly. The field was flooded. I went to the Scoutmaster and begged to go home. He let me go, and I arrived home wet and cold – and the next day I was at the Southport Flower Show.' The sense of escape was exhilarating. Scout camps in Scotland were particularly bracing, the boys wearing kilts for the whole week.

Charles Fraser ready to go off to scout camp in Lanarkshire, 1941

Camps and courses conformed to parents' visions of how they wanted their offspring to turn out. At the opposite end of the social spectrum, and of the rural/urban spectrum, from the Devon Christian Youth Camp, upper-class girls were being sent on fortnight-long Lucie Clayton modelling courses in South Kensington. 'It was another ploy to get rid of the three of us when we were in London,' said Henrietta Moyle, one of the Bateman triplets, whose mother had tried to keep them busy in Kent with the strawberry-picking job in the 1970s and was now trying to keep them busy in London. Far from learning to light fires and orienteer, these girls were being taught the essential social skills of how to get in and out of a car in the most elegant way possible, and how to apply make-up in layers. 'Inside a room in the house in the Cromwell Road,' said Henrietta, 'they'd installed two different sample car doors, each opening onto a car seat – one was a sports car and the other a more normal car, so not quite so low down. We had to practise getting in and out each one, lifting both our legs together and swivelling round.'

The London townhouse echoed to the sound of 'sit up!' 'Stand up straight!' 'Shoulders back!' These instructions came as a shock to the girls, who'd been perfectly happy in their Kentish country life, walking across the fields to the weir with the dog.

'Then in the afternoon, we had make-up practice. We had to cake ourselves with the stuff. There had to be a colour-contrast: blue eyeshadow with yellow on top, and lots of foundation and mascara. I remember thinking, Why on earth are we doing this? We were country bumpkins. We came out at the end of the day looking like clowns, and we walked home, feeling nervous of the punk rockers we passed on the way – they looked terrifying. But they weren't aggressive.'

*

For many, inland travels, like the ones we've seen in this section had to suffice through whole childhoods. British sea air and British field dew were considered adventure enough.

But in spite of the parental advice that 'going abroad is vulgar', some did long to touch foreign soil, attracted by rumours that the weather was more reliable there. We'll now turn to the lucky few who did go abroad.

PART V

INTERNATIONAL DEPARTURES

22

Journeys Abroad

Before we get into any dormobiles for our first longed-for foray into the land where they count in kilometres, we must return briefly to the boarding-school children of expatriates, whom we last glimpsed being ferried to and from Heathrow Airport by their UK-domiciled grandparents, or sometimes by a school matron let out on ferrying duty. What happened after those punctual chaperones had said goodbye to their charges?

Those children, about to fly home to their parents for the summer holidays, were beside themselves with excitement, as well as basking in a brief sensation of kudos. Their change in status was dramatic. After a school year of being the non-special ones, the objects of pity, who never went home at weekends or half-terms, and who received fewer letters and parcels than anyone else, they were suddenly the ultra-special ones: allowed to leave early to catch an aeroplane, and about be given – as a present – some of the thrilling paraphernalia of air travel, such as a miniature toothbrush-and-toothpaste pack.

They didn't look all that glamorous, corralled with a crowd of other children of expatriates in roped-off areas of airports, all dressed in their school uniforms. Drably dressed, starving hungry, penniless, and sometimes actually wearing labels, they looked more like displaced persons after the liberation of a prison camp.

As for the stardust of leaving school a day early, it didn't always happen like that, as Steph Worsley told me, recalling her journeys home from North Foreland Lodge to Nyasaland in the 1950s and early 1960s (her father was a Chief Secretary in the Colonial Service). 'Sometimes I had to leave a day later than everyone else, because the plane happened to be leaving a day after the end of term. I slept on my own in the dormitory after everyone else had gone home. I'd looked at all my friends' photographs of their huge English country houses – and I knew I was going home to a house with a tin roof. But I was terribly excited: I'd been counting down the days.' The great thing about her tin roof was that it was in such a hot climate that you could bake meringues on it.

Dizzy with a sense of release, even with the school matron still in tow, Steph was deposited at Heathrow and left with a group of other unaccompanied minors: 'the Africa crowd, from lots of different schools – some were only going as far as Nairobi.' The journey in the BOAC plane was a bit like a bus journey, with frequent stops to refuel and let passengers on and off. Aeroplane rules were not strict: the children were allowed to lie on the floor to go to sleep on the journey.

I noted that the main thing people remembered was what they were given to eat at the various airports. 'First we landed at Rome,' said Steph, 'and we were marched off for disgusting scrambled egg or a watery omelette. Then we stopped at Khartoum, where we were given lukewarm orange juice. Then we stopped at Nairobi, and then at Salisbury, where our little lot would spend the night in a hotel, supervised by an adult – perhaps a friend of someone's parents. The next day we took a tiny plane to Blantyre in Nyasaland, and by then I was really excited. I could actually see my parents waiting for me, tiny dots on the tarmac as we came in to land. Then we drove for fifty more miles along a road made of two strips of tarmac, to get to Zomba, where we lived in a house on the side of a mountain. There were no passing places on the road, so there were stipulated twenty-minute time slots for going up and down the mountain.'

As for what happened when they arrived, we'll come to the details in the next chapter on 'being abroad'. Steph had landed in the middle of her parents' increasingly miserable marriage.

'A kind of pen with a rope round it,' was how Angela Holdsworth described the unaccompanied minors' area at Heathrow where she was plonked, having been delivered there by her Camberley grandmother. 'If you had flown a thousand miles, you got a badge: your Junior Jet Club Wings. I did.' The children were also given logbooks in which to keep an archive of their flights. This was a thrill for the stationery-lovers, of which there were many. The fizzy drinks were exciting, if disappointingly warm: 'no refrigerator, or ice. You could buy a Coca-Cola in a hut at Nice and Malta airports – we got off every time the plane stopped.' Angela was an army officer's daughter, on her way to Tripoli, where there was 'quite a lot of fairly innocent wife-swapping. I saw my father snogging from time to time. I think they all felt quite liberated there.' The racy life in Tripoli was a profound change from life in her strait-laced boarding prep school at Stoke Poges, run by Miss Broome and Miss Bibby.

There was a sense of dazzlement at the sudden change from glamour-free boarding-school life to the world of foreign travel. That, combined with the prospect of seeing parents you hadn't seen for months, made the whole thing feel almost unreal. 'My father was Chief R E [Royal Engineer] in Trieste after the war,' said Joanna Barker (b. 1937), 'and there was an army scheme for children to go all over Europe for the summer holidays. We were assembled at Liverpool Street station and labelled with our destinations.' (This was at the beginning of summer 1948.) 'We took a train to Harwich, where we were put on an overnight troop ship to the Hook of Holland, sleeping in dormitories with three tiers of bunk beds. Then, after a marvellous breakfast of bacon and eggs in the transit camp, we were put onto the Medloc train – the Mediterranean Line of Communication. We were put in first-class wagon-lits with leather bunks and a washroom, and a chair in an alcove with a table and lamp. I shared with my brother. The troops just had hard seats. The train pulled into Cologne – and there was not a single bit of glass left in the station. The only things standing in that bombed-out city were the two towers of the cathedral. That train journey took twenty-four hours, and the train stopped for the troops to have ablution halts in the Alps. On the afternoon of the second day we reached Villach in Austria, and were taken to the gloomy Post Hotel for the night. The next morning we were put on buses and drove via Treviso to Trieste.'

The journey took four days. 'We arrived at our wonderful flat in Trieste, and the British Army had its own beach where we were able to go and swim and spend the whole day. But we lived on evaporated milk. The agriculture of Europe had been totally disrupted.'

*

Having parked those children on foreign soil with their semi-estranged parents, we can now turn our attention to the few adventurous British families of the 1960s and early 1970s, who, after weeks of mooching about in each other's company in the garden to the sound of the lawnmower, were preparing to go abroad for a family holiday, with their GB sticker on the boot.

As with so many activities in those days, these intrepid holidays were usually father-conceived and father-led. There were various motives for choosing abroad as a destination: for example, an irresistible attraction to a brochure photograph of an azure pool under an azure sky, or an urge to drive very fast, or trying to keep up with the neighbours, or knowing someone who owned a castle abroad. A sizeable proportion of early adopters of foreign holidays, though, were visionary but meagrely paid pillars of society such as schoolteachers or clergymen: well-read, with a deep knowledge of French Gothic architecture, and with good grammatical French, but not much money – and even if they had had money, there were still foreign currency restrictions till the mid-1970s. So these ones camped.

Their children tended to be unadventurous eaters, accustomed to predictable English food, so the easiest, as well as cheapest, course of action was to bring enough tins for the whole holiday. This meant packing a tin of baked beans for every single day they would be abroad: 'twenty-one tins of baked beans for our three-week holiday,' said Eleanor Oldroyd, vicar's daughter and eldest of three children, who travelled from the vicarage at Cleobury Mortimer to France every summer of the 1970s with her family.

'We did try the vicarage-swapping holidays in England,' Eleanor said, 'but they were a disaster: you were just landed with all the other vicar's problems. And then the three of us all got chickenpox by Lake Windermere.'

So, from the summer of 1972, they started going to France instead. 'My mother fitted the baked-bean tins around the wheel arch in the boot, along with the tinned mince and tinned Campbell's soup.'

That first summer they went to France with another clergy family, so there were six children, aged eight, seven, six, five, four and three – but it was stressful, because they chose the French Atlantic coast, and there was a huge Atlantic storm, and rain poured into the tent which had no inner compartment, and they tried to take no notice and keep the game of Monopoly going, but it was no good. One of the children refused to eat anything except Rice Krispies and fish fingers, and while they were away the other family got burgled.

From then on, the Oldroyds travelled on their own, by hovercraft from Ramsgate and car through France, staying with the grandparents in Margate on the way. 'My brother Martin was sick in anticipation of the hovercraft,' said Eleanor. The excitement was too much. 'Our mother tried to force cornflakes down us to settle our stomachs.' The children kept scrapbooks of each year's holiday, as instructed and encouraged to do by their parents. One of the items stuck into the scrapbook is a Hoverlloyd sick-bag, emblazoned with the words 'in case of sickness, please call stewardess for disposal'. It was Eleanor's younger brother Martin who insisted that this be stuck into the album: a more memorable souvenir to him than any postcard of a Gothic rose window.

Up and down the country, fathers with wanderlust were studying maps, thinking out these journeys, and the mothers, as always, were micromanaging the domestic details: 'packing packets of Smash and tins of corned beef and Spam under the bench seat in our Commer camper van', as Jim Rogerson recalled: his father was the headmaster of a secondary school in Barnsley, and his mother was a primary-school teacher – so, again, long holidays but not much money. 'We always went away for four weeks, to France or Spain.' The family of five would cook and sleep in their Commer van, which had a kitchen section at the back, with two gas rings, a grill and kitchen cupboards on the inside of the back doors. 'I slept on the front seat. Above me was a hammock hanging from the two sides of the windscreen, slung across to the partitions. My sister had a hammock in the roof. My parents slept in a double bed made out of the benches.' They put the extendable roof up every time they stopped, 'even if it was just to make a cup of tea'. The roof converted the van into something almost resembling a house.

The Rogersons and their Commer van

Off they drove from Barnsley, in their travelling cocoon of Englishness, Jim practising his skill at recognising makes of car by the shape of their headlights. 'I got it right nineteen times out of twenty.' They aimed to hit London at night, driving down Park Lane, following the signs to Dover. If you were coming from the north or west in those pre-M25 days you needed to drive through London. The actress Janet Dibley's chief memory of her family's 1960s journeys from Leeds to Holland was 'seeing London upside down', because she and her three siblings were lined up, asleep in their pyjamas, on the flattened back seats of their father's Standard Vanguard Estate, and their father woke them up, saying, 'This is London!' 'He didn't want us to miss London,' Janet said. 'I was half asleep and vaguely aware of the upside-down towers of Tower Bridge through a haze of Player's No. 6 smoke.'

When the family reached Dover, just before dawn, Janet's father parked beside Dover Castle and pitched a small tent, for two hours' sleep before driving onto the early ferry. Never let it be said that these fathers hadn't thought everything out.

In the list of fathers' habits, in the Fathers chapter, I mentioned the father who commandeered the dining-room table for months (not weeks – months) before the annual family motorcaravan holiday, planning it 'like a military operation'. This was another schoolmaster, Ted Amos, the father of QC Tim Amos; the family lived in Bedfordshire and Tim's mother Jean was a music teacher. A sign of the family's thriftiness and resourcefulness was that his mother cut out the chocolate box cover of a box of Terry's All Gold to re-cover her holiday diary. Tim's father had set his eyes further afield than France. The family drove all the way to Ankara in 1973, 'and there was a T-junction at Ankara, pointing in one direction to "London 3,400 km" and in the other to "Tehran 2,000 km"'. And my father, with his hand on the steering wheel, said to my mother, "Shall we, Jean?" They didn't, quite; but that 'Shall we, Jean?' stayed with Tim as an unforgettable glimpse of the possible: the world of the open road opening out.

At the Bedfordshire dining-room table, before the journeys began, Tim's father thought out the minutest details to do with insurance, and whether countries like Greece still required coupons for petrol, because petrol was rationed for tourists, and he knew there were different rules north and south of the Rome–Pescara autostrada line. As for the petrol-station siestas, he needed to know the precise timings in order not to be held up for three hours in the searing heat of an Italian, Greek or Turkish afternoon. His mother, meanwhile, was preparing the food. 'She worked on the basis of fresh food for the first two days, and from then on, it would be tins plus local produce. There was an awful lot of Spam.'

The setting-off operation was a notch more militarily organised than the usual drill of families leaving at crack of dawn to get to Clacton. 'On the night before leaving,' said Tim, 'all three of us children were put to bed in our pyjamas in the van on the front drive. Our parents drove off at 3 a.m. in order to catch the first ferry. When the van started moving, I woke up, and was lulled back to sleep, knowing that the van was moving towards the sea and our summer holiday.'

'The insane excitement of the car ferry: the epic feeling of a journey across the Channel,' as Simon Winder described the thrill of his family's journeys from Newhaven to Dieppe, en route to Brittany in the 1970s. Having tasted the exhilaration and the salty breeze of a sea crossing, he was unimpressed the following year when the family went on holiday to Wales instead. 'We visited the slate mine and museum. That holiday lacked the essential, almost religious ingredient of going on a boat. There was no transition. Driving to Wales just felt like an extended version of driving to Sainsbury's.'

Standing on the diesel-scented deck, watching the seagulls following the wake, watching the old land recede and the new land come into view, you felt as if you were going far, far away to a new world, where the bread would be long and thin and they drove on the opposite side of the road, or 'the wrong side of the road', as

Jane Adams's father put it. Families emerged from the ferry and started singing 'Drive on the right!' to the tune of the Toreador Song from *Carmen*. The first French advertisements painted on the sides of buildings beside railway crossings made a deep impression. 'Dubo, Dubon, Dubonnet.' That was a French pun to mull over as you ate up the first kilometres.

Kilometres – so fleeting, compared with miles. They seemed to make the whole world go by faster. The first thing many fathers did, in their ongoing drive to improve their children's mental arithmetic, was to remind them that a kilometre was five-eighths of a mile, 'so how many miles is it to Reims?' On terra firma after the rolling ferry trip, children sat wedged queasily in the back, slithering around on open sleeping bags, quietly trying to calculate the answer, and by the time they came up with it the distance had dramatically decreased. 'And my mother hissed to my father, "It's not pronounced Reams, it's *Rrrhaiiiiinse*",' said Caroline Barnet. 'She prided herself on her good French.'

The second thing fathers did, on the dot of 10 a.m. French time, was switch the car radio on to see if they could still tune in to the cricket. 'Dad could carry on listening to *Test Match Special* if we weren't too far south,' said Eleanor Oldroyd. But the moment came when the noise went buzzy and bits of French interference started mingling with John Arlott's commentary. Then they really were cut off from Britain. It was time to look forward to the first campsite or '*le camping*', pronounced in a French way; and thus to get acquainted with the French taste for simplistic gradations. The Michelin *Camping Caravanning* guide graded campsites in diagrams of tents: one tent meant showers and lavatories – 'and if they were footprint loos, we wouldn't stay there,' said Eleanor. 'We pushed Dad towards two tents and three tents. The swimming-pool ones were four tents. Red tents meant "in a more beautiful location".' The two-or-three-tent level seemed the perfect compromise for a clergy family: not miserable, but not flashy.

'As there were no photographs in the Michelin guides,' said

Catherine Mould, whose family drove to 'Mr Haigh's camp', an upmarket camping resort, with cottages, in the South of France in the early 1970s, 'all the hotels and restaurants were just in our imagination, and we fantasised about them.' Just looking at a Michelin-listed hotel with multiple turrets (denoting grandeur) and two or three Michelin rosettes (denoting good food) made everyone long to stop there – 'and we never did go anywhere that wasn't in the Michelin guide,' said Catherine. She was lucky in that respect. No Spam in their car, 'although my mother did always pack a box of essentials: English loo paper, English coffee, and marmalade and Marmite.' Michelin's simplistic division of the world's experiences into three categories – '*intéressant*'; '*vaut le détour*'; '*vaut le voyage*' – was captivating in its ruthless verdict-giving. For Michelin-inspired daydreamers, these categories became a useful hierarchy with which to rank later life's offerings.

Off these families drove, into the great land mass of 'the Continent', 'and suddenly the car becomes all that's left of the family,' said Simon Winder – 'a bubble of Britishness making its way across France.' 'If we saw another British car,' said Jim Rogerson, 'we'd flash our lights and toot our horn. My father drove along the *routes nationales* at exactly 56 mph: that was supposed to be the most efficient speed. [Another father's theory for our collection.] I sat in the middle at the front and filled his pipe with tobacco – he smoked as he drove.'

Child of the nouveau riche, Pippa Allen, meanwhile, was being driven through Germany at reckless speed by her father. 'I'd already been sick in the ferry from Dover to Ostend. Now we were in my father's Rover V8. He loved fast cars, and he always chose somewhere very far away, so we could drive there through Germany on non-speed-restricted motorways. The three of us were loose in the back, and my brother sometimes perched on the armrest in the front, changing gear for my father. My mother screamed at Dad to slow down.'

Austria was her father's preferred destination, because getting there required driving through a vast chunk of Germany at over 100 mph. 'If we got too unruly,' said Pippa, 'Dad would make us do kilometres into miles or litres into gallons.'

The ultra-trendy thing to do was to put your car on the plane from Lydd to Le Touquet. The magical pairing of those two place names had all the glamour that 'Shannon to Sharm El-Sheikh' has now. Two cars fitted onto the plane at the tiny Kentish airport, and over the channel it tottered, mothers silently panicking that the whole thing was far too heavy and must surely plummet under the weight of the two cars. It didn't. 'Then we stayed our first night at Le Crotoy on the Somme Estuary,' said Richard Worsley, recalling his 1950s family holidays as a schoolboy at Ampleforth. 'Le Crotoy was a kind of Frinton of northern France.'

So, what was it like, actually being abroad?

23

Being Abroad

On arrival at the house with the tin roof on the side of the mountain in Zomba, Nyasaland, Steph Worsley, freshly home from North Foreland Lodge after those multiple plane hops (this was a typical summer of the late 1950s), experienced what so many children in Britain also experienced on arrival home: ten minutes of joyous reunion with the parents, and then the realisation that they would not be devoting their summer to her entertainment.

In her case, though, there hadn't even quite been a joyous reunion: no full-blooded motherly hug. During the bumpy drive from Blantyre Airport, Steph picked up on the chill in the air between her parents: no better than last summer; if anything, worse.

'My mother was a bit aloof, and I never remember her being affectionate,' Steph said. 'She was too unhappy to think about it. My parents were stuck in mutual hatred of each other, but they refused to divorce. My mother was determined that my father wasn't going to get away. He had affairs, and she did. They kept busy, with an awful lot of parties and race meetings at the Turf Club. But my mother, a Norfolk girl, was never happy, and longed to be back here [we were talking in north Norfolk]. She was an unhappy woman in a terrible marriage, and she had migraines. My parents had awful fights. We'd see them throwing things at each other.'

The prospect for her summer holidays could have been dismal. But once again, as for children in unhappy households in Britain, daily release from domestic hell was possible and allowed. Steph embarked on the colonial version of running wild. Living around her in Zomba was a gaggle of other colonial children (some of them, for all she knew, also escaping from parental pressure-cooker atmospheres) who ran about and played all day. 'It didn't matter what our parents did – whether they were soldiers, police, Post Office, Scottish, Irish ... we were all one, and we all played together.' The subtext of that was that any snootiness among the grown-ups about the lowlier jobs of their neighbours was ignored by the children.

So, it was a kind of Thorpeness-in-Africa existence, with mountain pools to swim in instead of the sea, and ponies to ride instead of bikes, but with a country club to go to, to watch films and have hot chips, and a constant crowd of friends. Any activity seemed to be conducted within inches of a snake. 'Snakes were curled on the path, and hanging from the rafters in the loos. We didn't think about it. We climbed trees with snakes hanging all around us. We broke thermometers and raced the mercury across a tray. We played a lot of Monopoly.'

Steph Worsley (left) and her friend Jacky relishing the unsupervised freedom of their African summers

In the evenings, Steph went home for the meringues cooked on the roof by 'our lovely African cook', and she talked to him, as well as to the pets (dogs, cats and guinea pigs). They were the affectionate ones. 'But sadly my father dismissed the cook because he sent the witch doctor to cast a spell over another boy. I was heartbroken when he went.'

Another tin roof: 'We spent our summers of 1944, '45 and '46 in a cottage in the hills outside Shimla,' said Joanna Barker – the one who later went to Trieste when her father was posted there after the war. 'We led very British children's lives; my parents were tremendously British and they were terrified of us getting Anglo-Indian accents. We went up to Shimla on the train from Delhi: first a night train, then the "Puffing Billy", winding and winding uphill. My mother brought bottles of squash, and the corks popped out of the bottles as the pressure changed. The train stopped at stations all the way up, and we were given tea in little terracotta mugs: when you finished you threw them out of the window and they returned to the earth.'

It was just like England up in those hills – 'British weather, with deodar trees'. 'We lived in a cottage called Hermelina. You could see the Himalayas. There were separate quarters for the servants – we always had a cook, and faithful bearers who looked after us. My mother had mahjong parties, and the bearer came in carrying a silver dish with hot buttered toast and strawberry jam. We walked to church every Sunday and came back home to breakfast – sausages wrapped in chapatis. We went into Shimla, and my mother had coffee with her friends, and I read Desperate Dan in the English newspapers.'

The meringues in that existence were not baked on the roof but eaten with two-pronged forks at Devicos, the restaurant in Shimla famed for its excellent meringues.

Joanna Barker with her brother Julian and dog
Vicky in Shimla, 1943, on the way to a picnic

One final expatriate glimpse, before we return to the cross-Channel holidays of our 1960s and 1970s holidaymakers. This is a macabre scene, recalled by a boarding-school girl returning to her expatriate parents: 'My father was stationed at Hohne in Germany when I was thirteen to fifteen,' said Angela Holdsworth, who was by then at Cheltenham Ladies' College – this was 1962. 'We lived on a big army base, in a maisonette on two floors in Officers' Street, and it was wonderful – full of young people. For the first time ever I had really good holidays. There was a cinema showing English films, and parties at night, and suddenly it felt like *living*. It was a mile or two from Belsen, and a gaggle of us cycled to Belsen out of curiosity. The camp was desolate: beyond the perimeter fence, you could just see several huge mounds, each saying simply "Here lie 5,000 dead". We all felt an oppressive silence about the place. No birds were singing. The locals never spoke about it, and I don't remember seeing anyone else there.'

A strong sense of living, and a strong sense of death, side by side.

*

Back in the dormobiles and baked-bean-laden cars of those British holidaymakers who had got up ridiculously early, or sometimes not gone to bed at all, in order to catch the first ferry – how was everyone coping, now that they actually were abroad?

They varied in the depth with which they integrated with the country in question. You could be abroad in the topographical and architectural sense but very much still at home in the culinary sense. This was true of the Oldroyds, who, having looked round their first few French Gothic churches of the holiday, were tucking into their first camping supper: shepherd's pie, made by mixing a tin of mince with a tin of Campbell's condensed vegetable soup, and spreading a layer of Smash on top, all cooked on the camping gas stove with a grill for browning the mash. 'Baked beans were the accompanying vegetable every night,' said Eleanor. 'Once, my mother tried to substitute the baked beans with a tin of French *haricots blancs à la sauce de tomates*, but that was spotted.' The children did at least go to French boulangeries to buy breakfast, asking for '*un pain, deux baguettes et cinq croissants, s'il vous plaît, Madame*'. That felt exotic and exciting.

Then the obligatory scrapbook-keeping began. As only daughter and eldest child, Eleanor was the dutiful one where this was concerned, writing elaborate captions under the stuck-in postcards, such as (of the tympanum above the door of Autun Cathedral), 'On the left there is Heaven, and on the right there is Hell. Christ is seated in glory in the centre.' And, as a caption under a postcard of a tomb: 'The tombs of Philibert le Beau, husband of Marguerite of Austria, and his mother Marguerite de Bourbon.'

A parent must then have said to one of her younger brothers, 'your turn to write the scrapbook today', because the handwriting changes and so does the elevated subject matter. 'We watched the trains at the station. There are chewing-gum machines as well.' 'We went to a Renault garage to have a fuse mended. I like the Renault 5.' And, of a wine-tasting at the Château de Pommard, 'Mum and Dad tasted the wine but could not buy a bottle because it was too expensive (36 fr).'

Every summer of the 1970s, the holiday scrapbooks were kept up. When there weren't enough postcards to stick in, they stuck in the paper bag the postcards had come in, plus any tickets for museum entry. Even aged seventeen in 1979, Eleanor was still diligently recording church visits: 'When it started to pour with rain, we took shelter in the church of St Nicolas, which turned out to be extremely interesting.'

Sometimes they must have forked out for a Michelin 'four-tents' campsite, because there are a few postcards of these, showing bronzed French boys standing louchely on high diving boards above a huge campsite pool, under a postcard-blue sky. The scrapbook tells us, also, that there was a strict family rota for clearing the table, washing up, drying up and fetching the water. 'My brother Martin still has the camping scars,' said Eleanor: 'one on his face from running into a guy rope, and no thumb print from burning himself on the car lighter.'

Scrapbook postcard of a Michelin 'four-tents' campsite

An enterprising couple called Jim and Margaret Cuthbert tapped into the British need to live in as British a way as possible while camping abroad. They'd had been camping themselves and, as they were packing up, thought, What if we were to leave this tent here for others to use? In 1965 they started Canvas Holidays – an early form of glamping – and Anne Owen (from Shenfield) went on one in 1966. 'Guests were promised that on arrival everything would be ready for the first cup of tea,' she said, 'and when we arrived, it was.'

'We didn't eat out, partly because of the expense, but partly because we wouldn't have known what to eat,' said Jim Rogerson, whose family had driven all the way from Barnsley to Spain in the Commer van, stopping at Lourdes on the way (they were a Catholic family), and were now by the sea. 'Paella? What was that? We never had courgettes cooked with garlic, or anything like that. My mother's father was a blacksmith and my father's father worked on the buses. So, it was lettuce, cucumber and tomato.'

Fathers, mothers and siblings were settling into their assigned travelling roles. There was a lot of 'Will you children shut up and stop fighting?' 'My father's way of stopping us fighting on journeys,' said Tim Amos, was to say, "Let's see who can keep quiet the longest". We children sat in fuming silence till my brother piped up with, "I don't care if I lose this game. You took the wrong turning twenty miles back."' The first thing Catherine Mould did on arriving at Mr Haigh's camp near St Tropez was to try to find other people to play with instead of her own sisters: 'I wanted to ditch my own family as soon as possible. We all did.'

The Amos family was covering vast distances, driving from Bedfordshire to Greece or Turkey for four weeks. 'A good day was four hundred miles.' They were more gastronomically adventurous than some. The sublime moment came, after the first forty-eight hours of purely British produce, when Tim's parents returned to the camper van with something foreign to eat: 'our first German *Brötchen* with butter, and then, in Austria or Italy, a whole crate of peaches or fresh grapes. We would just gorge on them. Italy was where I first became aware of aubergines. My mother made ratatouille. A man in Bulgaria started talking to my father about the benefit of yoghurt – that was the first time he or I had ever heard of yoghurt. The man was saying, "I eat yoghurt because I want to live till the year 2000." That was in 1976.'

They ate out at a restaurant just once during the whole holiday – in fact, just once during the whole year, on Tim's brother's birthday on 24 August.

The Amos family in front of the Parthenon (no railings), 1970

*

Well-travelled though most of us are nowadays, we're still pleasantly startled when the 'wall of heat' accosts our faces as we walk down the steps out of an aeroplane into a hot country. For Kirkcaldy boy Harry Ritchie that sensation of being 'hit by heat', on arrival in Majorca for his first-ever foray abroad in 1969, almost knocked him over.

He was one of the lucky ones whose parents (both teachers) had taken the plunge and decided to go on an all-inclusive package holiday to a foreign country. 'It was too scary to go to Majorca on our own,' said Harry, 'so we went with our neighbours, a doctor's family called the Beatties. We booked the holiday through the travel agent: it included the flight, hotel and all our meals. That made it cheaper and doable.'

Having been hit by heat, Harry was then, on the first evening in the hotel dining room, 'shocked by fruit'. He had never seen a peach. When one was presented to him, his father said, nervously, 'make sure it's not rotten and doesn't have worms in it'. 'My father remained suspicious of fruit for the rest of his life,' Harry said. Real peaches, with their strange furry skins, their unequal squishy cheeks, and their genuinely poisonous inner stones, were shockingly different from tinned ones.

There was a mass-catering element about the all-inclusive holiday, 'an element of Pontin's', but this was what both families had expected and everyone liked it. 'Dr Beattie particularly liked the crème caramel, when the best pudding in Britain at the time was Angel Delight.'

'Swimming on Scottish beaches – this is so profoundly unpleasant,' said Harry. 'Being able to take your clothes *off* for a holiday, rather than having to put more on: that was wonderful in itself.' The two families relaxed in the extraordinary heat and the warm water, dabbing themselves with olive oil they'd brought along from the chemist's: 'you had to use a pipette'.

The British were thus discovering the delights of the Mediterranean: balconies, bare feet on hot sand, outdoor café tables. It was at this moment, in the mid-to-late 1960s, that family photograph albums went into colour. The photographs of chilly grandparents in coats and lace-up shoes on beach deckchairs changed to ones of family members in sandals, squinting into the blazing sun. 'Fell in love with EVERYTHING,' Valerie Grove wrote in her diary on arrival in Ibiza in the summer of 1963, having dipped her toe into the 'incredibly warm' Mediterranean. 'A few days later,' she told me, 'there was the transformation into blissful happiness on finding holiday romance with Geoffrey Conway-Henderson, who looked like Rupert Brooke. So, tra-la, the rest of the diary was all sun, sea, sand, Ambre Solaire, holding hands in the moonlight, and kisses under the stars.'

Seventeen-year-old Valerie Grove's transformation in circumstances, 1963: first, in her London garden, with her 'sun-hating boyfriend' ...

... and then, later that summer, on the beach in Ibiza with her sister Alison (right)

You just had to be a bit careful which package holiday you chose: 'My parents,' said Anne Owen, 'booked through the socialist magazine *The Tribune* to go on a package holiday to Viserba di Rimini on the Adriatic coast in 1964. 'The advertisement said that it would be "with like-minded people", so my parents thought they'd be having fascinating Fabian conversations with like-minded intelligentsia. Instead, it was a bunch of blokes in search of a pint.'

What did everyone do at outdoor café tables, apart from experience for the first time the sensuous pleasure of coffee foam on the tongue, or the urgent need to add eight spoonfuls of sugar to the eye-wateringly sour *citron pressé*? They watched the world go by, marvelling at the way foreign people just strolled about, not going anywhere fast; and they wrote postcards to relatives, friends and neighbours. 'I went to have my hair washed,' wrote the teen-aged Katharine Chadburn in her 1951 diary of a cycling holiday in Gouda, Holland, 'while Mummy posted the fifteen postcards we had written, and Susan finished her crossword and sent it to the editor of the *Sunday Chronicle*.'

It was at these tables that children stared into the middle distance, holding a Bic pen, trying to think of anything interesting to write to an aunt or grandmother. A good morning's work was at least ten stamped postcards dropped into a post box that looked like a litter bin. My Scottish grandfather, forced by his nanny to write a postcard home to his parents from the British seaside, and unable to think of a thing to say, managed a mere four words: 'The church is opposite.' That postcard-conciseness was extreme, but it epitomises the low interest level of postcards in general, both for the writers and for the recipients. The well-meaning drive for writing them was that you (or your parents, at least) wanted to show your loved ones that you were thinking of them – and also quietly to say, 'See what an exciting life we lead'.

As postcards were public property at the point of delivery, to be displayed on chimneypieces in the home country and turned around to be read by prying eyes, you couldn't write anything private on them. Nor was it the convention to ask any questions to the recipient about what they were doing. The postcard was a one-sided litany of sightseeing events – and writing them was another chore, along with keeping up the holiday diary or scrapbook. At least, with postcards, you were spared the thank-you-letter rule about having to go onto the second side of paper.

It was at this point in history, also, that 'The Glamour of Other People's Exotic Foreign Holidays' became an annual minor torture. Nowadays we experience this through Instagram, which has become Greek-sunset-central in the months of July and August. Then, it was just postcards and casual place-name-drops.

The aspirational families worked hard to keep up with the Joneses. 'I loved France,' said Julie Welch, 'and would have preferred to go to France rather than Spain. In Spain, the men were sweatier and gropier and the women were uglier. The Catalan women were spectacularly ugly – they all looked like Bretch, my housemistress, with their moustaches, black hair and white faces. But because our next-door neighbours, the Ides, went to Spain, we had to go to bloody Spain. My friend Jo Ide had mentioned to me that her family were going on holiday to Spain, and my mother had grilled me for details.' The Ides always seemed to be one step ahead, when it came to booking their holiday destinations, and they always let their destination be known to Julie's family just too late for them to book it for that year. 'Unfortunately, my mother's triumph in getting us to Spain the following year was short-lived, as she then found that Spain was old hat as far as the Ides were concerned: the next year, they told us they'd booked a holiday in Goa.'

When Julie said, of Spain, 'the men were sweatier and gropier', she was speaking from experience. 'We were staying in a posh hotel on the Costa Brava when I was fifteen,' she said. (This was in about 1953.) 'The man behind the bar was a sad-looking Spaniard called Fortunato, who had a grumpy looking wife. Everyone loved Fortunato. One morning, he brought me my breakfast on a tray in my room, put the tray down, and suddenly started snogging me. It was such a shock. I was just a naive English boarding-school girl. Fortunato – the man who was everyone's friend – was suddenly this horrible sex offender. I shooed him away – it was a bit like kicking a dog, and he stumbled out of the room. I didn't say a word to anyone about it. I was worried my father would horsewhip Fortunato if he found out, or that I'd somehow have been blamed for the whole thing.'

Pippa Allen's aspirational family, having been driven by their father to Austria at 100 mph, was now by a lake, 'getting horribly burnt. My entire back would crisp up, and all the skin flaked off over the next few weeks. My mother's idea of bliss was to put olive oil on and sunbathe all day: she didn't go into the water.' Jane Adams, the girl with strong vegetarian leanings who had suffered in British hotel dining rooms, was in a chalet halfway up a mountain in Switzerland, discovering the bliss of cheese as an alternative to meat. But the holidays were tense: 'my father was very controlling of all of us and he always had to be right. When he was communicating with people abroad, he spoke very loudly and slowly at them in English. He didn't have a word of German except "kaput". "My – car – is – KAPUT."'

Recollections of family members vomiting in foreign-holiday situations linger long in the memory. On that villa holiday in Spain, which Julie Welch went on with another family, the Easts, who had once lived in the same cul-de-sac in Essex and who, like the Welches, had gone up a bit in the world, 'I had to sleep in my parents' bedroom,' said Julie, 'because Di East had just started her period and "needed a room of her own", according to her mother. My father got pissed all the time, drinking gallons of wine from one of those Spanish glass-spouted vessels. I had to sleep on a lilo next to him and he got up in the middle of the night to be terribly sick in a bucket. I was told not to mention it.'

The loo in the villa, Julie said, 'was two footprints and a hole. One developed a good aim.'

France was so very French in those days, Spain so very Spanish, and Italy so very Italian. You still saw yoked oxen. Old ladies in long black dresses sat outside their front doors, or walked to church to the clanging of bells. It was all very foreign. 'I queued all morning and I still couldn't get any money,' one parent would complain to another, having spent hours in the wrong queue at a bewildering bank and still not managed to exchange the travellers' cheques. The foreignness was delicious for the more culinarily adventurous people I spoke to, who recalled reconnoitring where they might have supper that evening – going into crumbling old farmhouses that doubled as tiny restaurants, to discuss the menu with an old lady in an apron whose hands were black from shelling walnuts, and 'in the evening a delicious home-cooked feast would be produced'.

Those baked-bean-reliant families were missing out – but at least they were steering clear of food-poisoning risks.

*

The third version of 'being abroad' – foreign exchanges – was the most drastic of all – more extreme even than being an expat child or being on a family holiday with adventurous parents. You were cast adrift, on your own, into the bosom of a foreign family, and had to witness and take part in their weird habits.

We've already met a few foreign exchange girls hanging around in British families during the period of this book – the scarily sophisticated German one with long red nails who had to muck in with the Buxton family in Norfolk, and Natalie who was living it up in London with the Heathfield girls. Some parents believed it was good for their children to 'mingle with other cultures', and that the mild bore of having to entertain a foreign girl or boy for a few weeks would be worth it if it meant your own child then went to stay in their country for an equivalent length of time, to master a foreign language, absorbing it like a sponge.

'We always had German, Spanish or French people staying with

us in the holidays,' said Miranda Johnston, 'and we had to entertain them. Lidon fell in love with my brother, and mooned about.'
This was all part of Growing Up. I visited a large country house in
Stirlingshire in the 1970s and the French exchange girl had gone
missing. She was later found fast asleep on the compost heap. That
seemed to sum up the level of parental supervision in those days.

Then it was the British children's (usually young teenagers')
turn to be the ones who were sent into the foreign country. 'Our
exchanges were organised by our school,' said Miranda, 'and I was
sent to Marseilles to stay with a girl called Marie-Agnès.' This was
in 1974. 'The family wrote a letter to us saying they lived outside
Marseilles and had a swimming pool. When I arrived, I found the
pool was green and full of frogs and had never been swum in. The
mother had chopped the top of her foot off with the lawnmower.
The family ate tinned spaghetti out of tins. The most exciting
thing was that the whole family used to sit down together, with the
lights turned off, to watch *Charlie's Angels*, dubbed. Watching that
programme would have been anathema to my parents. I thought
it was really nice, that the family turned off the lights to watch
television together.'

Transported to another culture entirely, these shipped-off
teenagers had to cope, and they did, sometimes in the face of
profound homesickness. 'We went to visit Marie-Agnès's cousins,'
said Miranda, 'who were proper peasant farmers. I loved that.
They lived in one room and made their own clogs and gave me
a pair. I can still smell the woodsmoke and the cows.' Back in
Marseilles, Miranda took a moped driving test (she was thirteen),
'and the examiner said he'd pass me, as I was never going to drive
in France again.' She arrived home with a moped licence and a
strong Marseilles accent.

That was a typical foreign exchange baptism of fire. As
with courses and camps, these sojourns with foreign families
matured you at a vastly accelerated rate. Juliet Gardiner's foreign
exchange got off to a damp squib of a start, when she presented

her underwhelming house gift to the mother of her pen friend: 'I took a box of cornflakes to Le Bourget.' No foreign food or drink avoidance was possible here: Juliet was thrilled to be allowed wine topped up with water; the fourteen-year-old Ruth Deech, staying in the Pyrenees in 1957, was 'force-fed with horse meat'. Miranda France went, aged fourteen, to stay with a terrifyingly sophisticated girl called Concorde, who climbed out of her bedroom window to meet her boyfriend at night, and whose grandmother collected snails in her garden to cook and eat. Concorde induced Miranda to get her ears pierced, and took her to 18-rated films.

These nervous British girls came home more changed than their parents had perhaps intended. Depending on the family, those stays could engender a lifelong love of the host country, or a vow never to go there again.

In a suburb of Zurich, staying with a Swiss girl called Solveig for a whole month, Markie Robson-Scott developed a relationship with Solveig's brother Urs, purely out of boredom, and to impress the people at her boarding school. 'I didn't find him at all sexy or attractive,' she said, 'and he had a strange alien look about him.' This was the kind of thing that did happen in foreign exchanges, desperate homesickness calling for desperate measures. Markie and Urs made secret assignations, creeping along the corridor at night, past the parents' bedroom.

The trip was linguistically unhelpful, as Solveig's family spoke Swiss-German instead of German, and Markie couldn't understand a word. 'They all drank Nesquik at dinner. I'd never had it before, but I got quickly into strawberry or chocolate Nesquik. It made my face turn bright red – I think it was a milk allergy – which was very upsetting, as I was sitting right opposite Urs.'

It was excruciating. This depth of immersion into a foreign family's lifestyle took people far further outside their comfort zones than anything the parents had to undergo on their more cautious travels.

*

As the end of the time abroad approached, for all travellers, it was the done thing to bring a memento home to keep in your bedroom, to remind yourself, and to show off to others, that this exotic event had genuinely happened to you. 'We were allowed to buy one souvenir of our holidays,' said Anne McMullan, whose family usually went to Ireland or Somerset but once went to Provence. 'Souvenir-hunting was an important part of our holidays: spending hours looking longingly at small china animals and asking, "Can *that* be my souvenir?"' 'For us in Majorca,' said Harry Ritchie, 'the souvenirs had to be a sombrero, and a badge saying "Palma" to put on your anorak sleeve. Also, a bullfighting poster with your own name emblazoned on it, to stick on your bedroom wall: "Harry Ritchie – El Cordobés".'

Travel-weary but travel-proud, having covered 5,000 miles to Turkey and back, and now in a campsite in Cologne on the way home, Tim Amos wrote with his index finger on the back of the dusty dormobile the names of the far-away places they'd been to, 'to attract the notice of the other campers'. It was the post-foreign-holiday equivalent of Peter Stanford's sprig of heather on the chromium bars of the car radiator.

On the (British) ferry home across the English Channel, Jim Rogerson's father bought all the children a small gift from the ferry's on-board boutique – 'I still have one of them, a small telescope in a leather case,' said Jim. 'And we always had a silver-service meal in the ferry's restaurant: meat and three veg. My father wanted that. It was going to be a long drive back to Barnsley.' Having not eaten out during the whole foreign holiday, this was the perfect, safe and appropriate treat with which to round it off: the best way of celebrating, 'we're back'.

PART VI

THE END IN SIGHT

24

Reflections

Where on earth are they all?

The streets have fallen silent; the green bits at the edges of towns have fallen silent; the meadows and woods have fallen silent.

In my eleven years as a dog-walker, and as a devotee of *The AA 1001 Walks in Britain*, which frequently directs you along footpaths around the edges of villages and over stiles into fields, I have never once seen 'a gaggle of children' spilling out from the back doors of their houses, rushing over a hedge into a meadow that goes down to a stream – an event so frequently described to me while interviewing people for this book. I've hardly even seen a child of any description out unsupervised in a rural spot.

Of course, you see children playing in municipal playgrounds and skate parks, and on tennis courts and football pitches. These are designated playing areas; not the same as the non-designated bits of woodland, grassland and wasteland that have featured so heavily in this book. Perhaps, I wonder, as I walk the dog, someone has been murdered right here and the local children have been told to steer clear of it. Or perhaps they're at home playing on their screens. That's probably it.

We know it, in fact: we know that the increasing pull of indoors is caused by screens. We, who lived predominantly outdoor child-hoods, see today's generation growing up with predominantly indoor childhoods. ('Lucky them!' say some adults, who used to long to be indoors when they were turfed out on rainy days.) Home, which used to be a place to dream, to read, to invent, to play imaginary cricket matches with dice – has become a place of screen addiction. Home has become a place from which parents now have to drag their children to do something active, in order to make them engage with real life – hence the non-stop planned activities to fill in the blank days of the holidays: anything to get them out into the fresh air and away from their seeming torpor. It no longer feels safe to present a child with an unscheduled day.

What's more, in the years since screens began their work of put-ting an end to childhood summers as we knew them, the number of screens you need to drag a child away from has tripled. It's now a video-game screen, a laptop screen and a smartphone screen, all being referred to at the same time. Earphones for multi-play were recently added to the mix, bringing another layer of impregnability to the child whose creativity and imagination you are trying to keep alive. The person you're trying to drag out for a walk, bike ride or swim now can't even hear you.

Towards the end of the period of this book, the pull of screens began. Anyone who grew up in the 1960s and 1970s remembers the thrill or tedium (according to taste) of spending the afternoon watching a Western on someone else's television; and some of those 1970s Lake District 'fields' holidays I've described were known as 'no television holidays' by the already despairing parents. But, as we've seen, in those days programmes did at least end and you then went into the garden to act them out.

While home is no longer a 'safe' place to be – safe for a child's inner being – the outside world is also seen as less safe, and prob-ably is less safe. Those country lanes on which twelve-year-olds cycled off for the day are now death traps, and you wouldn't want your child cycling on them. The 'pool of blood' image that haunts parents' febrile minds – the dread of the policeman's knock to break the news that an accident has occurred – has put a stop to the mass turfing-out of the young into the outside world. It feels safer to have them at home and alive than out and dead, the death of their imaginations being preferable to the death of their bodies. As well as panicking about traffic accidents, today's parents worry (justifiably) about their children being abducted by strangers or joining violent street gangs and (perhaps less justifiably) that too much exposure to sunshine will give them skin cancer.

I wonder, hearing about the childhoods of the people in this book, whether their parents fretted and catastrophised as much as today's parents do. You would think they must have. Through the ages, to love a child has always been to live in constant dread of his or her death. But those mothers didn't seem to be nervous wrecks as they stood at their kitchen sinks waiting for their children to come in for tea. They should have been, perhaps: there was much less traffic (four million cars in 1950, over thirty million today), but a higher number of road deaths per year than there is now: they peaked in the 7,000s in the mid-1960s and are now down to the 1,000s. It's easy to think, It used to be a safer world, but it wasn't, when throngs of loose children were crossing roads without looking, and Sunday drivers went out for a spin after an alcoholic lunch. But there was a perception of safety: a general belief among parents that 'they're with their friends, so they'll be all right'.

Do today's back gardens even have holes in their hedges so children can go in and out of each other's gardens whenever they like? That, as well as the spilling out onto meadows, embodies the porousness I've tried to capture in this book; children spontaneously interacting with each other without the event having to be designated a 'playdate'. I hope back gardens do, but I must say, staring nosily into them on walks and from train windows, I haven't seen much sign of this. Gardens seem alarmingly empty of children. The most common back-garden sight is a trampoline with a safety net round it, looking forlorn in the back corner, covered in dead leaves, with nettles pushing up under it, like some abandoned item in the ghost town of Prypiat.

As for the great British tradition of playing out – the hopscotch, skipping, doorbell-ringing and general hanging-out on pavements till dark on summer evenings – I saw that tradition die out in my very own west London cul-de-sac. When I first arrived, thirty-five years ago, there was a patch of wasteland at the far end, which attracted crowds of loose children from all over the neighbourhood. Nine houses were built on the site in the late 1980s. Still, the children in our street played out on the road, welcoming the newcomers from those nine houses. The sound of 6 p.m. on a summer evening was the babble of children's voices briefly drowned out by Concorde flying over. Two sisters, Joanne and Katie at No. 8, used to knock on our door asking whether our son Toby could play out. He could, and did. Once, in gratitude for their sweetness, and wanting to give Joanne and Katie what I thought would be a treat, I took them to Legoland for the day, along with my sons. It didn't work. They would all have far preferred to be playing on the pavement, unsupervised. That would have been true freedom, while this expensive excursion was a sort of glamorous captivity. They were relieved to get home and back out onto the tarmac.

Then Joanne and Katie's family, the linchpins of the street, moved away to live near their grandparents in Dorset. I was outraged. How could those girls, who embodied the very spirit of the street and rarely went out of it, be the ones who were moving away, while we, the Legoland-goers, were staying put? Gradually, after they left, everyone started staying indoors more and more.

Now I look for signs of playing out, wherever I go, and breathe a sigh of relief whenever I see any sign of street-playing: chalk marks on the pavement, or a goal-shape painted onto a wall, or two hoodies lying a goal-width apart on a common, or – very rare – a front door kept open.

'We moved to the country especially so our children would have a big garden to play in, but they hardly go out into it.' This is something I've heard from friends and acquaintances. If children are hardly going into their own gardens, except when called out for the barbecue, they certainly aren't spilling out into the brambly, stinging-nettly, wild world beyond the garden, except when called out for a family walk. Nor are they going around with their *Observer's Book of British Wild Flowers* to learn the names of everything that grows. The lifelong love of, and knowledge about, nature, which was instilled in so many of my interviewees by those outdoor months, has changed to a different kind of love of nature among today's young people – environmental campaigning. It's wonderful that they care about saving the planet. They are far more politically aware and socially responsible than the previous generations were, and they are deeply knowledgeable from extensive reading of online articles. But can they tell a deadly nightshade berry from a blackcurrant?

Genuinely, I've heard it said that today's children don't leave the house in the holidays except to go to a restaurant or an airport. This is an extraordinary change from the state of affairs evoked in this book, where children never went to restaurants or airports, but were out of the house all day. To be widely travelled but not to know the back alleys and paths of your own neighbourhood seems odd. The Trumper's man (in his eighties) summed up his generation's affront at the travel expectations of today's young: 'My grandsons – they're spoilt rigid, in my book. They won't be satisfied with staying in England for the holidays any more. This little blighter says, "I want to go back to Antigua."'

Little blighter indeed, but it's partly the parents' fault, as we've all got caught up in travel competitiveness in the age of affordable air travel; and some of us, deprived of global travel in our child-hoods, now want to travel all over the place ourselves and take the children with us (although this urge is perhaps starting to be damped down in the age of flight-shaming and pandemics). We feel we're failing them if we don't send them back to school in September with at least one enviable answer to the question 'Where did you go in the holidays?' Again, it's marvellous that children have travelled to so many places and experienced so many different cultures by the time they're eighteen, but are they really better informed than they would be if they'd been out loose and unsupervised in their local multicultural environment? Don't they reach adulthood slightly world-weary, lacking that motivational yearning to go to Paris or New York that galvanised the previous generation into financial independence?

*

I tried to dig up clods of melancholy as I probed people about their childhood summers. There was a fair amount of it, as we've seen – loneliness, detestation of siblings, boredom, sense of parents' unhappy marriages, disappointing holiday accommodation, bad weather, unspecified dreads and longings. But I have to say, the overriding memory was of a sort of easy, un-self-conscious, cotton-wearing happiness. Even if memories are selective, tending to edit out the bad stuff, it tells us something about humanity that this overwhelming sense of having had happy, free, unspoilt childhood summers sustains vast swathes of the population.

Why do we feel nostalgic for days when we had less, were more neglected, and didn't travel far? I think it pleases us, as we live through adulthood in a state of perpetual financial anxiety, to remind ourselves that, for children, happiness is not dependent on money, material wealth or privilege. That's what these descriptions of summers do remind us. Open space, free time and an idea: those are the chief requisites of happiness, plus there being someone loving in the background, even if it's not your own mother. With a jam sandwich in your pocket and a tree (or slag heap) to climb at the back of the village for the day, you could be just as happy as a child with a heated swimming pool in a des-res or in the grounds of a stately home – if not more so, as you were even more free. The simple fact of being at liberty to roam, and properly a part of your local neighbourhood – that was true richness of life.

The doctrine of thrift, on which so many British families

lived and thrived, inculcated children with a sense of modesty, helpfulness, respect and a sense of duty. The hand-me-down clothes, rusty old bikes, threadbare carpets, thin old towels, non-crenellated buckets and plain ham sandwiches that adorned people's mid-twentieth-century summers are looked back at as badges of honour. They announce: 'I became the strong, independent, imaginative person I am without materialistic propping-up.' Thrift could and did, though, have its negative side: a kind of puritan abstemiousness, which could make for very dreary living conditions, as we've seen, with some of the mothers' lives of unglamorous drudgery, their flavourless cooking and their rigid avoidance of 'vulgar' indulgences.

As for creativity, all of us who have waited for a delayed train and killed the time by playing a game on our phones have been thankful that we've lived to see the Death of Boredom. The utter blankness of there being literally nothing to do, which the children in this book had to wake up to each morning and deal with, without the cushion of electronics to fall back on, has been replaced by the constant availability of something to do.

Out of that blankness, creativity had to come. As Archbishop Stephen Cottrell put it, 'I believe the greatest creativity arises out of that attentive nothingness.' 'There's a problem with creativity now,' said Giles Fraser, 'a sameness about entertainment.' Not that today's young people aren't (sometimes) highly creative – and this is even more impressive than it used to be, because in order for them to write their novel, read their way through a whole library, paint their picture, or become good at their musical instrument, sport or hobby, they've had to fight against electronic temptations, rather than against mere nothingness.

'You just wanted to gorge,' said Jamie Buxton, recalling his rereading of comics in the 1960s. That's what those summers made (and still make) possible: gorging. Today's gorging can all too easily be eighteen hours a day on a single video game: such total absorption that, as has actually happened, a child doesn't notice for five hours that another family member has had a heart attack in a different room. In the age of this book, the gorging came in multiple varieties: intellectual gorging, sporty gorging, handicraft gorging, musical gorging or low-brow gorging, but whatever it was, you emerged at the end as some sort of expert, even if it was just having become very good at ping-pong.

'There were days that felt very long, weeks that felt very long,' said Colin Burrow. Time could indeed hang heavily. Some I spoke to, who lived through those months of uneventfulness, vowed never to be bored again or to inflict boredom on their own offspring. Others are sustained by the memory of just being at home with nothing much planned. 'It's still my favourite thing, to have a free day,' said Debora Robertson. Of being at home, Giles Smith said, 'I feel the pull of that house in Colchester in summer, the doors and windows open in the evening, and I just feel incredibly warm and comfortable when I think about it.'

I think that warm, reassuring feeling of windows and doors being open at home on a long summer evening sustains millions of us.

As for the lashings of fresh air, here's one example of its effect in shaping someone's adulthood. 'Because of the love of outdoors that I got from those camping trips,' said Neil Herron, 'I did a degree in geography at Newcastle University and my dissertation was on solute levels in Lunedale in Teesside. I had one interview for Scholl Shoes, but I didn't want an indoor job. I saw an ad for a labourer at Sunderland fish quay, and I put it in my pocket so nobody else could apply. I did that job for twelve hours a day, six days a week, and then started a business as a market trader at Park Lane Market in Sunderland.'

That seemed to sum up the motivating effect of those summers of frugality and not too much parental attention. They got you up and out.

Just as sustaining is the deep and abiding love that people have for places they went back to every summer of their childhoods.

'When my father died,' said Neil, 'we scattered his ashes at the riverside in Cotherstone where we used to go camping.'

There was nowhere on earth that meant more to those brothers than that spot by a river, an hour's drive from home, where they'd returned again and again for their summer holidays – some of the holidays only a day long, but it felt like infinity.

Neil aged ten, fishing at Cotherstone

25

Paradise About to Be Lost

Aand so, through all the length of days, September came into view.

It seemed extraordinary, as well as horrifying, that some shops seemed to take pleasure in advertising the prospect of going back to the unmentionable place beginning with 's'. Children shuddered at their first sighting of the words 'BACK TO SCHOOL' emblazoned on a shop window, or, if they were in France, '*LA RENTRÉE*'. Why make such a song and dance of it? And why would anyone want to dress a mannequin in school uniform?

A chill in the air; the grass dewy in the mornings and evenings; the curtains being closed at 7.30; these were the first tell-tale signs that paradise was about to be lost. Then, it would be casually dropped into the conversation that you were going to be going to the dentist in a few days' time. ('Haircut, went to the dentist, he *did* hurt,' wrote Elizabeth Millman in her diary for 11 September 1935, skating over the self-pity.) Then it would be mentioned that you were going on a trip to 'town', and you knew it was not for fun but to buy new school clothes.

Barkie and Pi, who ran The Yews as a holiday home, were *in loco parentis* for all these duties, taking the girls all the way from Somerset to the uniform shop in Cheltenham and back, if need be. 'The local dentist in Taunton,' said Sheila McGuirk, 'said to us, "I can tell you're Yews-ites: your hair smells of peat smoke."'

The intrusion of all this into people's summers is remembered so vividly that, decades later, it can still make them feel sick. 'I remember getting really sad about two weeks before the end, and not being able to eat,' said Henrietta Petit. 'People said to me, "Make the most of it – you've still got two weeks left."' 'I felt ill – really sick,' said Felicity Shimmin. 'with this cold, clutching feeling of desolation. The local summer shows – the Shepton Show and the Frome Show, in late August and early September – those were the harbingers.' 'I still resent the ebbing away of summer,' said Libby Purves. 'I feel a panic coming on. The thought of getting back into a pleated skirt and blouses tucked in was dreadful. But at least I got a new pencil case.' 'The prospect of going back to school felt like going back to prison,' said Jilly Cooper.

Stepping off from a world of timelessness back into a world of time made hearts jolt and stomachs churn. Could you carry on as before, once you knew the end was in sight? Rumer Godden thought you could. In *The Greengage Summer*, she wrote, 'the holidays would be over, but there were still three and a half weeks to go, and at Les Oeillets each day was like a year. Twenty-three days, twenty-three years. Who bothers what will happen in twenty-three years?'

But as soon as you became re-aware of what date it was, having totally lost touch with the date in the depths of August, it was somehow the end of innocence. You couldn't quite re-enter the timeless paradise. 'I have a recurring dream,' said Philip Mould, 'that the end of the holidays is in sight – but there's still a week to go. Just a week.' However hard you tried, it was impossible to trick yourself into thinking that a week at the end was just like a week at the beginning. They were quite different things, in the way that a place looks different depending on whether you're arriving at it or leaving it.

Feelings of nausea could overcome you. 'The smell of new

shoes in the shoe department in Peter Jones was horrible,' said
Ben Thomas, 'and I had my hair cut way too short. And then, the
name-taping began.' Quietly, mothers sat by their sewing baskets,
calming their own nerves as they meditated on their children's
names in turn, striving to obey the clothes-list injunction that
every item must be named. The sight of the clothes list was terrifying for those about to go back: a reminder of the mercilessness
efficiencies of the other world. Teenaged girls who'd had summer
jobs working in shoe shops now had to succumb to having their
own feet measured, and doing five clumping steps to the mirror
and back, to check the new shoes fitted.

Then the trunk came down from the attic. No longer was it
a 'vessel of salvation', something you would want to sleep inside.
It was now a vessel of doom, and, again, its leathery smell was
revolting.

*

It's easy to recreate that feeling of dread. Now imagine that, as well
as living with the end-of-summer-holidays tummy ache, you're
gathered round a wireless set on 3 September 1939. There's a split
second of hope, as Neville Chamberlain opens with an upward
inflection as he touches on the ultimatum. Then comes a down-
ward inflection in his voice. 'I have to tell you now that no such
undertaking has been received.'

So, as well as school-dread, you now have to live with being-at-
war-dread. Not a nice start to September.

'3rd Sept,' wrote Elizabeth Millman in her diary: 'No church.
Listened to Chamberlain. War declared at 11.15. Awful day,
small dinner.'

There was a mass loss of appetite on that day, especially among
school-returners. 'In the summer term,' said Peggy Thomas, who
went to school in Birmingham, 'we'd had an evacuation rehearsal:
meeting at the appointed meeting place and marching to the local
railway station. But on the day war was declared, I was in Abergele.

The coaches were all booked up and I couldn't get home.' The result was that the thirteen-year-old Peggy was driven to Ashby de la Zouch in Leicestershire by the person next door who happened to come from there and had a car, and Peggy suddenly found herself billeted in a tiny bedroom in a 'modern semi' with a horrible couple called Mr and Mrs Bentham, who made her skivvy for them. She stayed for two years, going to the local school. 'I had to get up, take the family their tea in bed, cook their breakfast, and do the washing-up, every morning before school.'

Peggy Thomas, aged sixteen, evacuated to Ashby de la Zouch, outside one of the schools there that took in evacuees

That was what happened: people were caught like rabbits in headlights at the places where they happened to be at that end-of-summer-holidays moment. That moment when life changed is remembered like the still of a film. Charles Fraser was in church, in the manse pew, as son of the minister. 'The beadle, Jimmy Mackie, walked in, in the middle of my father's sermon. He went up into the pulpit and whispered the news to my father, who announced it. I remember my mother crying. That very afternoon, a dispatch rider drove up the drive to the manse and gave my father his calling-up papers. He became padre to the Cameronian Scottish Rifles.'

'I was helping my mother dust the dining-room table when we heard the news,' said Jean Lunam, born in Lancashire in 1922. 'We were at Borth,' said Henry Villiers. 'At the very moment war was declared I fell off a breakwater and broke my arm. We never went back to Cardigan Bay.' His wartime summers would be spent staying near cousins in Sussex, lodging in a nearby pub.

'We were still on holiday at Sutton-on-Sea on Friday 1 September,' said Walter Balmford, 'but we started driving home on Saturday, stopping off to listen to the news in Melton Mowbray on the way – we didn't have a car radio. By Sunday we were back home in Birmingham, gathered round the radio in the dining room.'

'We were staying at Nethy Bridge Hotel in the Cairngorms,' said Sandy Stephen. 'Everyone gathered round the wireless in the lounge. I knew we were going to win. We were the goodies and the goodies always win.' For him, as for Tom Stacey, life was about to get more exciting, as their prep schools were evacuated to remote places: his from Edinburgh to Perthshire, and Tom Stacey's from Kent to the wild hills of Argyllshire. 'I'd never seen such natural beauty,' said Tom Stacey. 'My life opened up like a flower.'

'I was staying with my grandparents at Barrhead, near Glasgow,' said Murray Maclean, who was a teenage helper on Christian camps, 'and I remember them saying the word "inevitable" a lot; war was "inevitable". On the day it was declared, a friend and I took a tramcar to the local loch. It looked ghostly: the swings and roundabouts were all chained up as it was a Sunday, and the boats were chained up. My parents phoned through from where we lived in Surrey, and said to my grandparents, "it's better if you keep him there". So I enrolled in the local school.'

'We were staying at one of the farms belonging to [the historian]

G. M. Trevelyan's family in Northumberland,' said Nicolas Barker. 'My father was convinced that the first thing the Germans would do would be to destroy the bridges over the British rivers. He knew that our nursemaid Gladys Fincham's brother had a big Humber car, and he rang him to ask him to drive up from Cambridge to collect us.' He did – and they managed to get back home before the expected bombing of the bridges.

I collected moments when current affairs crashed into blissfully oblivious childhood or teenaged summer consciousnesses. As well as Daniel Finkelstein getting caught up in Watergate while on holiday in Scotland in August 1974, Katie Thomas said, 'I took golden syrup mixed with cocoa powder up to a friend's treehouse on the day of Mountbatten's funeral.' (5 September 1979.) Mary Miers recalled one of her cousins being 'inconsolable with grief on South Uist for a whole week when Elvis Presley died.' (16 August 1977.) Jenny Taylor said, 'I was caravanning in East Yorkshire on the day of the Great Train Robbery.' (8 August 1963.) But nothing could match Sunday 3 September 1939 for bad news just before the beginning of term – as well as before lunch, of which little was touched on that day.

※

For lonely children, or those living in unhappy households, as well as for children who simply loved school, the prospect of going back could be a happy one. 'Going back to school was fine by me,' said Pippa Allen, who was sick of the unhappy atmosphere of home. 'My mother said things like, "If you go and visit your father I'll make sure you never see your brother and sister again." School was an absolute godsend, because I could get away from home.' 'The only thing that redeemed going back to school,' said Jilly Cooper, 'was seeing your friends again. Apart from that, it was a nightmare: missing the ponies, dogs, cats, parents and the lovely valley.'

Markie Robson-Scott, through those long lonely summers in Bonchester Bridge, had prepared herself for going back to

Badminton School so much, so obsessively, that she almost spoiled
the reality. In her diary she wrote, 'I don't think I want to go back
to school. I've thought about being in Group III [the next class
up] so much that it's now worn off, I mean the excitement. Oh
dear, even seeing Kiwi [her pash] doesn't hold the excitement it
should.' She was right: you can pre-smother an experience by over-
rehearsing it in your head.

Generally, as well as the sickening dread there was a seam of
excitement in people's hearts at the thought of starting in a new
class, a whole level more senior than you were last year, and vastly
improved at whatever accomplishment it was that you'd mastered
during the summer months. Parents did try to soften the blow. On
our last day in France in the early Septembers of the 1970s, my sister
and I were given pocket money to go to Monoprix to buy French
stationery, which seemed glamorous compared with English stationery. A pack of French felt pens arranged in rainbow formation
was something to gloat over, and was consolation of a sort.

'In the last week of the summer holidays', said triplet Henrietta
Moyle, my parents took each of us out on our own, in turn, for
supper at the Romantica restaurant in Canterbury.' That was a
once-in-a-holidays treat: to have the full beam of parental attention
on you alone, for the duration of a whole restaurant meal. This was
deep bonding, and an hour and a half of concentrated empathy,
before the girls were sent off for another year at boarding school.

'Going back to Halidon House in Stoke Poges from Tripoli
aged ten,' said Angela Holdsworth, 'my main thought as I left my
parents was, "I hope they'll be all right when I come back". I never
worried that my propeller plane would crash, but I did worry that
some ill would befall my parents while I wasn't looking after them.'

One can imagine all too well the feelings of Steph Worsley and
other colonial children like her. They would have to do, in reverse,
every step of the long-drawn-out journey that had brought them
home. 'We all hated the thought of going back to grey England
and to school rules,' Steph said, 'after our wild summers in Africa.

I longed to be allowed to go to school in Salisbury [now Harare], as some of my friends did – that would only have been an hour away by plane. But my parents thought a British education was best – or perhaps it was just a matter of "out of sight, out of mind". I cried from the moment I woke up, on the day I knew I was going back.'

After giving a final tearful hug to the pets, she had to do the drive down the mountain, the flight hops from Blantyre to Salisbury, Salisbury to Nairobi, Nairobi to Khartoum, Khartoum to Rome, Rome to London: all a travesty of travel as it was going in the wrong direction. 'When I got back to North Foreland Lodge, the Gam [that was the nickname of the kind headmistress, Miss Gammell] asked me, "Why are you always on the penance table?" – that was the table you had to sit at if you'd misbehaved. I told her, "I'm like this because my parents don't seem to care." She said, "You'll become a stronger person because of this, and that's how you must think about it."'

Steph Worsley, aged eleven in 1958, at Blantyre Airport in Nyasaland,
about to step onto the first of the three planes that would take her
back to school

'How was your summer?' Caroline Wyatt's friends asked her when she arrived back at Woldingham in September 1978. 'Not very good. My mum died,' Caroline replied. 'They were all very sympathetic,' said Caroline, 'but they couldn't quite deal with it. I was marked out as "different". There was a special assembly held for me, which was a really sweet thing of the school to do – but suddenly I was looked at by everyone with sympathetic eyes.'

When Harry Ritchie got back to school in Kirkcaldy, he realised that no one else in his school had been abroad, except him and the Beatties. 'I stood out like the Hitler Youth: blond hair, deep suntan – the only guy with a tan in my class.'

Transferring from one world to the other could be seamless. Elizabeth Millman goes from home life back to school life with hardly a jolt in her 1930s diary prose. 1936: 'Tidied room and packed my things. Back to school. I do like Nancy Eden, I don't care if nobody else does.' 1938: 'Last day of hols, did flowers, helped mow lawn, tea in garden, get ready. Back to school, sleep in 26 with Violette, Annette, Cynthia and Gay. Cynthia sick about 11 o'clock.'

For Marianne More Gordon in 1946, going back to school was not seamless at all. Returning to England at the end of summer, after six weeks in Northern Ireland, felt like walking into another life. It was a completely different world.

Goodbye to the cobbles, goodbye to the horses, goodbye to the gentle grandmother. It was a long drive back to Hertfordshire along the tarmacked roads lined with new ribbon development.

Fresh from that wistful journey home, and feeling very nervous, the fourteen-year-old Marianne arrived a few days later for the first day of term as a new girl at Ware Grammar School in Hertfordshire. She was wearing the wrong dress, bright yellow when it should have been green-and-white check, and one of her aunt's white WRNS shirts rather than a regulation school shirt, and a blazer that had been worn by her mother during the one term that she had attended any school. The blazer was the wrong style and colour for Ware Grammar School. After six weeks of carefree unselfconsciousness in peaceful, remote, beautiful Ireland, Marianne was suddenly overcome with self-consciousness, horribly aware that she stood out.

The girls had to stand up in class one by one to give the alarming form teacher their full name.

'What's your name?' barked the teacher to Marianne.

Marianne stood up, and announced, 'Marianne Lucia Perronet Thompson-McCausland.'

As she spoke the words, she could feel the whole class turning round to stare at her, in her wrong clothes, with her too-long name.

Autumn term begins. British summer time ends.

Acknowledgements

This book could not have been written without the generosity and kindness of my interviewees, who gave up their time to talk to me. I'm immensely grateful to them, as well as to friends and acquaintances who suggested people I might talk to, introduced me to them and steered me towards them. Huge thanks to: Jane Adams, Douglas Addison, Charmaine Alder, Alice Allen, Pippa Allen, Tim Amos, Evelyn Armstrong, Elaine Ashton, Susan Baldwin, Joan Borg, Walter Balmford, Joanna Barker, Nicolas Barker, Caroline Barnet, Elisabeth Beccle, Jamie Blackett, Joan Borg, Linda Bowley, Humphrey Boyle, Nicky Bradford, Alan Brown, Susan Brown, Celia Burns, Colin Burrow, Jamie Buxton, Vanessa Buxton, Marie Byng, Dugald Cameron, Josie Cameron Ashcroft, Bubble Carew-Pole, Bill Carroll, Rita Carroll, Caroline Chichester-Clark, Violet Child, Alan Collins, Jane Corry, Harry Cory-Wright, Shirley Cotter, Eileen Cottrell, Stephen Cottrell, Dave Coupland, Caroline Cranbrook, Kathleen Crawley, Candida Crewe, Jilly Cooper, Amanda Craig, Kevin Crossley-Holland, Anna Dalrymple, the late Hew Dalrymple Robert Dalrymple, Andrew Davey, Bolla Denehy, Ruth Deech, Frankie Devlin, Janet Dibley, Johann Dickson, Pat Doyne-Ditmas, Mark Dunfoy, Sabine Durrant, Elfrida Eden, Annabel Fairfax, Daniel Finkelstein, Phoebe Fortescue, Miranda France, Ann Fraser, Charles Fraser, Fiona Fraser, Giles Fraser, Kit Fraser, Olivia Fraser,

Susan Gardham, Juliet Gardiner, Anthony Gardner, Derren Gilhooley, Mark Girouard, Jonathon Green, Hester Greenstock, Mark Greenstock, Evelyn Griffin, Kate Grimond, Trevor Grove, Valerie Grove, William Gulliford, Enid Hales, Edward Hall, Bill Halson, Penrose Halson, Paul Hansford, David Hartshorne, Cathy Hawkins, Neil Herron, Annabel Heseltine, Diana Holderness, Angela Holdsworth, Richard Holloway, Bridget Howard, Catriona Howatson, Malcolm Innes, Rachel Johnson, Miranda Johnston, Peter Julian, Ursula Keeling, Jackie King, Jenny Landreth, Julia Little, Ann Lindsay, Angela Lynne, Lucinda MacDougald, Morag MacInnes, Murray Maclean, Jennifer McGrandle, Sheila McGuirk, Anne McMullan, Grace McNulty, Rochelle Madill, Andrew Makower, Katharine Makower, Peter Makower, Sonia Malcolm, Dorothy Matthews, Rachel Meddowes, Mary Miers, Philip Moore, Joanna Moorhead, Anne Millman, the late Elizabeth Millman, Marianne More Gordon, Hervé de la Morinière, Lizie de la Morinière, Leila Moshire, Honor Mottram, Catherine Mould, Philip Mould, Henrietta Moyle, Harriet Mullan, John Mullan, the late John Julius Norwich, George Oaks, Eleanor Oldroyd, Ali O'Neale, Tara Odgers, Anne Owen, Ian Oxley, Jayne Ozanne, Marnie Palmer, Jean Parfrey, Allison Pearson, Victoria Peterkin, Henrietta Petit, Georgina Petty, Camilla Presland, Irene Protheroe, Libby Purves, Issy van Randwyck, Les Ranson, Phyllis Reed, Jasper Rees, Alex Renton, Alice Renton, Noreen Rimmer, Audrey Roe, Dorothy Rice, Harry Ritchie, Debora Robertson, Markie Robson-Scott, Jim Rogerson, Charles Ropner, Jo Ropner, Emily Russell, Sue Sabbagh, Nicholas Sagovsky, Abby Scott, Ben Scrimgeour, Christian Scrimgeour, Mary Ann Sieghart, Gillian Shephard, Felicity Shimmin, Simon Shimmin, Lucinda Sims, Ian Skelly, Dennis Skinner, Caroline Slocock, Andrew Smith, Giles Smith, Peter Smith, Nicholas Soames, Gabrielle Speaight, Tom Stacey, Peter Stanford, Sandy Stephen, Anne Stockton, Peter Susman, Jenefer Tatham, Cicely Taylor, Jenny Taylor, Veronica Telfer, Sally Terris, Ben Thomas,

Katie Thomas, Peggy Thomas, Maurice Tonks, the late Henry Villiers, Fred Walker, Nick Weeks, Julie Welch, Rowan Williams, Bee Wilson, Simon Winder, Peter Witchlow, Hazel Wood, Mia Woodford, Richard Worsley, Steph Worsley, Caroline Wyatt and Philip Ziegler.

Thank you to my agent Sophie Scard at United Agents, to my editor Richard Beswick at Little, Brown, and to David Bamford, Richard Collins, Hayley Camis, Viv Lipski, Kimberley Nyamhondera, Emily Moran, Bekki Guyatt and Marie Hrynczak at Little, Brown – all a delight to work with.

Thank you to the lovely staff at my two writing-haven cafés: Le Pain Quotidien on Parson's Green, and the No Name café in Sandwich, Kent.

To my husband Michael, our sons Toby, Charles and Francis, my mother Claudia Maxtone Graham, my sister and brother-in-law Livia and Joseph Sevier, and my nephew Joe Sevier – deep thanks for your love and support.